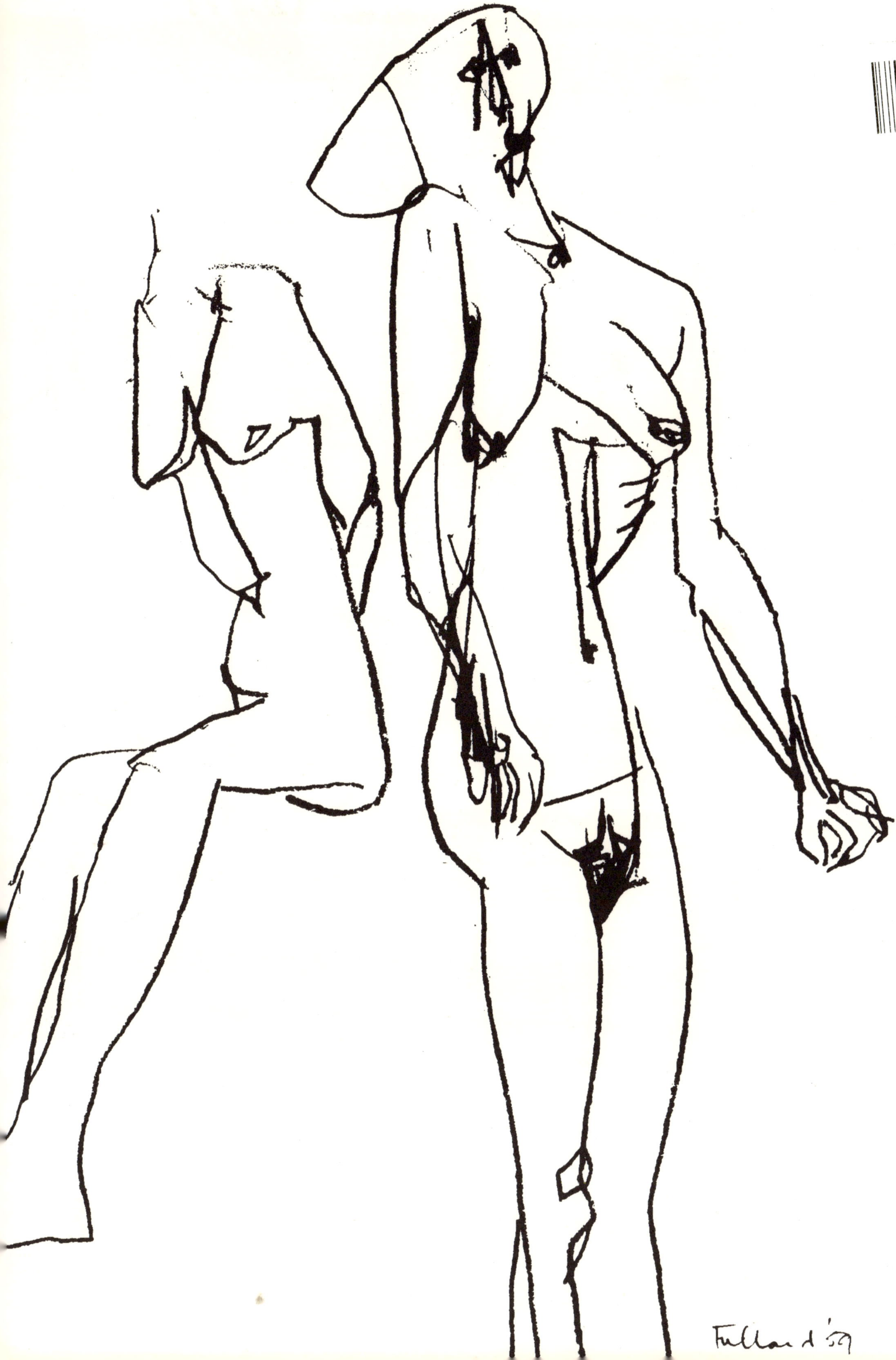
Fullard '59

Assembling the Absurd:

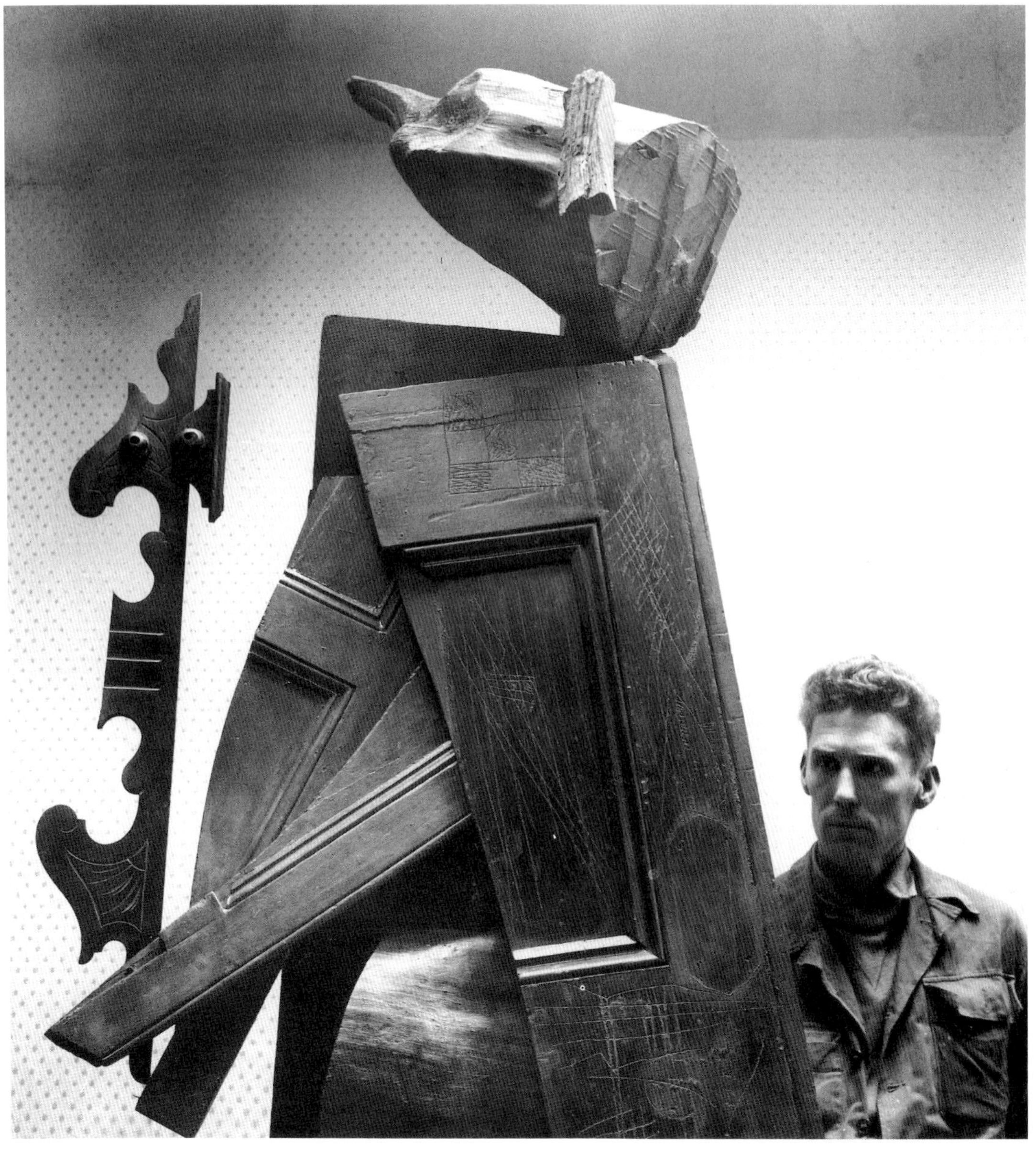

The Sculpture of George Fullard

Gillian Whiteley

The Henry Moore Foundation in association with Lund Humphries Publishers, London

First published in 1998 by
The Henry Moore Foundation
Dane Tree House
Perry Green
Much Hadham
Herts SG10 6EE
in association with
Lund Humphries Publishers
Park House
1 Russell Gardens
London NW11 9NN

British Library Cataloguing in Publication Data
A catalogue record for this book is available from the British Library

ISBN 0 85331 736 4

Distributed in the USA by
Antique Collectors' Club
Market Street Industrial Park
Wappingers Falls
NY 12590
USA

Designed by Ray Carpenter
Typeset by Tom Knott
Origination, printing and binding in Singapore under the supervision of MRM Graphics

ENDPAPERS
Nude Women 1959
Pencil on paper

FRONTISPIECE
Fullard with **Woman with flowers** 1959-60 (Cat.39)

For Danny and Alex

Contents

Photographic credits

The author and the publisher have made every effort to trace the copyright holders or owners of works and photographs. If any institutions or individuals have been incorrectly credited, or if there are any omissions, we would be glad to be notified so that the necessary corrections can be made in any reprint.

All numbers refer to Plates

Ernest Adsetts 5, 9, 10, 16
Arts Council Collection, Hayward Gallery, London Jacket back, Endpapers, 51, 65, 76, 85, 92, 111
Bretton Hall, University College Collection, Wakefield 61
Pamela Chandler 7, 12, 20, 22, 30, 72
Conway Library, Courtauld Institute of Art 8, 14, 21, 35, 50, 55, 60, 77, 78, 82, 83, 86, 87, 96, 99, 100, 102, 118, 119, 120, 121, 122
A. C. Cooper 6
Crispin Eurich 51, 75 (archive photograph obtained from the artist's estate)
Mary Farnell 13, 15, 31, 37, 103, 115
Ferens Art Gallery, Hull 89
George Fullard's Estate 34, 73, 75, 91, 97, 98
Jerry Hardman-Jones Jacket front, 1, 25, 26, 27, 29, 33, 38, 39, 56, 57, 59, 62, 63, 66, 67, 79, 81, 89, 90, 93, 95, 117
Martin Koretz 68 (archive photograph obtained from the artist's estate), 84
J. Lewinski 80
Valerie Macready 88, 101
Manchester City Art Galleries 64
Frank Monaco Frontispiece, 2, 3, 11, 17, 18, 19, 36, 47, 48, 52, 58, 61, 70, 76, 104, 113, 114, 116
New Art Centre Sculpture Park, Roche Court, Salisbury 94
Norfolk Museums Service (Norwich Castle Museum) 28
Garrick Palmer 94
Sheffield Galleries and Museums Collections Jacket front, 1, 25, 26, 27, 55, 62, 63, 66, 79, 80, 109, 114, 117
Stoke-on-Trent City Museum and Art Gallery 48, 49
Tate Gallery, London 32, 75
Patrick Thurston 53, 69, 71, 74
John Webb Endpapers, 4, 105, 106, 107, 108, 109, 110, 111
Gillian Whiteley 54
Jonty Wilde 23, 24, 40, 41, 42, 43, 44, 45, 46
Yorkshire Sculpture Park 23, 24, 40, 41, 42, 43, 44, 45, 46

Acknowledgements

Many individuals and organisations have given their time and support to this project. The author would like to thank all those who have enthusiastically and warmly given their recollections, information, material and critical comment.

I am especially indebted to Irena Fullard for her tireless generous assistance with the provision of information and photographs and for the insightful suggestions and commentary she has offered.

Particular thanks also to Ernest Adsetts, Ray Arnatt, Phyllida Barlow, John Berger, David Brown, R. Butler, J. Clements, Alan Cole, Andy Croft, Peter de Francia, Colin Fullard, Derrick Greaves, Leslie Duxbury, Ivy Harper, Michael Harrison, Paul Hogarth, Gordon House, Steve Hurst, the late John Lloyd, Kay Maclaren, John Mills, Frank Monaco, Brian Ord, Susan Parkinson, Clive Philpott, Adam Pollock, the late Philip Pollock, Ray Rasmussen, Jasia Reichardt, Jim Richardson, Matt Rugg, Jeanetta Sindall, the late Bernard Sindall, Jack Smith, Neville Strong, Paul Swales, R. H. Waites, the late John Warren Davis, Ian Welsh, John Willett, John Wragg and Chris Yetton.

The following galleries, museums and archives have been helpful and responsive in providing access to works, supplying information and photographs: Aberdeen City Art Gallery; Arts Council of England; Bovington Tank Museum; Bretton Hall University College, Wakefield; Bristol City Art Gallery; Brotherton Library Special Collection, University of Leeds; Chelsea School of Art; Conway Library, Courtauld Institute of Art; Ferens Art Gallery, Hull; Glynn Vivian Gallery, Swansea; Hatton Gallery, University of Newcastle; Henry Moore Centre for the Study of Sculpture, Leeds; National Museum of Labour History, Manchester; Manchester City Art Galleries; Mappin Art Gallery, Sheffield; New Art Centre Sculpture Park, Roche Court, Salisbury; Norwich Museums Service (Castle Museum); Royal Academy of Arts; Royal College of Art; Sheffield Galleries and Museums Trust; Sheffield Hallam University; Southampton City Art Gallery; South London Gallery; Stoke-on-Trent City Museum and Art Gallery; Tate Gallery, London; Yorkshire Sculpture Park, Wakefield.

For kindly permitting the reproduction of extracts of published work, thanks to: John Berger; Cynthia Berry; Derrick Greaves; HarperCollins Publishers Ltd; Barbara Hayman; David Lee, editor of *Art Review*.

I am particularly grateful to Ben Read for his help and advice. Above all, thanks to three special people: Geoff, for providing unending support, music and late-night talks; Danny and Alex for their patience and for being the perfect antidote to life in the attic.

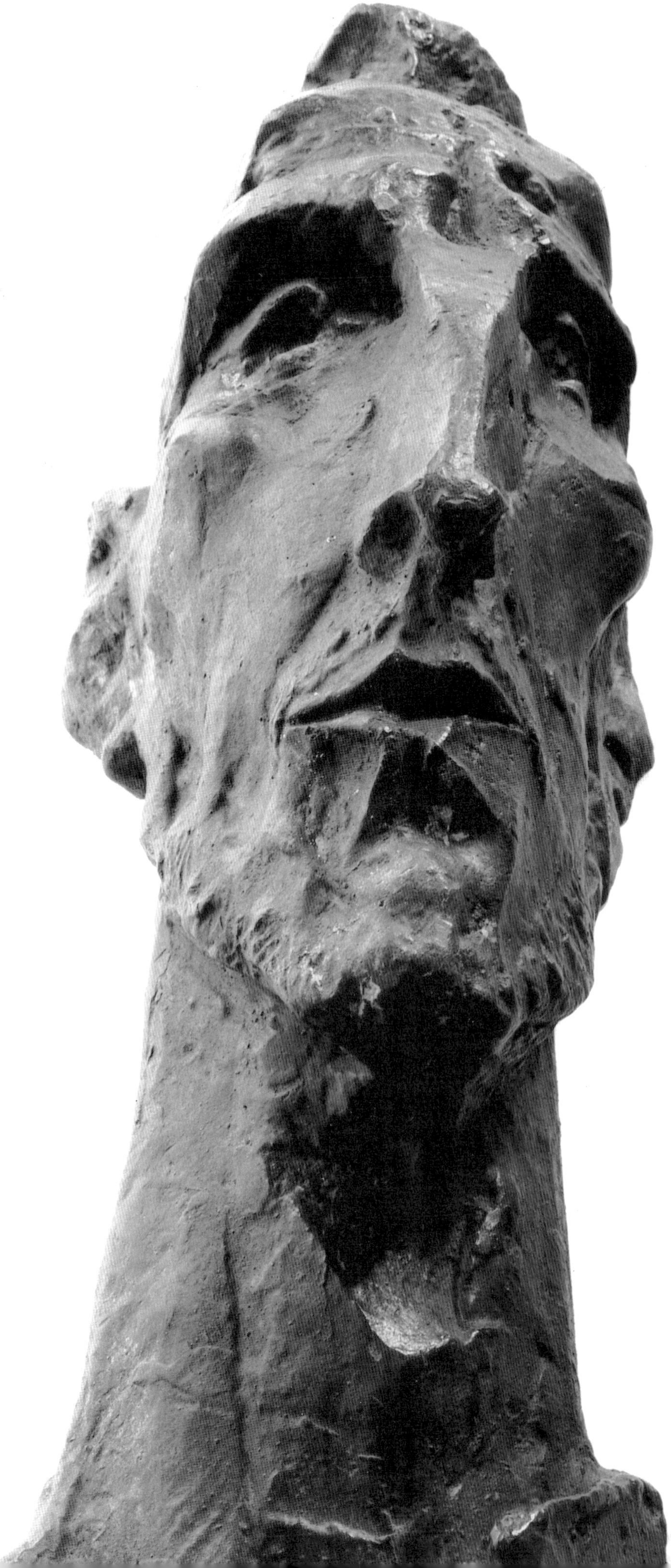

1

Introduction

Plate 1 (Cat.26)
Walking man 1957 (detail)
Bronze
183 x 24 x 48.3 cm

Art is an implement of realisation in a universal sense and of self-discovery in the personal sense. Sculpture, for me, is compelling in the way it requires, paradoxically, that the complex quality of being, which is intangible and elusive, be given tangible form ... Instead of dreaming a dream it is like *making* a dream piece by piece ... like putting together a jigsaw puzzle whilst simultaneously inventing the picture ....

George Fullard[1]

Fullard's comments about the nature of art and sculpture provide a fitting introduction to his work. In his view, sculpture was about giving physical form to intangible things – the *making* of the dream. It was also part of a process of self-discovery. The analogy of the jigsaw puzzle is particularly apt given his use of assemblage in the 1960s. More importantly, the 'picture' which the artist was 'simultaneously inventing' might represent Fullard's own life as, for him, sculpture involved not only self-discovery, but also *re*covery of the self and one's personal past.

In the 1950s, John Berger recognised that Fullard's work was 'unusually and profoundly personal, yet at the same time unusually observant'.[2] Reviewing his memorial exhibition in 1974, another critic wrote that, to some, his idiosyncratic assemblages of the 1960s had been regarded as 'personal to the point of quirkiness'.[3] His work was certainly distinct from the celebrated abstract constructions of the 'New Generation' of sculptors of the mid-1960s. Although his sculpture was included in most of the important exhibitions of contemporary art of the decade, for many reasons, some of which will be explored in this study, his work was never fully appreciated in his lifetime and few works had been sold when he died. Following his earlier support of Fullard's work, in 1984 Berger looked back at the endeavours of a small group of artists, writers, poets and thinkers of the 1950s and commented pointedly: 'By intention, with imagination, and with clumsy anger and dreams of those who see what the privileged ignore, we were close to those without power. None more powerfully and poignantly than George Fullard whose exceptional work still awaits proper recognition.'[4]

In addressing Berger's plea, this study will explore the subjects, themes and techniques with which Fullard worked. On the surface, he clearly had distinct preoccupations: the human figure, war and, later, the sea and nautical objects. The changes of subject broadly correlate with the moves from modelling to assemblage and construction. However, to reduce his œuvre in this way, masks the real continuities and discontinuities in his work. Underlying the nominal subjects there were deeper and darker themes: survival, both as an artist and as a human being; a profound concern with the loss of innocence and the transition to adulthood; the inventiveness of the child, of the untutored, of the 'primitif'. His late works, although apparently simple, are surprisingly complex and enigmatic. These seascapes – or are they dreamscapes? – play with nostalgia and sentiment; their simplistic appearance disguises rather than displays. As ever, nothing is quite as it seems. These works are both intentionally ambiguous, and reflect the artist's own ambivalence: Fullard teases with double-meanings and wit but, at the same time, conveys an uneasy pensiveness and melancholy.

Biographical information may facilitate understanding of an artist's work but, equally, it can also obfuscate. In Fullard's case, there was a vital connection, a symbiotic relationship: the life and the art were inextricable. Intimacies, memories and experiences are woven into the details and minutiae of his sculpture in such a way that it becomes an exploration of personal history, neither as a sentimentalisation of the past nor as mere catharsis, but always with a strong sense of irony. Knowledge of the circumstances and events of the artist's life, therefore, is essential to understanding the work which in some instances takes on an almost narrative quality. The sculpture tells life-stories.

Other twentieth-century sculptors have been equally absorbed with the particularity of their own past: Louise Bourgeois, a sculptor admired by Fullard, has been described as an artist who 'returns compulsively to the past'.[5] Fullard shared the idea that art should draw on lived reality and experience – life rather than art should be the impetus. This link was emphatic

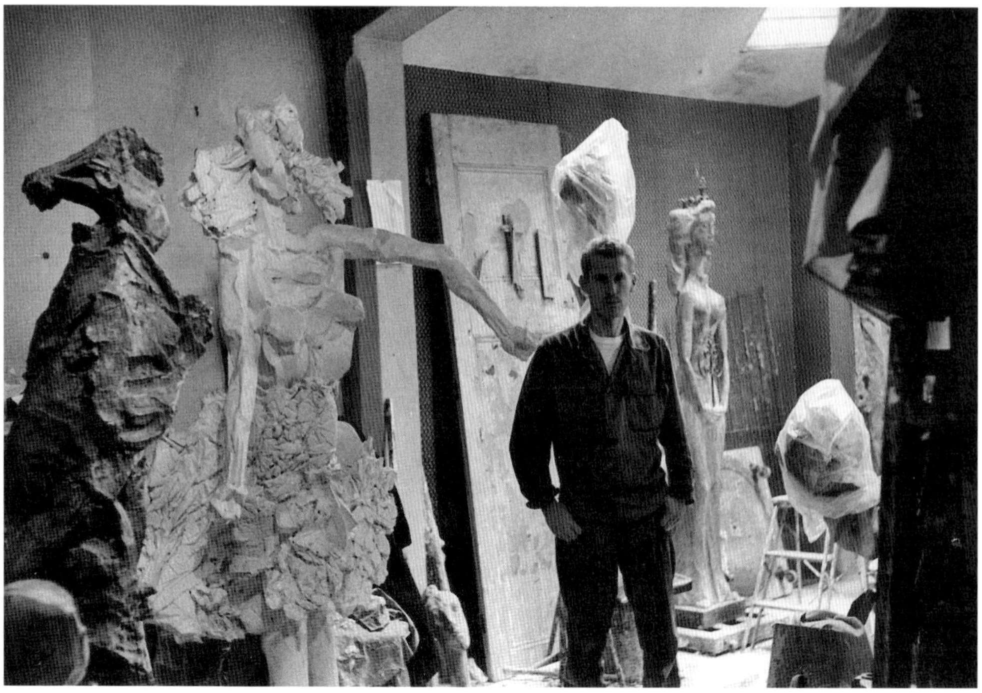

Plate 2
Fullard in his studio at Park Walk in May 1958 surrounded by various works. The plaster *Angry woman* 1958 (Cat.30) stands in the foreground.

in his work, his writings and his conversation: 'Forget the idea that Art is somehow inferior to Life. Art is Life. We live Art. That's what it's all about.'[6]

The individual artist has, historically, been given primacy in the writing of art history. The celebratory monograph which centres on the life and career of the artist has become something of a cliché. Proclaiming the 'death of the author', Roland Barthes constructed a critique which privileged the reader, or viewer, urging us to ignore the individual creator and concentrate on the work itself. Similarly, Michel Foucault famously declared 'what difference does it make who is speaking?'.[7] Whilst acknowledging that, of course, various interpretations can be brought to the sculpture which Fullard made, many other possible readings are lost to those who have no knowledge of the personal history of the artist. In an obituary, John Russell described Fullard as an artist who relived experiences from his own past which other people would perhaps have preferred to forget.[8] Fullard's own past, paradoxically, was a psychic present which he remade and recovered through his assemblages. Further, the self-conscious, purposeful nature of this aspect of his work must be kept in mind. We need to remember that Fullard saw himself, as he frequently remarked, as '*sculpting his own auto-biography*'.[9]

This survey of the artist and his work of necessity includes extensive biographical material. It also places his work in a critical context alongside that of contemporaries. Sculpture, like all other cultural practices and objects, is neither made nor received in a social or political vacuum. An awareness of the historical and political circumstances of the post-war period is vital to understanding the reception, production and exhibition of Fullard's work – for example, his associations with Social Realism in the Cold War and the effects of art history and art criticism historically dominated by a modernist view.

This study attempts a marriage of contextual narrative and critical analysis. Hopefully it will also serve as a belated tribute to an artist who, as Berger noted, deserves not only wider viewing but 'recognition' – with all the problems contained in that notion. This volume provides a place for revaluing an artist whose work continues to have relevance to us at the end of the twentieth century: a non-conformist, independent sculptor of diversity and idiosyncracy. A maverick absurdist who recognised a transcendence immanent in life's quotidian details.

NOTES

1. Unpublished notes by the artist, undated, probably mid-1960s, private collection.

2. J. Berger, 'George Fullard', *New Statesman*, 6 September 1958, Vol.56, No.1434, pp.274-6.

3. F. Crichton, 'London Letter', *Art International – The Lugano Review*, 15 November 1974, XVIII/9, p.37.

4. J. Berger in J. Spalding (ed.), *The Forgotten Fifties*, exh. cat. Sheffield 1984, p.46.

5. S. Morgan in S. Morgan and F. Morris, *Rites of Passage – Art for the End of the Century*, exh. cat. Tate Gallery, London 1995, p.54.

6. Comments reported to the author by Leslie Duxbury, painter and print-maker, fellow student at the Royal College of Art and lifelong friend of Fullard's; letter 23 May 1995.

7. See R. Barthes, 'The Death of the Author', (originally published 1968) in S. Heath (ed. and trans.), *Image, Music, Text – Roland Barthes*, 1977 and M. Foucault, 'What is an Author?', [1969] in P. Rabinow (ed.), *The Foucault Reader*, Harmondsworth 1984, p.120.

8. J. Russell, 'Mr George Fullard, sculptor of distinction' (obituary), *The Times*, 5 January 1974.

9. Author's discussions and correspondence with Irena Fullard, the artist's widow, 1995-8.

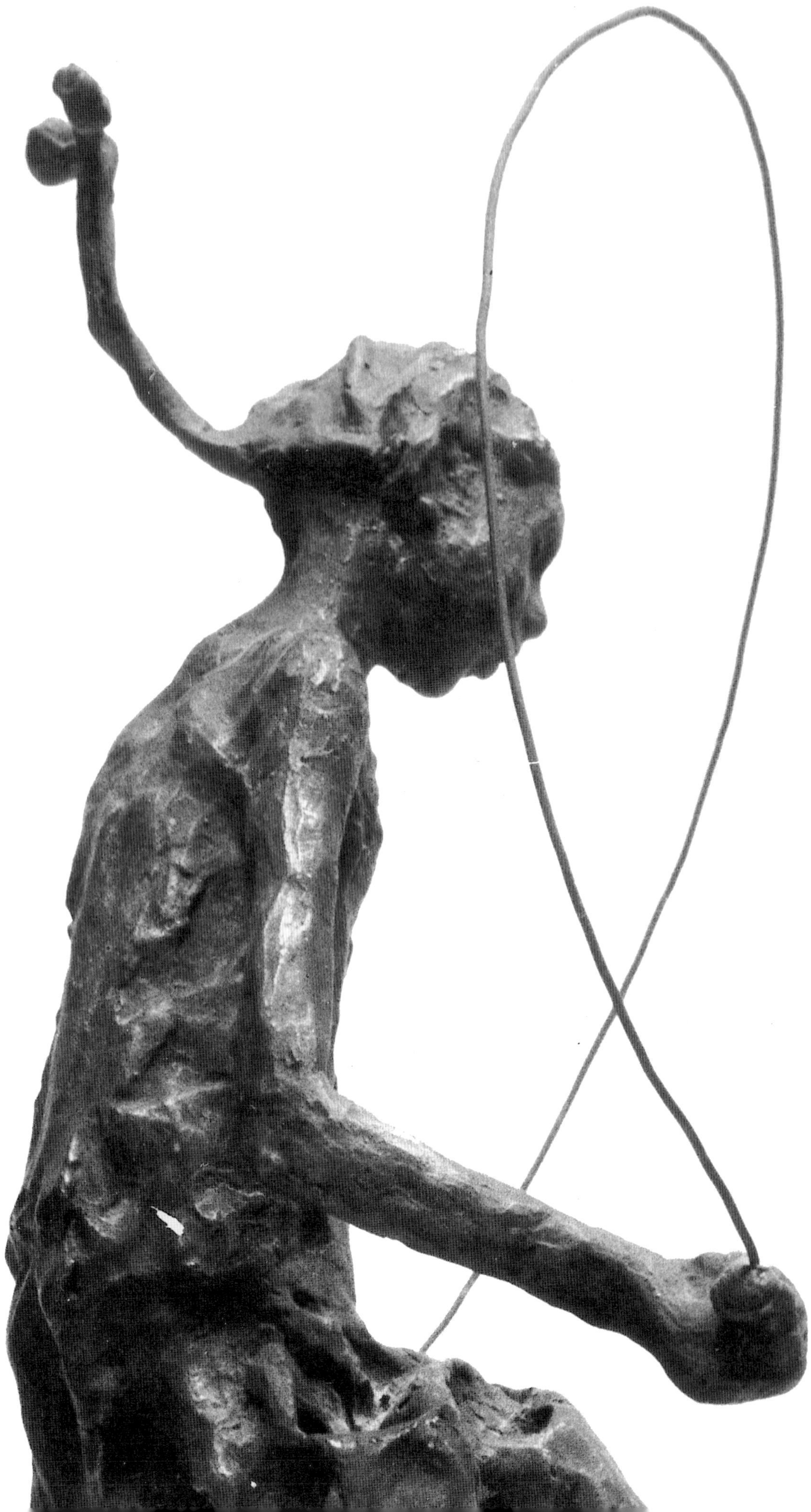

2

Early years and training 1923-47

Street games and remembrances

Plate 3 (Cat.15)
Skipping girl 1955 (detail)
Bronze (edition of three)
33.7 x 15.5 x 15 cm

As adults, we might look back to childhood days with fondness, nostalgia and yearning – to an essentially irretrievable time of innocence and freedom from responsibility. But growing into experience is bewildering and painful. Fullard closely identified with a particular generation of young people: those born between the two world wars. In 1959, in an occasional notebook he kept for jotting down ideas, he wrote of this generation as one caught 'between two fires', sometimes bewildered but unremittingly burdened with the tragedy and loss of both wars.

We are born as part of the tragic hangover of the First World War – the mysterious cataclysm that smote our elders. Mysterious because though recent to our own parents it was in the unknown void before our own life began. Era of war widows in church on Armistice Day. Legendary uncles killed at Ypres, Arras, the Somme and Paschendale [sic]. Stories of Mespot, Zeppelin raids, Richthofen's flying circus. Fathers with wound scars and souvenirs – medals fading on ribbons. That was the spirit of fascinating past just beyond our grasp.[1]

His later artistic preoccupation with war resulted not only from his own direct experiences but also from the strange mixture of fascination and grief felt for the older generation's involvement in a more distant war. Family war stories of horror and heroism were integrated into the everyday games of his youth and later informed his artwork too.

His sculpture shows a preoccupation with childhood: many of the war assemblages refer to games or infancy in their titles and images. They draw on the view that innocence was lost forever after the mass slaughter of young men in the First World War. Fullard felt – as had Baudelaire, Rilke and Klee – that children had a special kind of inventiveness and creativity, to which an artist should aspire. In Fullard's late 'sea series', a childlike vision predominates and many of these works have titles which relate to the nature of temporality and, implicitly, the process of ageing. They also relate specifically to his own childhood. In one of his last interviews, when asked about these works, Fullard recalled the time when, as a child, he felt that he was 'free to play 50 parts in one morning, to fly, to sail'.[2] The time and place of his own youth evidently held special significance for the artist. What is more, the events and circumstances of his early life profoundly influenced Fullard's work. Most importantly, by 1945, he had a store of images and experiences on which he continued to draw until his death in 1973.

George Fullard was born on 15 September 1923, the youngest of six children. The family lived in Darnall, a working-class district in Sheffield, largely occupied by coal-miners and steel-workers. Although in 1934, the Fullards moved to a council development a little way out of the city, it was to the backyards of his earlier childhood that he later referred. The physical nature of this built environment had made a strong impression on Fullard. On being interviewed in 1963, he described his boyhood as 'like living in a sculpture'.[3]

Recollections of childhood games and of life in the terraces inform his later sculpture. *War game* 1962 incorporates, on one side, a backdoor and steps, and on the other, something resembling a fireplace. In this work, Fullard combines two potent symbols of working-class life – the scrubbed steps and the family hearth – encapsulating the dignified struggle to maintain a clean, warm home regardless of low wages and poor living conditions. Whilst it is a sculptural caricature of a 'back-to-back' dwelling it might also have been inspired by the bombed-out streets of the 1940 *blitzkrieg* – an instant playground for a child's game of hide-and-seek.

In an environment where individual privacy was rare, the labyrinthine 'closes' of the east end of Sheffield provided the main space for social activity, whether entertainment, play, work, petty crime or just for the passing of time. The idea of 'street life' – with all its implications of class and social background – was especially important to Fullard and it affected his character and concerns as an artist. Popular cultural activities and his early memories of such experiences meant a lot to him: in an occasional notebook, he had jotted the words 'cinema', 'toys' and 'gangs' among a page of notes headed 'my cultural background'.[4] He maintained a predisposition for *kitsch* which perhaps came out most of all in his love of popular songs. The trite banalities of such songs held a tacky charm and raw truth. The engagement with 'real life' was something he emphasised repeatedly, frequently stressing that, as far as he was concerned, those people who had not spent their childhood on the street 'lacked reality'. For him, they remained 'beings of another race …'.[5] His social background played a crucial part in the make-up of his own artistic sensibility.

Fullard's early student sketchbooks feature typical street scenes: one drawing shows a young boy entranced by a street fiddler, a wash drawing of the old 'rag market' area of Sheffield depicts a busking duo – a flautist and banjo-player. Another drawing shows a group of drunks propping each other up by a lamp-post.

Trade union militancy and communist politics were an integral part of Fullard's early family life. His father, a coal-miner, was well-known locally as a political agitator and a communist who had played an active role in the 1926 General Strike. His activities brought serious financial problems to the family as he was blacklisted for organising a strike of pit deputies in 1934. Despite

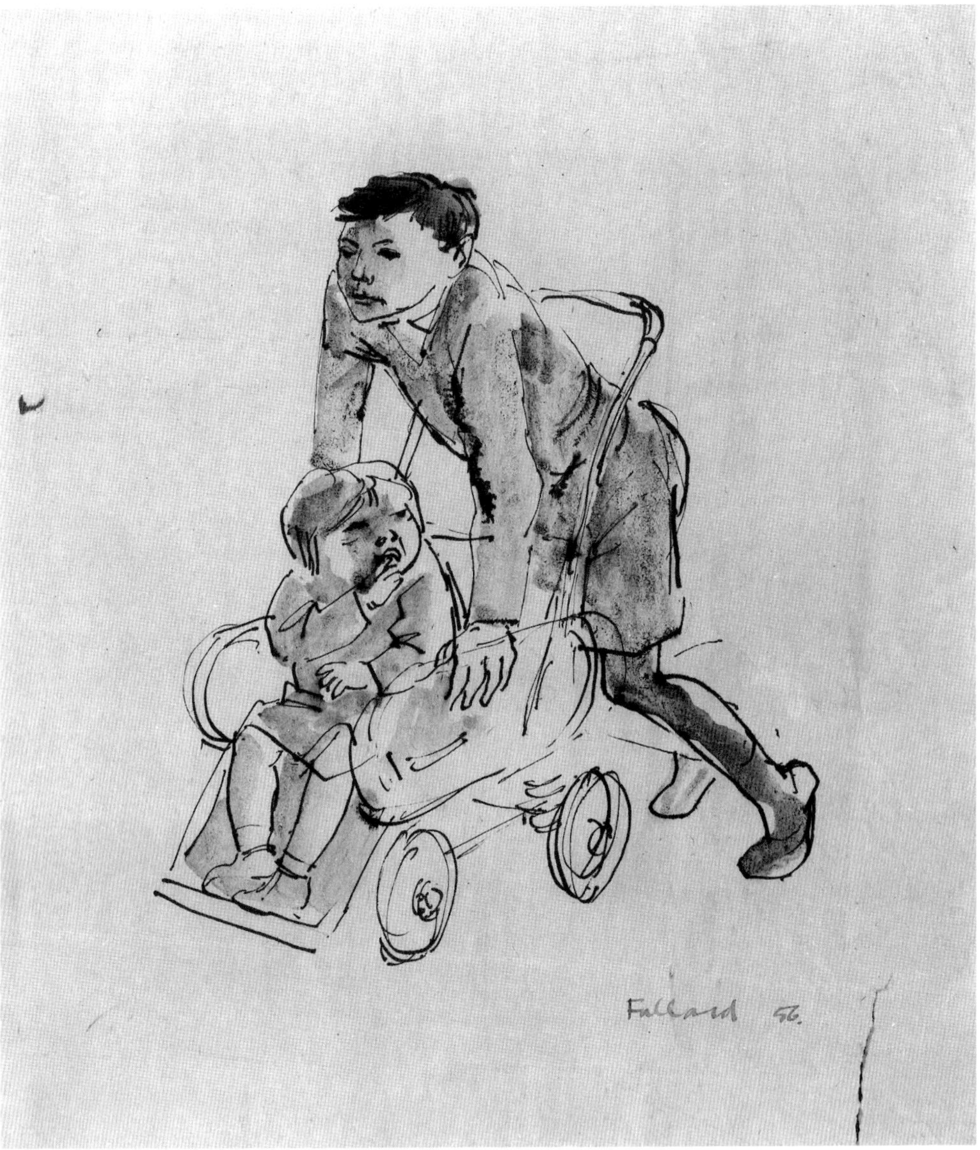

Plate 4
Boy with pushchair 1956
Ink on paper
Private collection

having little formal education, Fullard senior wrote book reviews and articles for the socialist press, such as *Tribune* and the *Left Review*, and, just before the war, submitted a novel of working-class life to the publisher Victor Gollancz. He also wrote a number of 'agit-prop' plays which were performed locally. The dialogue in the plays expresses the dignity, resilience and humour of working-class life; all qualities which surface in Fullard's sculpture of the 1950s and 1960s.[6]

His family's involvement in communist politics was not unusual, given that mass unemployment and poverty were key issues in Sheffield in the 1930s and, further, that the local party was noted for the strength of its organisation. However, the Italian invasion of Abyssinia in 1935 and the Spanish Civil War galvanised anti-fascist feeling and spurred Fullard to become active in the youth wing of the local party branch. Growing up in an atmosphere of militant anti-capitalism affected his work in a number of ways, contributing to his frequently expressed view that, as an artist, integrity and commitment to one's work were fundamental values. An expectation of comradeship and loyalty also informed Fullard's later work as a teacher.

Politics may also have provided Fullard's introduction to art. He was probably more familiar with the George Grosz-like satirical cartoons in the *Daily Worker* or the *Left Review* than with more traditional art-historical 'masters'. These periodicals commonly featured satirical illustrations by the three James's: Boswell, Fitton and Holland, or the graphics of radical artists such as Frans Masereel.[7] Nevertheless, it seems that a perceptive Headteacher at the Darnall Church School recognised Fullard's artistic abilities and persuaded him to apply for the Sheffield College of Arts and Crafts, which he entered in 1937, as a full-time Junior student.

The work which has survived from Fullard's time at Sheffield College of Arts and Crafts shows a flair for rapid line drawings and an empathy with life on the streets. His sketchbooks are, significantly, full of images of ordinary people going about their everyday business – miners walking to and from work, children playing, harassed mothers, boys wheeling prams of junk. Some of these images recur in the figures he modelled in the 1950s and in his early wooden assemblages of *objets trouvés*. Fullard's *Woman with flowers* of 1959-60 echoes an earlier drawing of a second-hand furniture dealer, or pawnbroker, with his jumble of piled-up wooden chairs, tables, wardrobes, picture frames and mirrors.[8]

Importantly for Fullard, the inter-relationship of art and war dates from his time at Sheffield College. The declaration of war was made in an atmosphere of increasing tension and anxiety among the student population. After the bombing of the college buildings in the *blitz* on Sheffield in December 1940, students were placed on 'Home Service' and met in small groups around the city to work on various projects designed to contribute their artistic skills to the war effort. Notably, Fullard's sketchbooks document a war-damaged city. Fire-fighters, soldiers and bomb-site debris were frequent subjects. Fullard's interest in the place of the 'insignificant' figure caught up in historic events remained a constant through to his later work.

The final, and most important, event of this period was Fullard's direct experience of war on active service in Italy. Having gained a place at the Royal College of Art in 1942, Fullard enlisted as a trooper in the 17/21st Lancers, a mechanised cavalry regiment. Following several months training at Robertville in Algeria, the regiment was involved in the protracted battles for Monte Cassino in Italy. The monastery was taken on 18 May 1944.[9] However, the following day, as forces advanced to break through the Adolf Hitler Line, Fullard's Sherman tank took a direct hit from a German shell. With a severely damaged shoulder, chest injuries and serious head wounds, it was thought unlikely that he would survive. After months of convalescence, he recovered nevertheless, and was invalided out of the army.[10]

Fullard considered a range of options on leaving his regiment. He briefly thought of becoming involved full-time in politics. Undoubtedly, his social concerns and political sympathies were just as important to him after the war and, indirectly, informed his work. However, he never resumed his involvement in organised politics to the same extent, believing that he could achieve more through his artwork than he could through any formal political connections.[11]

The artist's own experience of war had been both formative and individually traumatic. The circumstances of his survival took on an immense, almost mythic, significance. When, in 1959, Patrick Hayman invited Fullard to write an article about making sculpture, he chose to entitle it 'Sculpture and Survival', describing how a completed work is not merely made, but rather that, '... it emerges as a survivor out of a phase of action ...'.[12]

Fullard's experience of war was intensely private yet universally that of a generation caught 'between two fires'. He survived yet remained preoccupied. This is evident most of all in the drawings and assemblages of the 1960s in which he explored images and ideas which directly relate to war.

Fullard's relationship to his childhood and youth was complex. The outward circumstances of his life suggest that he was clearly able to leave the past behind physically and socially: he never considered returning to Sheffield to live or work, he had no particular contact with regimental veterans and never revisited Italy.[13] One might suggest that he had no need to return. His awareness of social class, memories of street politics, a strong identification with family history, a fascination with childhood games and the war – all these had shaped a vocabulary readily accessible to the mature artist. Yet there is an ambivalence about Fullard's relationship to his own past. He was a metropolitan artist not a localist and, whilst remaining emphatically rooted in his own biography, he could always ironise his past with panache and urbanity.

Ambleside to Kensington

Fullard was part of a unique generation of students who, as a result of the war, studied during a period of transition and upheaval. After his war service he took up his place at the Royal College of Art in January 1945. In particular, he witnessed both the rural isolation of the exiled Royal College in Ambleside and, subsequently, its post-war return to London.[14] This left a legacy for his later work and for his personal life. At the RCA, Fullard developed his interest in the human figure and his exceptional modelling abilities with clay – though, paradoxically, the latter increasingly proved a source of frustration. Also, these years held special significance as Fullard formed lasting relationships with a number of fellow students, and later shared houses and studios with various ex-RCA painters and sculptors, some of whom became staff colleagues at Chelsea School of Art in the 1960s.

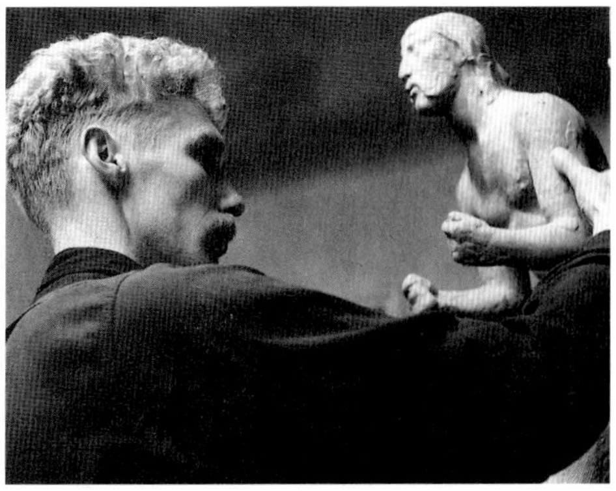

Plate 5
Fullard modelling a work, probably while at the Royal College of Art.

Following the bombing of the RCA buildings in London, the whole establishment had decamped to Ambleside in 1940 for the duration of the war. Whilst some students were inspired by the rural surroundings, others felt miserably isolated and were acutely aware of how remote they were from libraries, galleries and museums. In 1943, *Picture Post* featured an article about the college, dispelling the idea of it as an 'artistic idyll'.

> Here among the lakes is the ideal setting for an artist. The quiet atmosphere of lovely tranquil things and beautiful surroundings, material at hand and in abundance to sketch ... but the disadvantages of this exile far outweigh these considerations. The equipment at [the students'] disposal is often inferior and makeshift. Everyone suffers from lack of outside stimulus and competition.[15]

The reporter noted that the student population was largely made up of women and ex-servicemen, most of whom had been demobilised or discharged from the forces as invalids.[16] Many, like Fullard, had to cope with the physical and psychological effects of recent frontline fighting and the transition from parade ground to student life is evidenced in the memoirs of Arthur Berry, a fellow Ambleside student who became one of Fullard's closest friends. According to Berry, Fullard quickly acquired a reputation for talking at length about life, politics and art:

> I usually sat at a table with students from the Sculpture School. One of these was a young, blonde-haired, blue-eyed, ex-tank soldier, George Fullard. He was the leader of the group and was fierce in his opinions and at that time a great admirer of Rodin, and through his conversations I was introduced to the world of sculpture and the conflict between Rodin and Maillol ...[17]

The sculptural polarities embodied by the work of Maillol and Rodin had engaged artists and students since the turn of the century. The expressive handling in works by Rodin, such as *Tête d'Iris* and the *Gates of Hell*, especially appealed to Fullard who was not attracted by the stark heavy classical feel of Maillol's figures. Fullard's admiration of Rodin persisted, directly influencing, in particular, a later series of large modelled heads made around 1960. At Chelsea, Fullard urged students to study Rodin's work and, when the distinguished Rodin scholar, Albert Elsen, lectured there in the 1960s, it was one of the few occasions on which Fullard categorically demanded that students attend.[18]

Plate 6
The wood-carving class at the Royal College of Art in 1946. Fullard is working on the female figure at the front right with Ernest Adsetts sharing the bench.

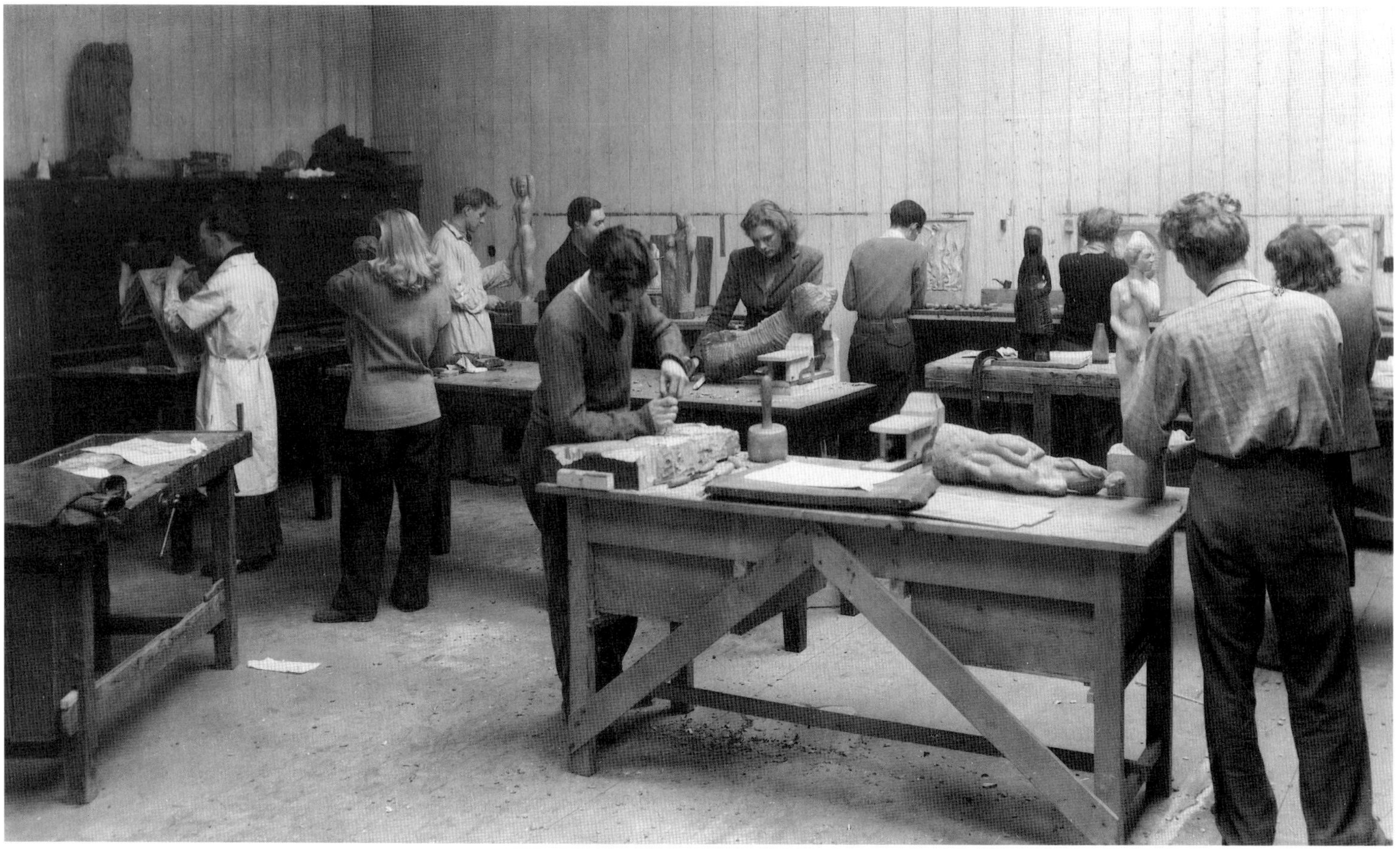

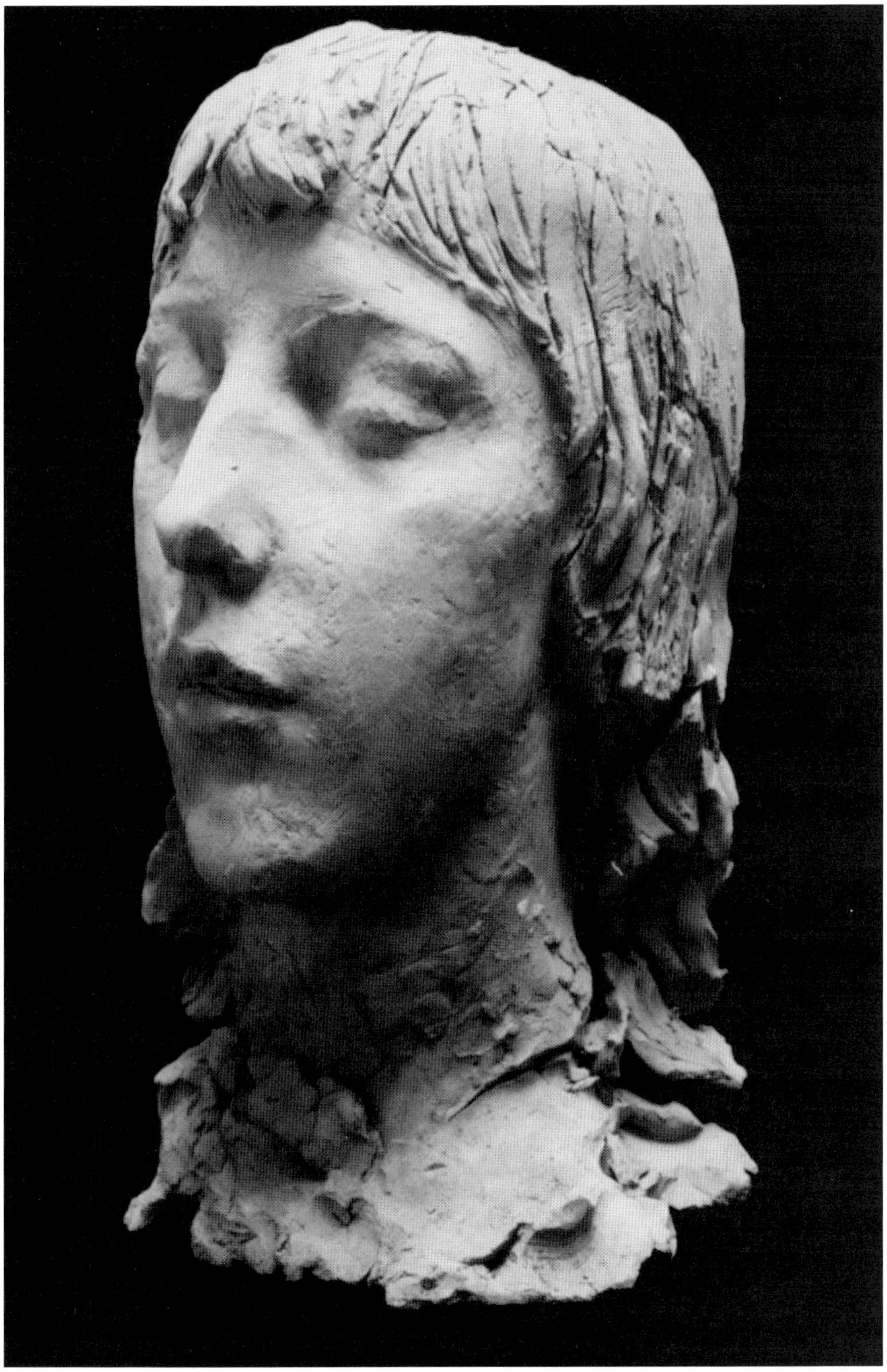

Plate 7 (Cat.1)
Female head 1947
Clay
34.3 cm (height)

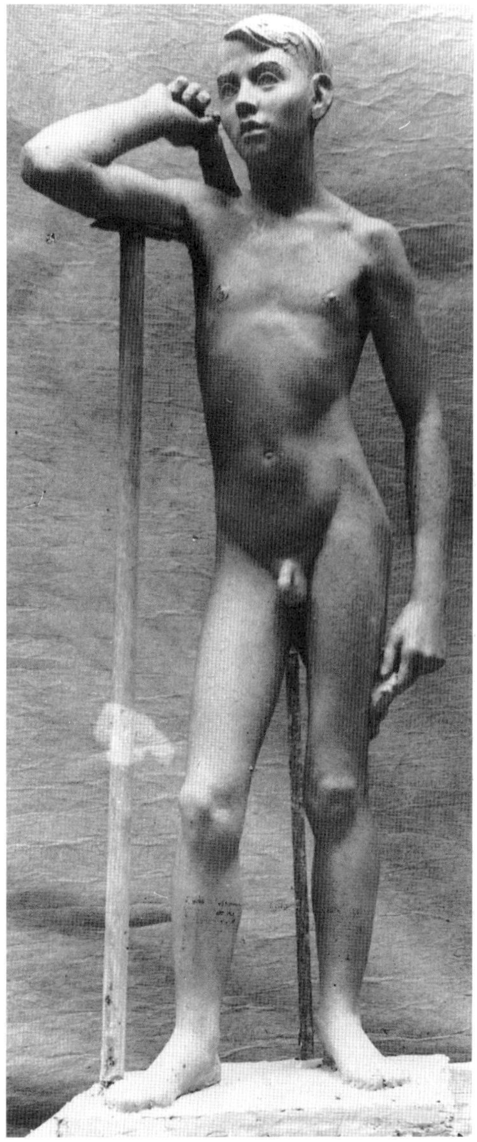

Plate 8 (Cat.2)
Young bather 1947
Clay
Dimensions unknown

Whilst Ambleside students debated the relative merits of Rodin or Maillol, it seems that interest in more contemporary European developments in art was not particularly encouraged as, according to Berry and Duxbury, the staff in the Sculpture School largely ignored the work of their own century. Ironically, one of the leaders of the European avant-garde, Kurt Schwitters, had sought refuge in Ambleside and was working on his final *Merzbau* in the mid-1940s.[19] However, the war had severely restricted information about other artists, shortages had curtailed publications and there were few exhibitions by major contemporary European artists until after 1945.[20] It is likely, therefore, that few RCA students, including Fullard, would have been aware of Schwitters' significance anyway.

The Sculpture School did, however, provide Fullard with an opportunity to develop his earlier interest in the human figure, as prospectuses for the Ambleside period show that this was the central focus. Professor Richard Garbe, a frequent exhibitor of work in horn and ivory at the Royal Academy, headed the School, assisted by Herbert W. Palliser, sculptor in stone and bronze. Besides modelling in clay, students were instructed in casting and pointing techniques and, highlighting the 'progressive' character, prospectuses expressly noted that carving, in marble, stone and wood, was as an 'integral part of the course'.[21]

The return to London in 1946 meant that students at least had access to museums, libraries and galleries but accommodation in the ramshackle college huts on Exhibition Road was, for many students, distinctly less inspiring than Ambleside. Indeed, Christopher Frayling has described the college as having 'the depressing atmosphere of a down-at-heel ivory tower'.[22] Susan Parkinson, a sculpture student in Fullard's year, recalls being instructed in techniques, and in surroundings, that would have been more suited to the 1890s.

> In those days the women's life room was separate from the men's, which seemed to be full of fountains and things, covered in dolphins etc.... I thought I had come to the leading edge of modern sculpture and here we were in the mid 19th century – the Albert Memorial would have been at home inside there instead of across the road in the Park ...[23]

In 1946, Garbe retired and was replaced, on Henry Moore's recommendation, by Frank Dobson. Although the focus on the human figure remained, separate drawing classes ended and a more relaxed working environment was created, in which students and teachers could exchange ideas informally. Dobson welcomed students to his studio where Moore and Epstein were frequent visitors.[24]

Unfortunately, all the sculpture which Fullard made at the RCA has been lost or destroyed but the photograph of *The young bather*, dated 1947, a life-size clay figure made for his RCA diploma, shows a finely modelled classical subject. His talent for modelling won Fullard a three-month travel scholarship to Paris where, in 1947, he spent much of the time studying the work of Rodin.[25] It also enabled him to take on various artistic projects of a more 'commercial' character into the 1950s, often with the assistance of 'Jock' Stewart, Ernest Adsetts and Leslie Duxbury, all ex-Ambleside students.[26] Signally, Fullard

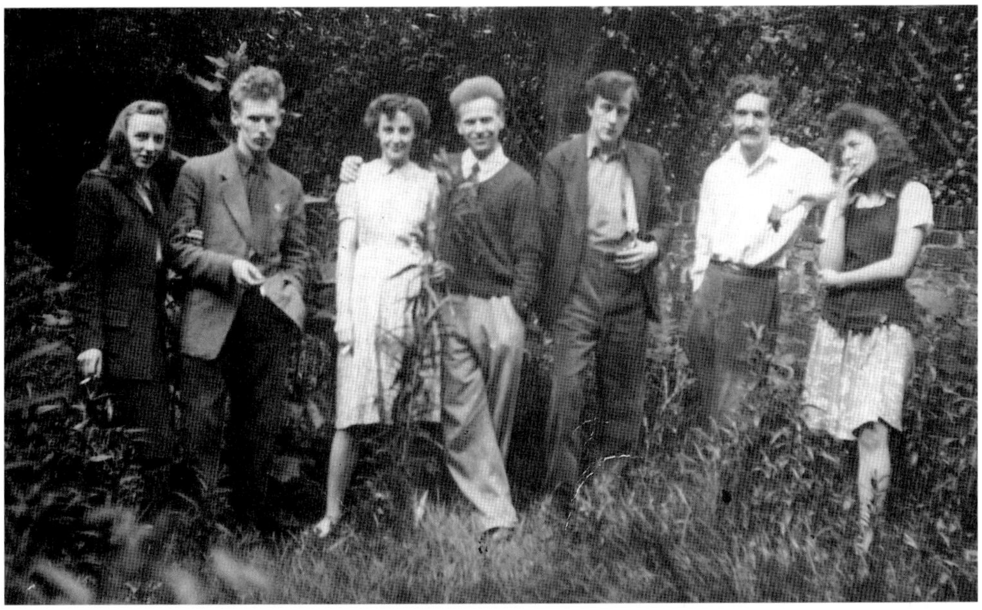

Plate 9
Some of the residents in the garden at Pembroke Road in 1946. From left to right: Irena Fullard (née Corcoran), George Fullard, Joan Dudley, Geoff Dudley, Arthur Berry, Leslie Duxbury, Erica Porter.

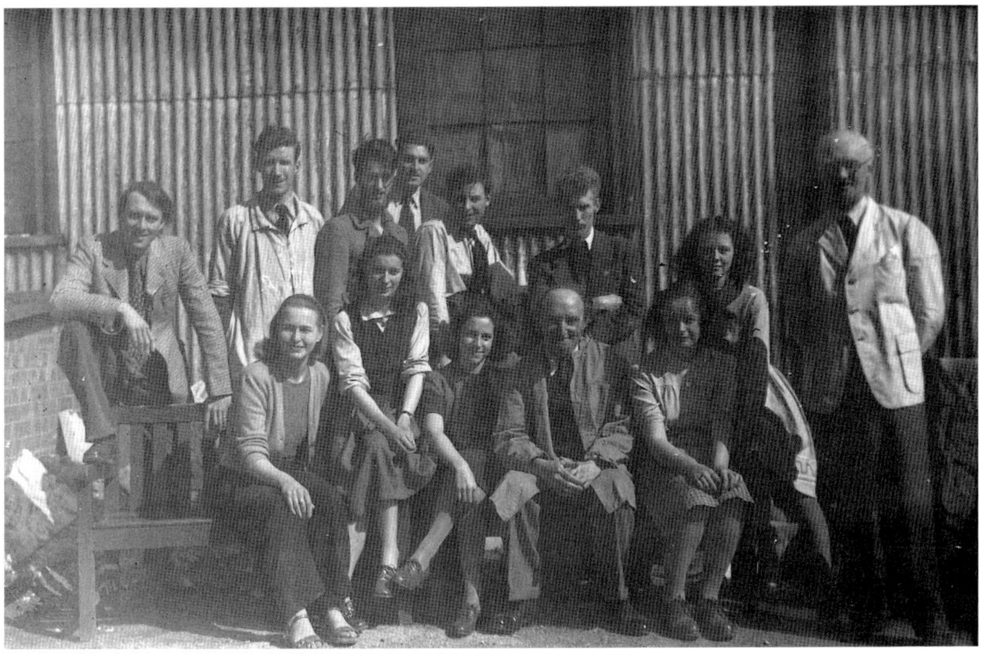

Plate 10
Students at the Royal College of Art in South Kensington. Fullard is standing behind Frank Dobson (seated centre-front) with Herbert W. Palliser standing on the far right. Sculptor Douglas Wain-Hobson, is the third from the left.

later felt that such technical skill and facility came to be a hindrance rather than an asset. Leslie Duxbury comments:

> George's talent was obvious. He was a fluent draughtsman and a superb modeller, hard-won … by tremendous hard work and awesome concentration. His facility bothered him throughout his career. He would try to stem this apparent easiness by using recalcitrant media and methods, even working with one hand only – the wrong one. And in the end he realised it didn't matter, it was just something he had to work through.[27]

According to Duxbury, Fullard was more impressed, in this period, by the work of older students, Douglas Wain-Hobson and Arnold Machin in particular, than by Garbe or Dobson. Dobson's work had sympathy with 'classical' sculpture and students have recalled his distinct disdain for the 'baroque', represented for him, by Rodin: a view with which Fullard is unlikely to have accorded. However, Dobson's influence was strong and others have remarked on the way in which sculptors subsequently fought to resist his style – including Fullard.[28] In some of Fullard's early work, since destroyed, one can detect a familarity with the modernised classicism of Dobson's terracotta work.

Being part of the exiled generation of art students, whose experiences were shaped by war in various ways, encouraged a kind of camaraderie among those who graduated at the end of the 1940s. In 1946, Fullard married Irena Corcoran, a former design student, and moved into a dilapidated property in Pembroke Road which they had acquired from an insurance company for a peppercorn rent on the understanding that they would repair the extensive bomb damage. Various Ambleside veterans, along with a number of other RCA students, lived and worked there for a couple of years.[29]

At the RCA Fullard's early interest in ordinary people and street life as subjects for drawing developed into a sculptural preoccupation. Although he later preferred to work from memory and rarely drew from life, he always found the human figure a limitless source of inspiration – 'in sculpture an inescapable challenge'.[30]

Whilst some of his later assemblages include pieces of roughly hand-carved wood, the idea of carving – in the vein of the 'truth to materials' school of the 1930s – had little appeal for Fullard or, indeed, many of his generation. Respectful rejection was, perhaps, an inevitable process for young sculptors under the shadow of Moore who was acclaimed as a national public figure after the war. Yet, despite viewing his own technical facility in modelling as a hindrance, Fullard nevertheless revelled in the freedom which clay offered and expressly commented on this in his writing.[31]

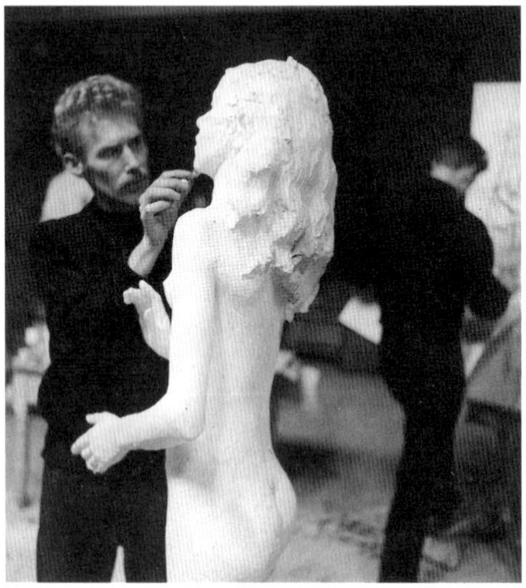

Plate 11
Fullard working on *Young girl* 1954-5 (Cat.14) at Fawcett Yard studio with Derrick Greaves in the background.

Overall, Fullard may have absorbed more than he rejected from his time at the Royal College. Later, however, he expressed little faith in the whole notion of 'learning' to be an artist. He maintained a deep respect for craftsmanship and skill but, fundamentally, he believed that becoming an artist could not be achieved through 'training'. Paradoxically, given his leading position at Chelsea in the 1960s, he was of the view that art-school training was insignificant and inconsequential when set beside the realities and experiences of life.

Fittingly, although he spent many hours studying Rodin's sculpture during the 1947 French sojourn, Fullard's own Paris drawings show a return to the 'streets' and 'real life'. His sketches of an old woman begging on the pavement and the two workers, with their berets and satchels, perusing political street posters bear witness to a continuing preoccupation with the quotidian.[32] There is an economy of line, a confidence about the fluidity but these figures could easily have been the miners he drew in Sheffield ten years earlier.

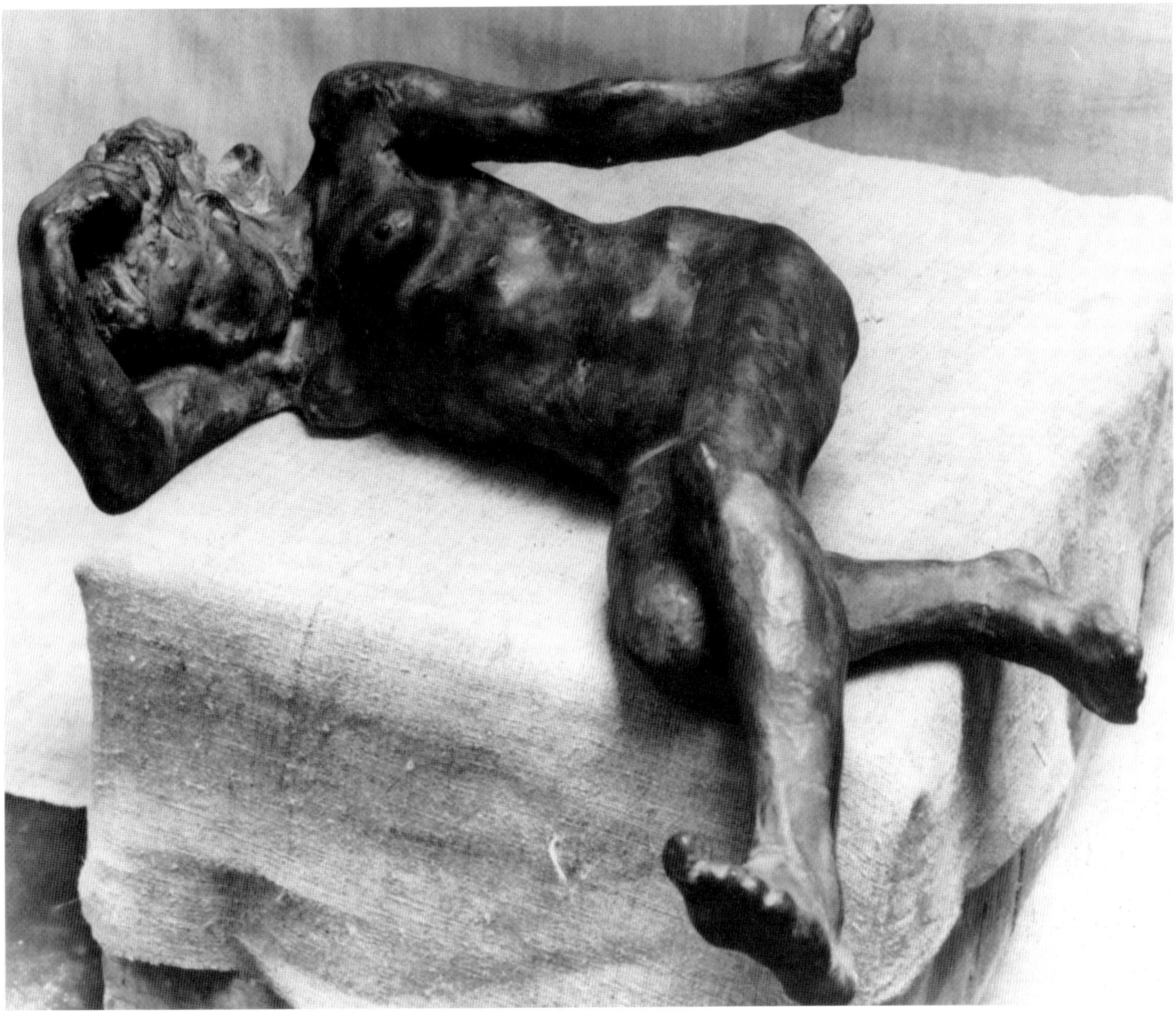

Plate 12 (Cat.4)
Reclining nude 1947
Plaster
Dimensions unknown

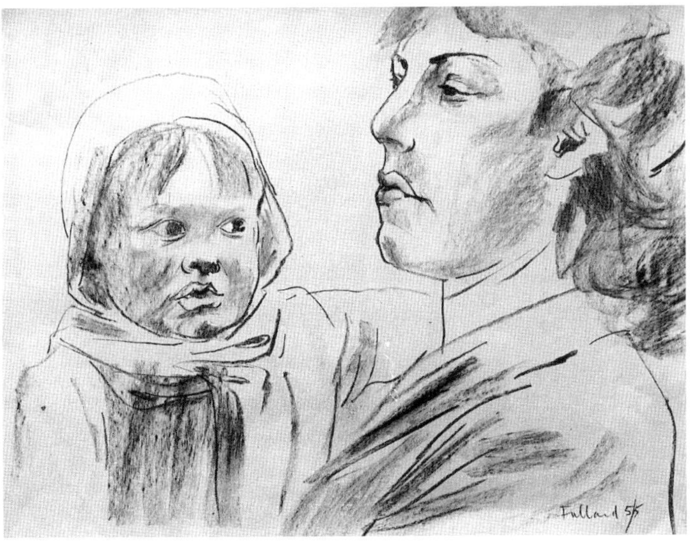

Plate 13
Mother and child 1955
Charcoal on paper
Private collection

NOTES

Information about the artist's early life has been gathered through discussions and correspondence of the author with a number of individuals, in particular Irena Fullard, Colin Fullard, Hettie Tomlinson, Neville Strong, Jim Richardson 1995-8. Also see Betty Hunt Papers, University of Sheffield archive; Local History Department, City Library, Sheffield; J. Spalding, *George Fullard Drawings*, exh. cat. London 1982; D. Alston, *George Fullard – Student to Sculptor*, exh. broadsheet, Graves Art Gallery, Sheffield 1993.

1. Notes by George Fullard, dated 23 September 1959 in private collection. One of Fullard's uncles was killed in the 1914-18 war; his father enlisted in 1915, was wounded at Ypres and demobilised in late 1918.

2. *Observer*, 2 January 1972.

3. C. S. Spencer, 'Sculptor in search of the labyrinth, George Fullard' in *Studio International*, July 1963, Vol.166, No.843, pp.8-9.

4. Notes by George Fullard, dated 1959 in private collection.

5. Comment is quoted from notes made by Irena Fullard, dated February 1985. The popular songs of the 1930s and 1940s were later important for Fullard; George Formby was a particular favourite. Students, colleagues and friends were familiar with Fullard's 'repertoire' and he would often instigate singing sessions at Chelsea. Also, he was an avid fan of American films of the period – 'gangster movies' and the 'western' genre had a special appeal. Author's discussions with Chris Yetton, Phyllida Barlow, Derrick Greaves, 1995-8 and correspondence with Steve Hurst 1996-7. The author has also had access to an audio-tape of the 'Chelsea Sound', a tape-recording of a session of singing, led by Fullard, made in the early 1970s.

6. George Fullard senior's plays centred on the problems of tenants in squalid housing with profiteering landlords and the hazardous working conditions created by private coalmine-owners. His three act play, *Clogs*, was performed in December 1938 at the Montgomery Theatre in Sheffield by the Left Theatre Club; the cast included two of his sons.

7. The *Daily Worker* and *Left Review* (1934-8) were regularly read in the Fullard household. Frans Masereel, a Belgian artist-member of the Association of Revolutionary Artists and Writers, was internationally renowned for his graphic work such as the posters and leaflets he designed for the Spanish Republican cause.

8. Access to Fullard's student sketchbooks and drawings is available through the multi-media CD-ROM project, *Complexity and Contradiction*, a project based at Hallam University, Sheffield.

9. For a general account of the regiment's part in the battle see F. Majdalany, *Cassino – Portrait of a Battle*, London 1957 and Lt Col R. L.V. ffrench Blake DSO, *The 17/21st Lancers 1759-1993*, London 1993. The trooper's viewpoint has been informed by the author's correspondence with R. Butler and J. Clements, both 17/21st veterans.

10. Regimental records show that Fullard was wounded on 19 May 1944. One of Fullard's closest friends, a wireless operator, gave an eye-witness account of the surprise attack on the tank-crew who were dismounting from the vehicle at the time. Fullard was partly through the turret cupola hatchway when the gun mantelet was struck. Letter, dated 22 June 1997, to the author from R. H. Waites who served in the same squadron as Fullard.

11. Fullard and Neville Strong joined others in action to support squatters in Sheffield, demonstrating against the lack of homes. In 1946, Fullard was involved in similar actions in Holland Park, London when attempts were made to evict squatters from apartments in Kensington. He later made drawings (now in private collection) of demonstrators being confronted by mounted policeman at this event. Discussions with Irena Fullard and Neville Strong 1995-6.

12. George Fullard, 'Sculpture and Survival', *The Painter and Sculptor*, summer 1959, Vol.2, No.2, pp.9-12.

13. There is some evidence that Fullard may have been planning to return to Monte Cassino as, while in hospital just before he died, he expressed such a wish: author's discussion with Frank Monaco 1996.

14. R. Woof (ed.), *The Artist as Evacuee – The Royal College of Art in the Lake District 1940-45*, exh. cat. The Wordsworth Trust 1987 provides useful information and commentary on this period.

15. *Picture Post*, 3 July 1943; also see various newspaper cuttings in the Royal College of Art archive, including one from the *Cumberland and Westmorland Herald*, 26 February 1944 which reports on Percy Jowett's BBC radio broadcast about the RCA experience in Ambleside.

16. In January 1945, Fullard was fit enough to begin studies at the RCA – though with a permanently damaged left shoulder which impeded him throughout his life. In a letter (Royal Academy of Arts archive) dated 6 April 1957, to Paul Hogarth, Fullard mentioned his physical difficulties: 'a slight case of anti-tank shell altered my left arm to something resembling a cork-screw which however useful for opening bottles is useless for weight-lifting and any that is necessary in the course of my work, I achieve by cunning, patience, levers and ropes and a quiet prayer to God.'

17. Arthur Berry, *A Three and Sevenpence Halfpenny Man*, Kermase, Staffs 1986, p.180. Berry, painter, poet and playwright, was a visiting lecturer at Chelsea School of Art in the 1960s, with a reputation among friends and students as a raconteur.

18. Author's interviews with Brian Ord (March 1996), Ian Welsh (February 1997) and Kay MacLaren (December 1997), former sculpture students at Chelsea School of Art. Fullard also held the work of Donatello in high regard.

19. In a letter to the author, dated 23 May 1995, Leslie Duxbury confirmed Berry's view and noted that students were unaware of the presence of Kurt Schwitters (1887-1948). Interestingly, in 1984 the inaugural exhibition of the newly refurbished Hatton Gallery at the University of Newcastle upon Tyne featured a reconstruction of Schwitters' *Merzbau* (known as his *Merz barn*) from Ambleside alongside a major retrospective of Fullard's work.

20. Art collections in London and provincial towns had been removed for safety during the war. One of the first major exhibitions of 'moderns' in London came in 1946 with the Matisse and Picasso shows. They had a huge impact, attracting crowds of viewers. Duxbury has noted, in a letter to the author, 23 May 1995, that they set students 'arguing for days and nights'. Also see A. Bowness, *Painting, Sculpture and Drawing in Britain 1940-49*, exh. cat. Whitechapel Art Gallery, London 1972.

21. Royal College of Art Prospectus 1939/40 and abridged prospectus for 1945/6, Royal College of Art archive. 'Direct carving' had, of course, been associated primarily with the modernist sculptor, Henry Moore, but, by the 1930s, Garbe had made a considerable contribution to the acceptance of carved sculpture at the Royal Academy and clearly wanted to encourage and train young sculptors at the RCA in carving as well as in modelling and casting techniques. See B. Read, *Sculpture in Britain Between the Wars*, exh. cat. The Fine Arts Society, London 1986.

22. C. Frayling, *The Royal College of Art – One Hundred and Fifty Years of Art and Design*, London 1987, p.128.

23. Letter, 11 January 1997, to the author from Susan Parkinson, fellow sculpture student.

24. N. Jason, *The Sculpture of Frank Dobson*, London 1994, pp.96-100.

25. Fullard and his wife Irena, stayed in an attic room at Hôtel d'Alsace. Fullard spent a lot of time studying Rodin's work first-hand at Hôtel Biron. Other visits were made to the Louvre, Jeu de Paume, Vézelay and Chartres. Letters to the author from Irena Fullard, November/December 1997.

26. See later – '**"Famously unacceptable" – sculpting in a Cold Climate**'.

27. Letter, 23 May 1995, to the author from Leslie Duxbury.

28. Author's discussion with John Mills, March 1997. Mills, who taught sculpture with Fullard at St Albans School of Art at the end of the 1950s, had studied at the RCA.

29. Residents at Pembroke Road included Frederick Brill (taught at Chelsea 1947-79), Geoff Dudley (taught sculpture at Chelsea and took over Headship after Fullard), Ernest Adsetts (a native of Sheffield who had attended the Sheffield College of Arts and Crafts), Sydney Birnie 'Jock' Stewart, Annesley Tittensor, Arthur Berry (visiting lecturer at Chelsea), Leslie Duxbury and Irena Corcoran (who married Fullard July 1946). From a slightly later RCA generation were two other Sheffield-born artists, Derrick Greaves (*b.*1927) and Jack Smith (*b.*1928 – also taught at Chelsea).

30. George Fullard, 'Sculpture and Survival', *The Painter and Sculptor*, summer 1959, Vol.2, No.2, p.9.

31. See later – '**Transcripts of writings by George Fullard, 5 Working with clay**'.

32. A series of Fullard's Paris drawings are among items in the Tate Gallery Archive, Ref. TGA 752.

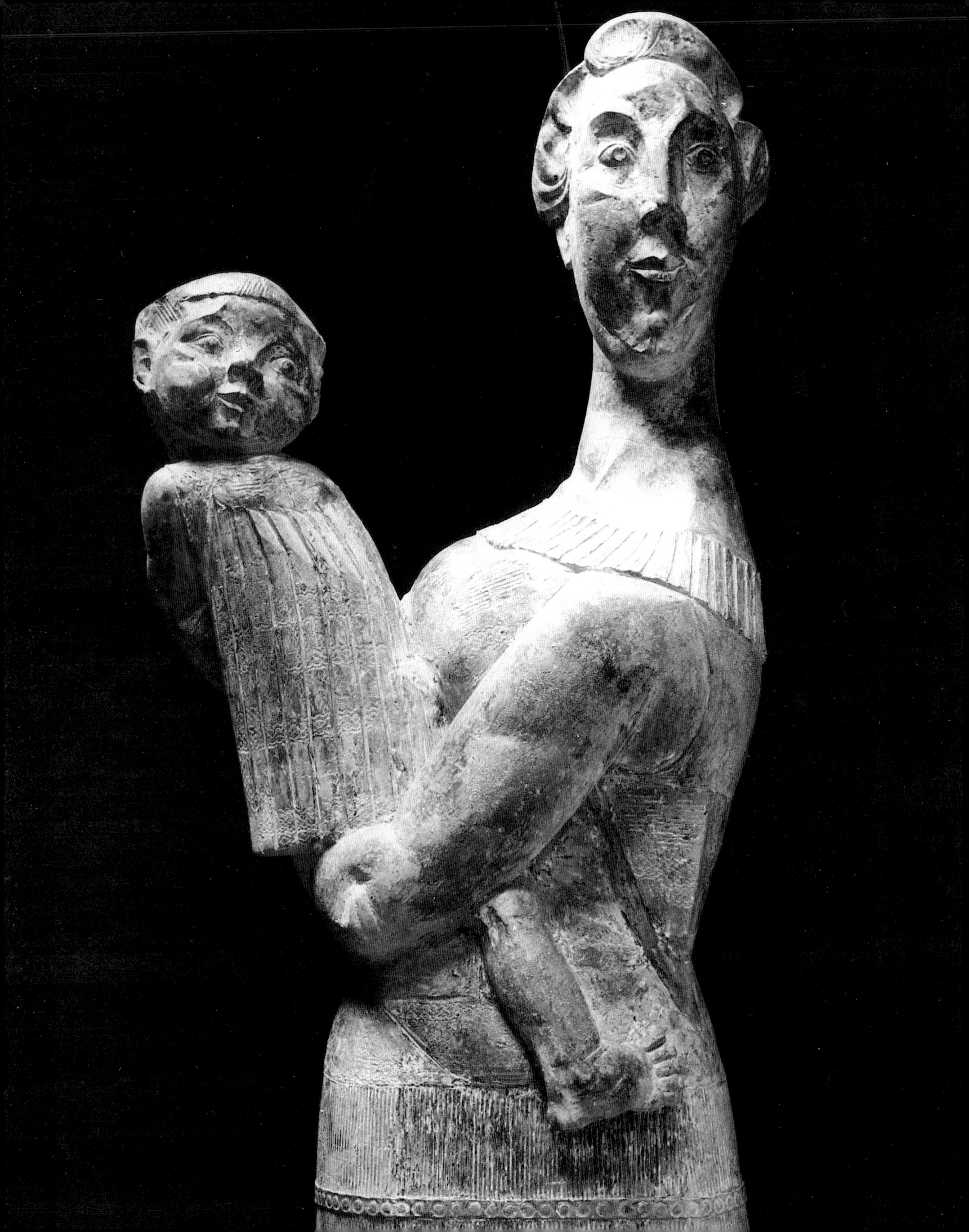

3

'Famously unacceptable' – sculpting in a Cold Climate

Plate 14 (Cat.19)
Mother and child 1956 (detail)
Concrete
142 x 59 x 37 cm

Reviewing Fullard's first solo exhibition held at the Woodstock Gallery in London in 1958, John Berger declared that he regarded Fullard as the best young sculptor working in Britain at the time, for the way he dealt with 'modern life'.[1] He identified a certain spirit, a 'sculptural dignity', which Fullard's work shared with that of sculptor Ossip Zadkine, whose remarkable Rotterdam Memorial, *La ville détruite*, erected in 1953, had been hailed as a modern tribute to human suffering and tenacity. Berger's writing on art became a focus for controversy but his critical support was important to Fullard's career in the 1950s. Towards the end of the decade, Fullard began to show in group exhibitions and public and private collectors started to take an interest in his work. However, the post-war climate had been distinctly 'cool' for Fullard; despite the opportunities provided by the rebuilding and regeneration of Britain, the early 1950s were difficult for many artists struggling to make a living from their work. More importantly, the political background of the Cold War is especially relevant to any consideration of Fullard's work of this time. A few years earlier, Berger had described Fullard as one of a handful of 'famously unacceptable' artists whose work had humanist qualities and social realist connections.[2] The effects of Cold War polarisation on artistic practice, critical presentation, patronage and reception was considerable. 'Realist' and 'humanist' were much more than merely descriptive terms. They marked a polemical territory that had political reverberations and implications for those associated with them, including Fullard.

In the immediate aftermath of the war, with a new Labour government under pressure to meet the aspirations of post-war Britons demanding homes, jobs and prosperity, the prospects for growth in the arts were promising. The wartime upsurge of public interest in art events and exhibitions was further developed by the setting up of the Arts Council of Great Britain. There were new patrons, such as the London County Council, which commissioned works for public sites, organised open-air shows of sculpture and purchased works for schools and new housing projects.[3] British sculpture received major acknowledgement when, in 1948, Henry Moore won the International Sculpture Prize at the Venice *Biennale*. This interest deepened in 1952 when eight

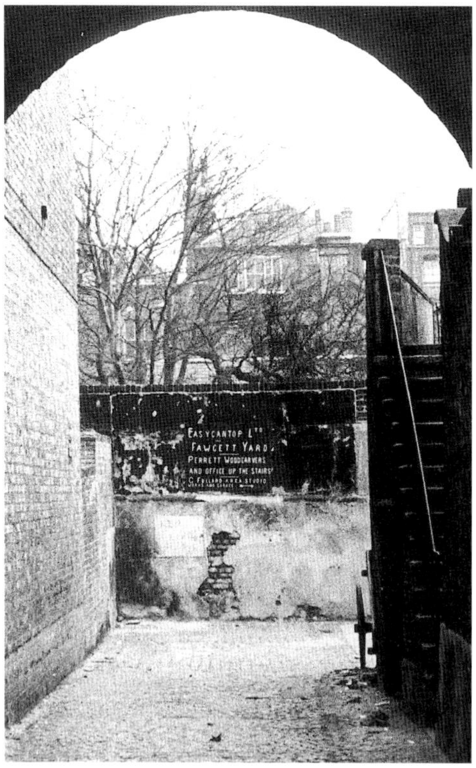

Plate 15
View of the entrance to the Fawcett Yard studio in the mid-1950s.

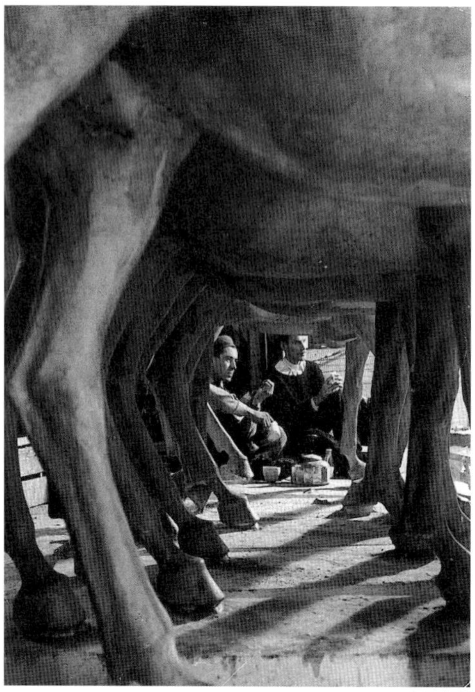

Plate 16
Ernest Adsetts and Fullard in the 1950s.

young British sculptors showed at Venice to international critical acclaim.[4] Richard Calvocoressi has described the years between 1945 and 1960 as the period in which Britain experienced the biggest renewal of interest in public sculpture since the Victorian era, commenting that by about 1960 it had become commonplace for observers to rejoice in the health of British sculpture.[5]

The Festival of Britain in 1951 was part of this 'renewal' and provided numerous commissions for artists and sculptors. The Festival was intended as a mid-century celebration to mark the end of the age of austerity and served to focus a burgeoning national interest and patriotism. Events were certainly popular with the general public: in London, almost nine million people visited the 'Skylon' and other exhibits on the south bank of the Thames. Inevitably, perhaps, the Festival also attracted criticism – both at the time and after the event. Michael Frayn, writing in 1963, cuttingly described the tone of the Festival as 'philanthropic, kindly, whimsical, cosy, optimistic, middlebrow ...' and was very critical of its claims to have been the 'people's show'.[6]

Although Fullard and his circle of friends were somewhat cynical about the overall aims of the Festival, they were able to take advantage of the work it provided. Fullard and Ernest Adsetts won a commission to make a half-life-size model of an Iron Age group for one of the pavilions celebrating the history of Britain. Fullard and Adsetts, assisted by fellow ex-Royal College artists 'Jock' Stewart and Leslie Duxbury, also worked on some large-scale coloured plaster pheasants for a garden feature designed by Hans Tisdall.[7]

Festival events gave a temporary fillip to the lifting of post-war gloom but 1951 did not mark the end of 'austerity'. Bomb-sites, rationing, the black market and conscription persisted – the 'affluent society' was, as yet, unknown. The optimism of the immediate post-war years appears to have been short-lived on all fronts, including in the field of the arts. In London, there was a shortage of materials, studio space, galleries and patrons. Julian Spalding comments on these general problems in the exhibition catalogue *The Forgotten Fifties* citing, for example, the painter Prunella Clough's recollections of the period as one 'when you got your head down and worked', with no easy roads to fame and no publicity machine.[8]

John Bratby, looking back in 1962 on the generation of ex-servicemen who had crowded the art schools just after the war, wrote about the archetypal young London artist of the time: 'Private Honer' was typically determined to avoid teaching and equally determined to paint or sculpt; 'Private Honer is all over this country; 30 to 40; an ex-serviceman with a sterile studio; biding his time and being resentful in his thousands. A few clutter Chelsea, living on their wives, being inactive geniuses – but most of them are like Honer.'[9]

Bratby's caricature reveals common difficulties for artists in London in the 1950s. Like Honer, Fullard was an ex-serviceman living in Chelsea, relying to some extent on his wife's income from a variety of acting and secretarial jobs. In a bid to avoid having to teach and to finance his own work, Fullard took on various commercial projects. In the early 1950s, Adsetts and Fullard spent five months working on a lucrative, but extremely demanding, commission to model and cast four life-size horses. Fullard made props for stage and film sets, including a Buddha, fifteen feet in height, made of clay reinforced with lath and plaster, for the film, *Seven Years in Tibet*. He also made a number of tem-

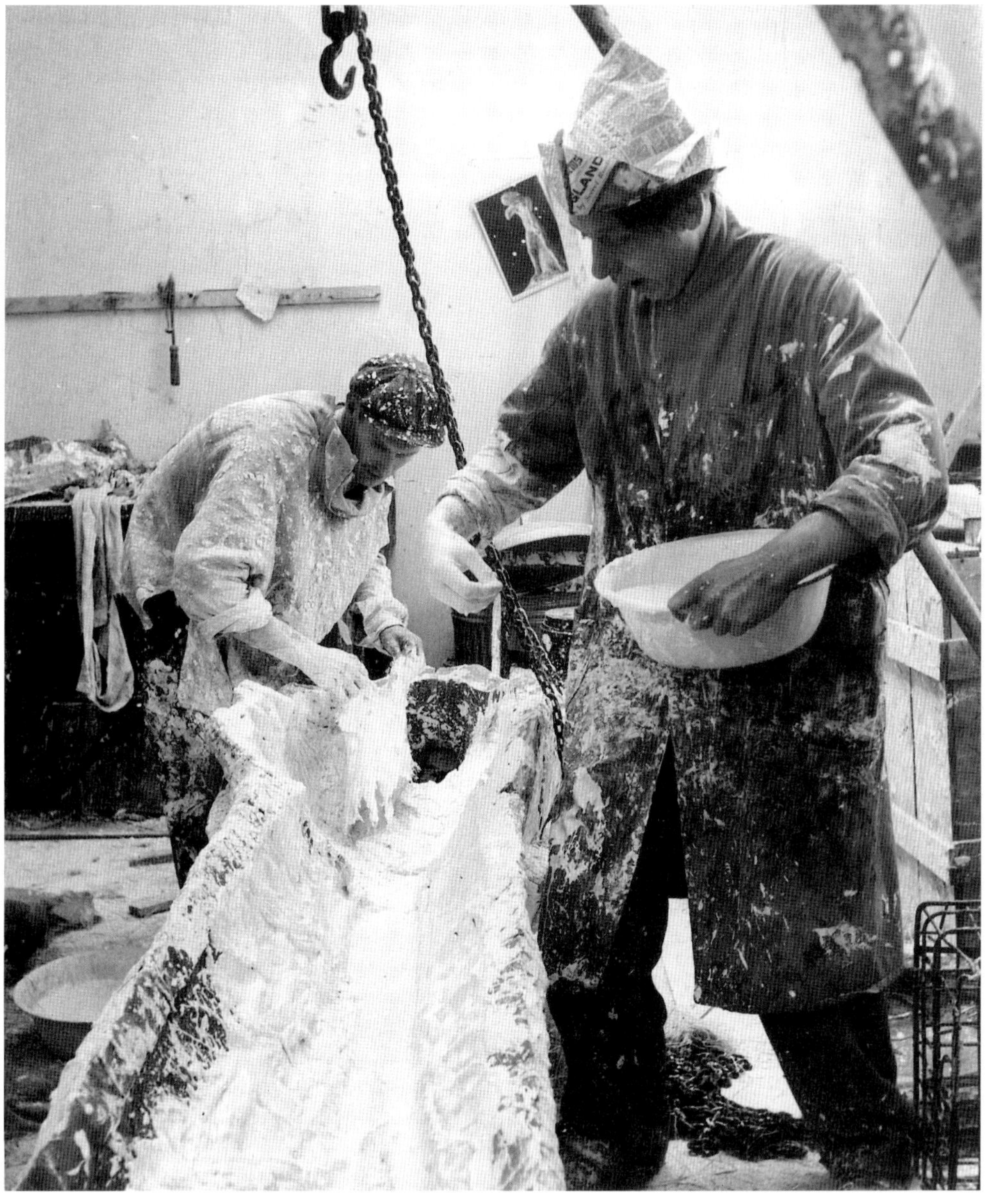

Plate 17
Fullard and 'Jock' Stewart. The makeshift 'paper-helmet', worn in the studio by sculptors, is the kind often made by children. It was a common feature of much of Fullard's later sculpture and drawings.

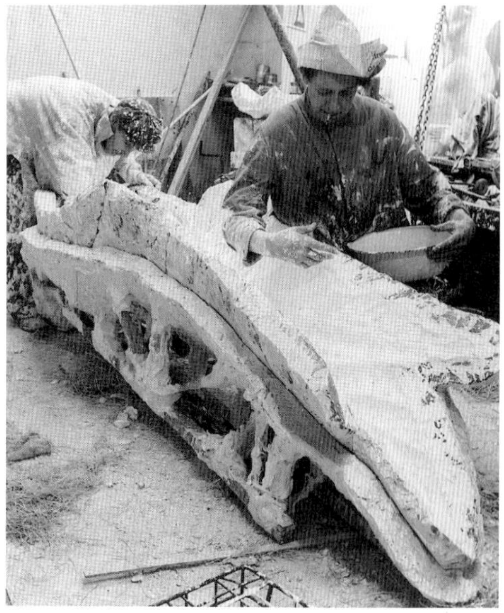

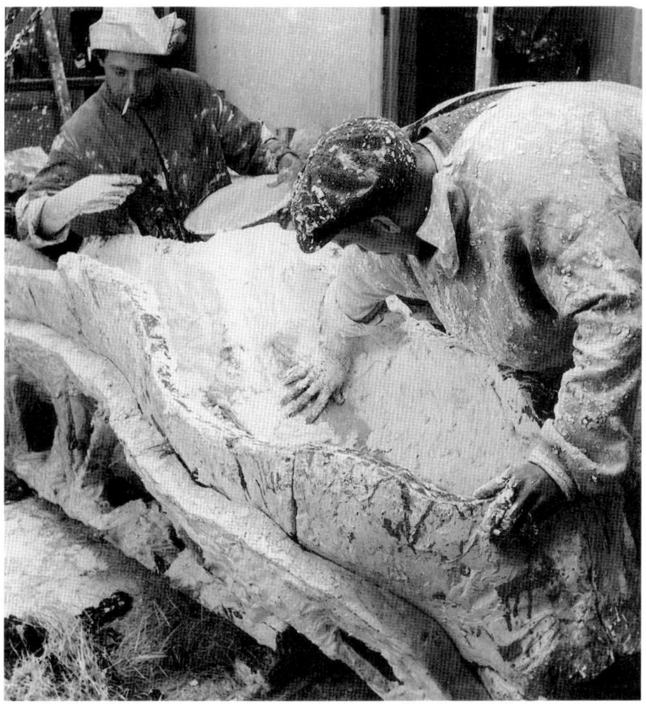

Plates 18 and 19
Fullard and 'Jock' Stewart working in the mid-1950s.

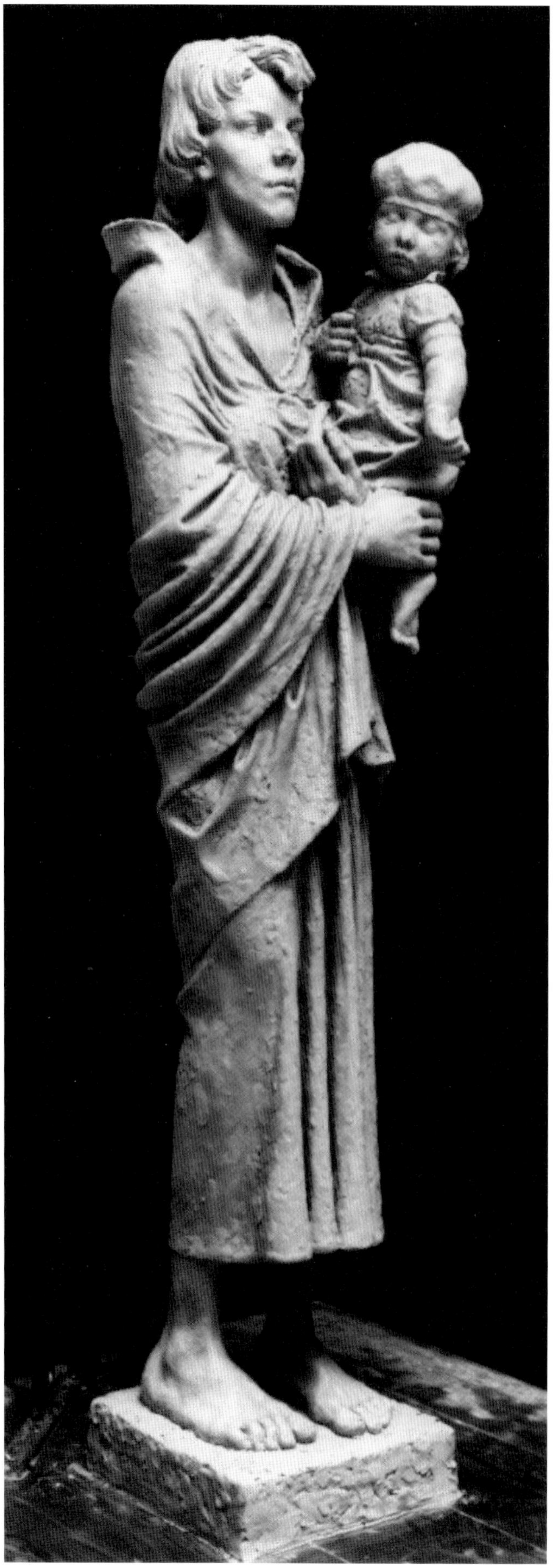

Plate 20 (Cat.6)
Mother and child 1949
Clay
175.3 cm (height)

porary pieces for annual events such as the *Ideal Home Exhibition*.[10]

In 1956, the left-wing journal *Tribune* featured an article, 'Art in a Cold Climate', which focused on the continuing problems faced by sculptor Fullard and painter Derrick Greaves.[11] Fullard had rented premises in Fawcett Yard after running out of studio space at his home in Park Walk, Chelsea where the Fullards had lived since 1950. Fawcett Yard, a former dairyman's yard just off Fulham Road, was far from ideal with unreliable plumbing, no heating, a leaking roof and high rent due to the scarcity of such accommodation. Greaves remembers it as a dilapidated mews with three or four enormous dark, cobbled stables,

> ... there was a gap between the tin roof and the boundary wall of about two feet which, when it rained, gouted water into our work areas. In torrential downpours rivers used to form between the cobbles and froth away into the main drain of the street. This meant that George's sculpture and my canvasses had to be strategically placed in order to avoid recurring Niagaras.[12]

The *Tribune* report drew attention to the particular financial burdens on sculptors as they usually had to pay for casting works before they had any guarantee of sale. Large-scale works – such as Fullard's *Mother and child* 1956 which was illustrated in *Tribune* – were expensive to cast in bronze. Often, they were not particularly welcomed by galleries, who preferred smaller, more saleable items – the kind which might, as noted by the reporter, 'fit nicely on a mantelpiece'. Consequently, at this time, most of Fullard's work was cast, if at all, in cement or plaster.

Despite the problems referred to in the *Tribune* article, the middle of the decade represented something of a turning point for Fullard's artistic career. A year earlier, Greaves had introduced the young Marxist art critic of the *New Statesman*, John Berger, to Fullard. He was immediately impressed by his work and went on to support Fullard in various ways. In 1956, he selected his work for one of his *Looking Forward* exhibitions of realist art at the South London Gallery; in 1957 he suggested Fullard for a major show of British contemporary art which travelled to Moscow and in 1958 he chose Fullard as one of four artists shown in another exhibition of graphic art in London.

In 1955, in an article entitled 'Social Realism and the young', Berger identified Fullard as one of a group of young social realist and humanist artists which included Jack Smith, Derrick Greaves, Edward Middleditch and Ralph Brown. In Berger's view, these artists had encountered undeserved difficulties in showing and selling their work: difficulties which could not be explained away by the general austere circumstances of life in the early 1950s. Describing them as the 'famously unacceptable', he wrote:

> Dealers complain that their work is unsellable because too large and too sordid; critics interpret it in terms of contemporary violence, a love of ugliness or (with a dab at their mouth with a white folded handkerchief) Social Realism; collectors, even if they are appreciative, are doubtful how they can house their works; public gallery officials remember with relief that all these artists are still under forty – the age of decision for Buying Committees.
>
> Their work described objectively *is* cumbersomely large, totally lacking in charm, raw, nearly always proletarian in subject matter and possibly somewhat aggressive ...[13]

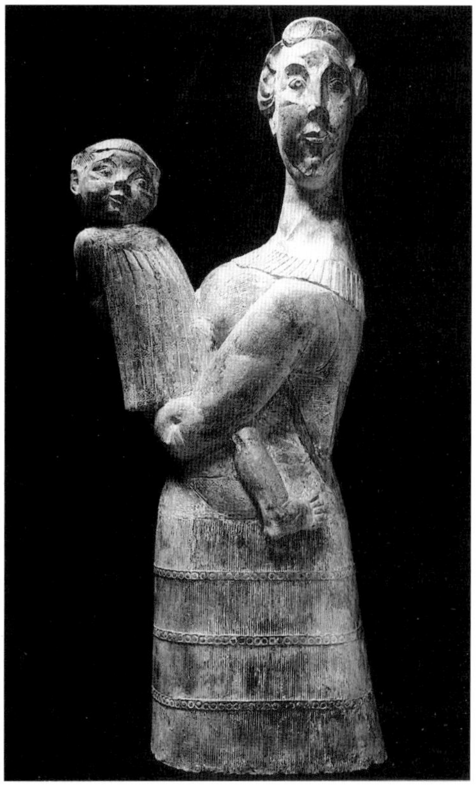

Plate 21 (Cat.19)
Mother and child 1956
Concrete
142 x 59 x 37 cm

OVERLEAF
Plate 22 (Cat.5)
Portrait of Andy Tittensor 1948
Bronze (edition of two)
35.6 x 22.9 x 25.7 cm

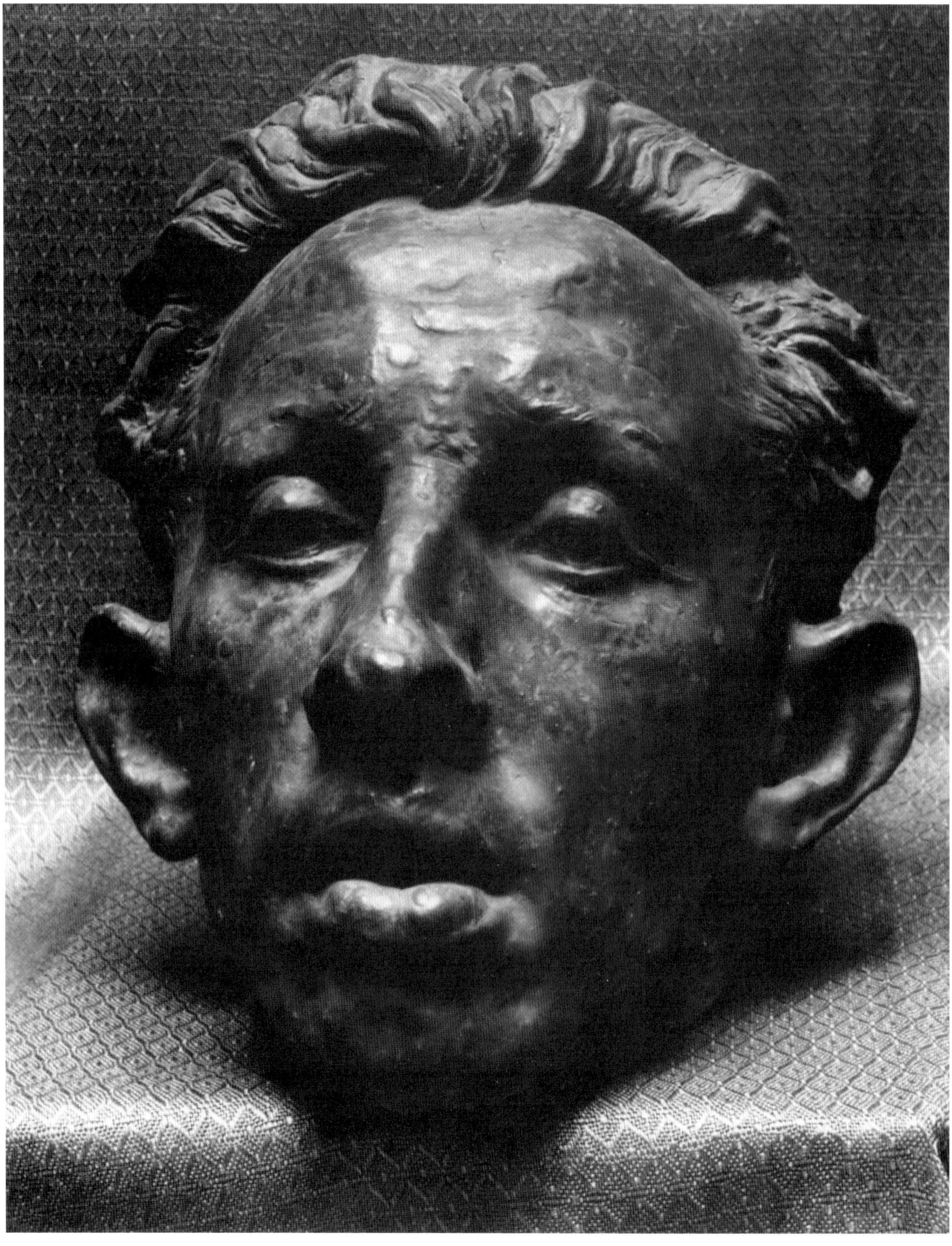

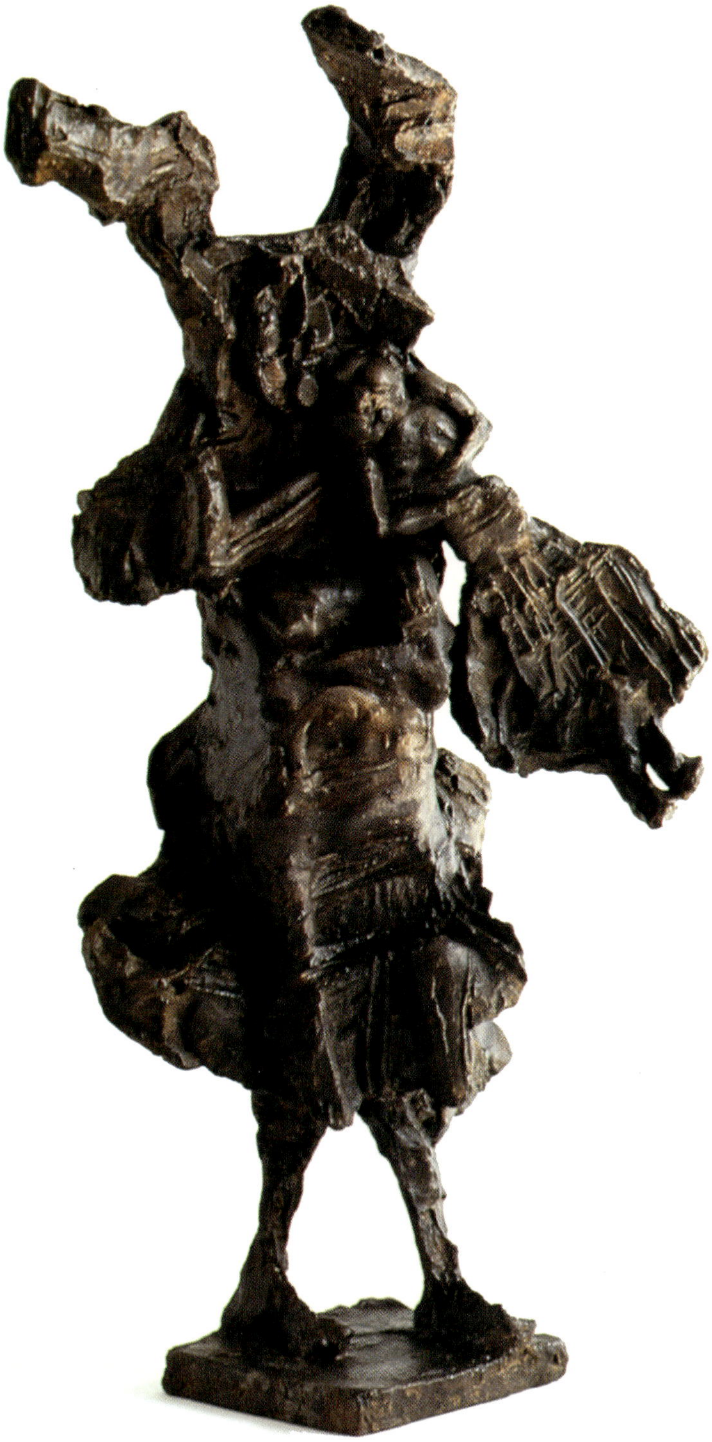

Plate 23 (Cat.27)
Storm 1957
Bronze (edition of three)
49.5 x 22.3 x 12.7 cm

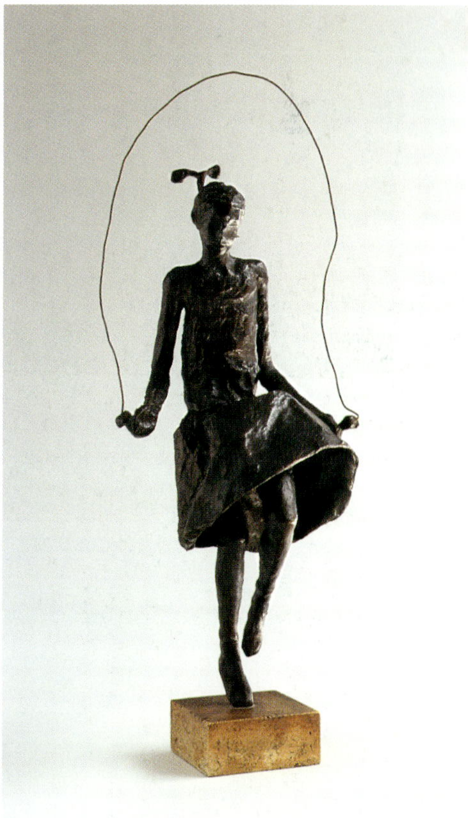

Plate 24 (Cat.15)
Skipping girl 1955
Bronze (edition of 3)
33.7 x 15.5 x 15 cm

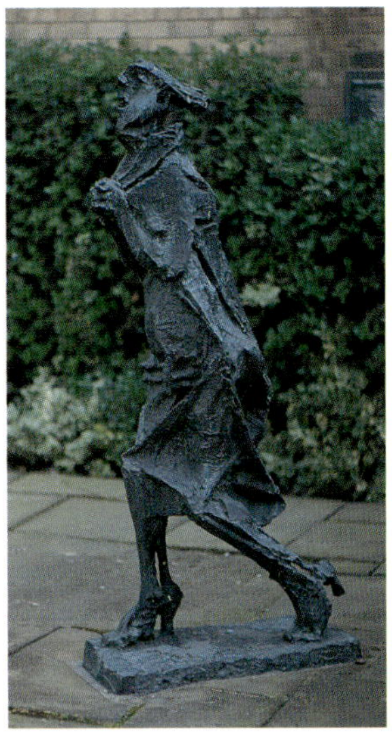

Plate 25 (Cat.28)
Running woman 1957
Bronze
213.5 x 122 x 85 cm

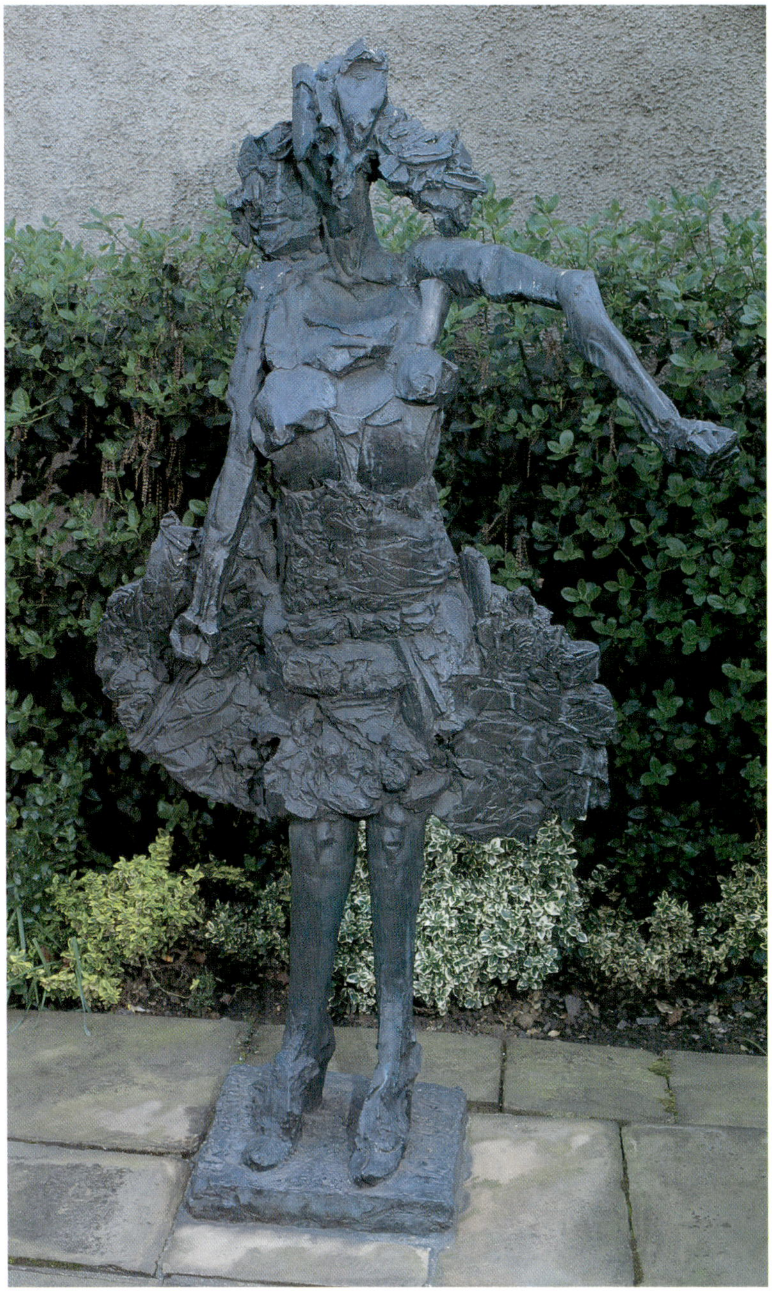

Plate 27 (Cat.30)
Angry woman 1958
Bronze
213.5 x 122 x 85 cm

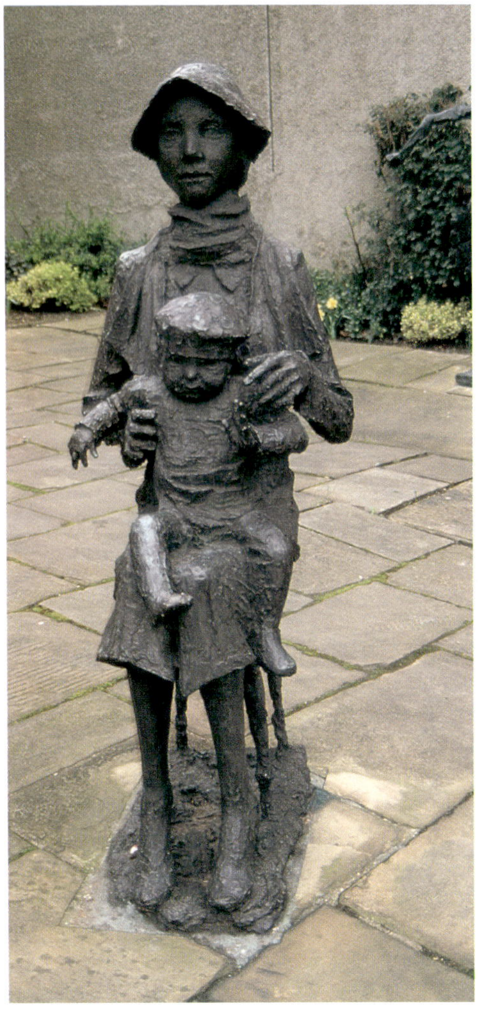

Plate 26 (Cat.21)
Mother and child 1956
Bronze
163 x 66 x 66 cm

Plate 28 (Cat.31)
Mother and child 1958
Bronze
163 x 66 x 66 cm

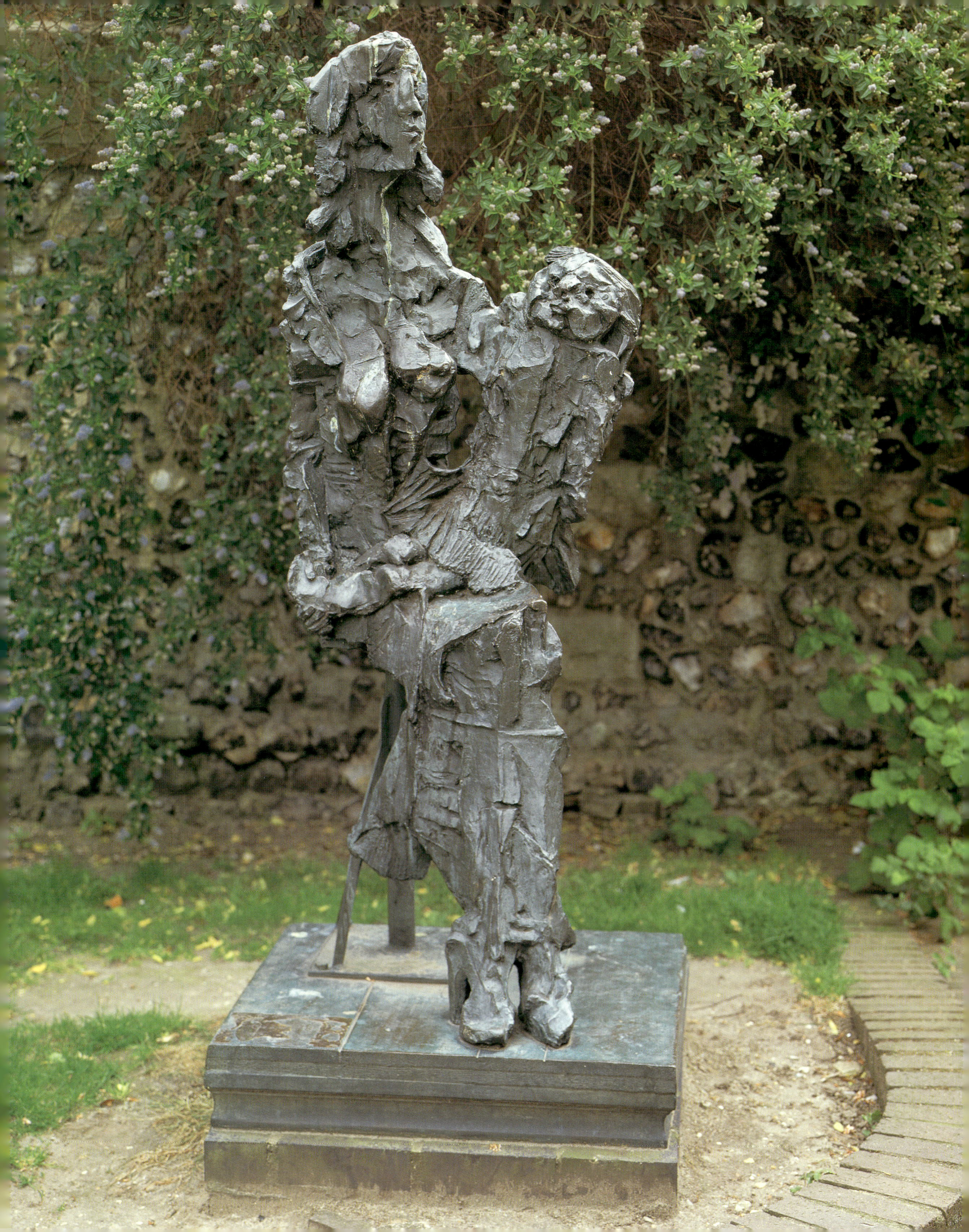

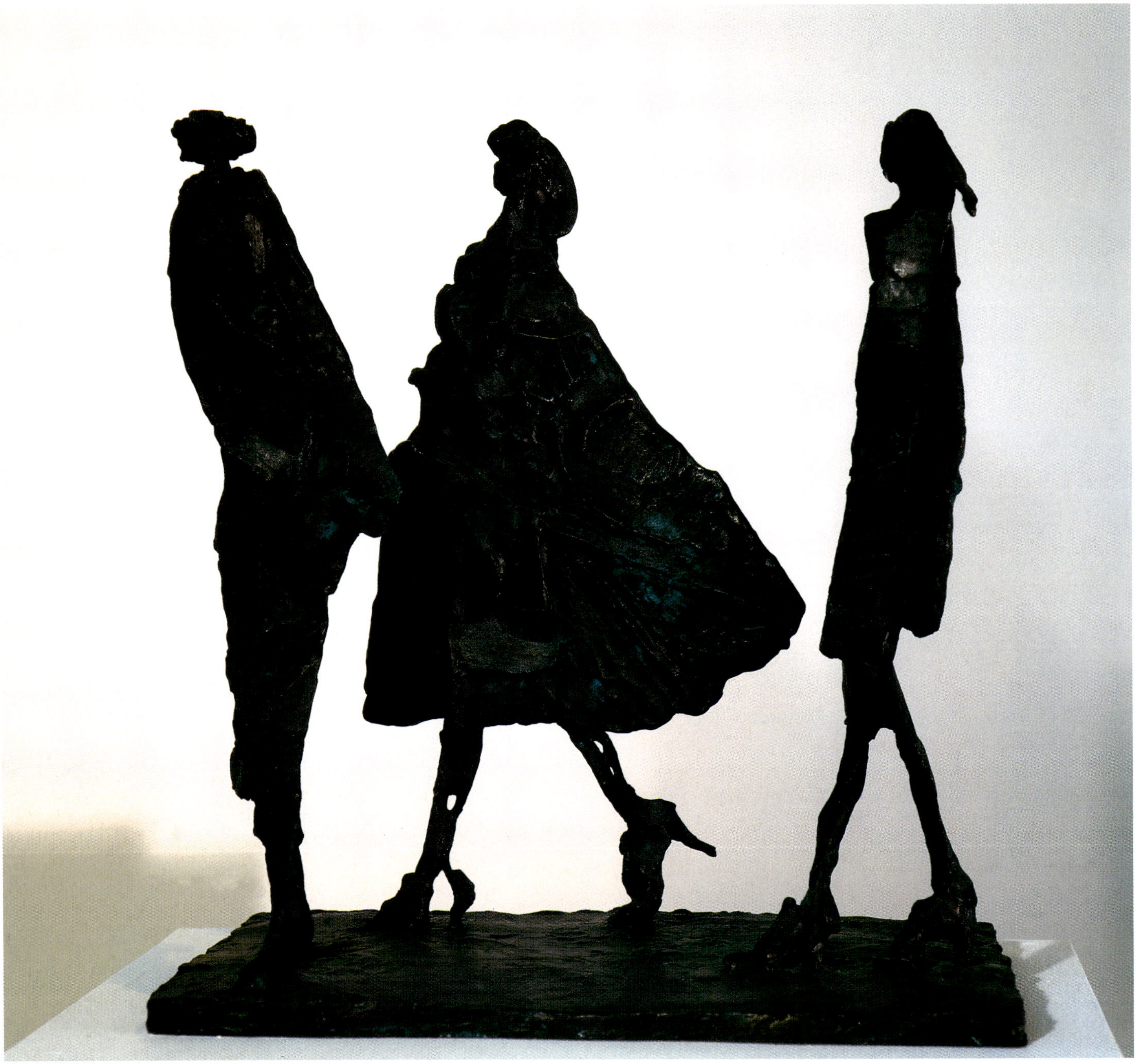

Plate 29 (Cat.33)
Three women 1958
Bronze
55.7 x 55.7 x 33 cm

Plate 30 (Cat.7)
Politicians early 1950s
Clay
Dimensions unknown

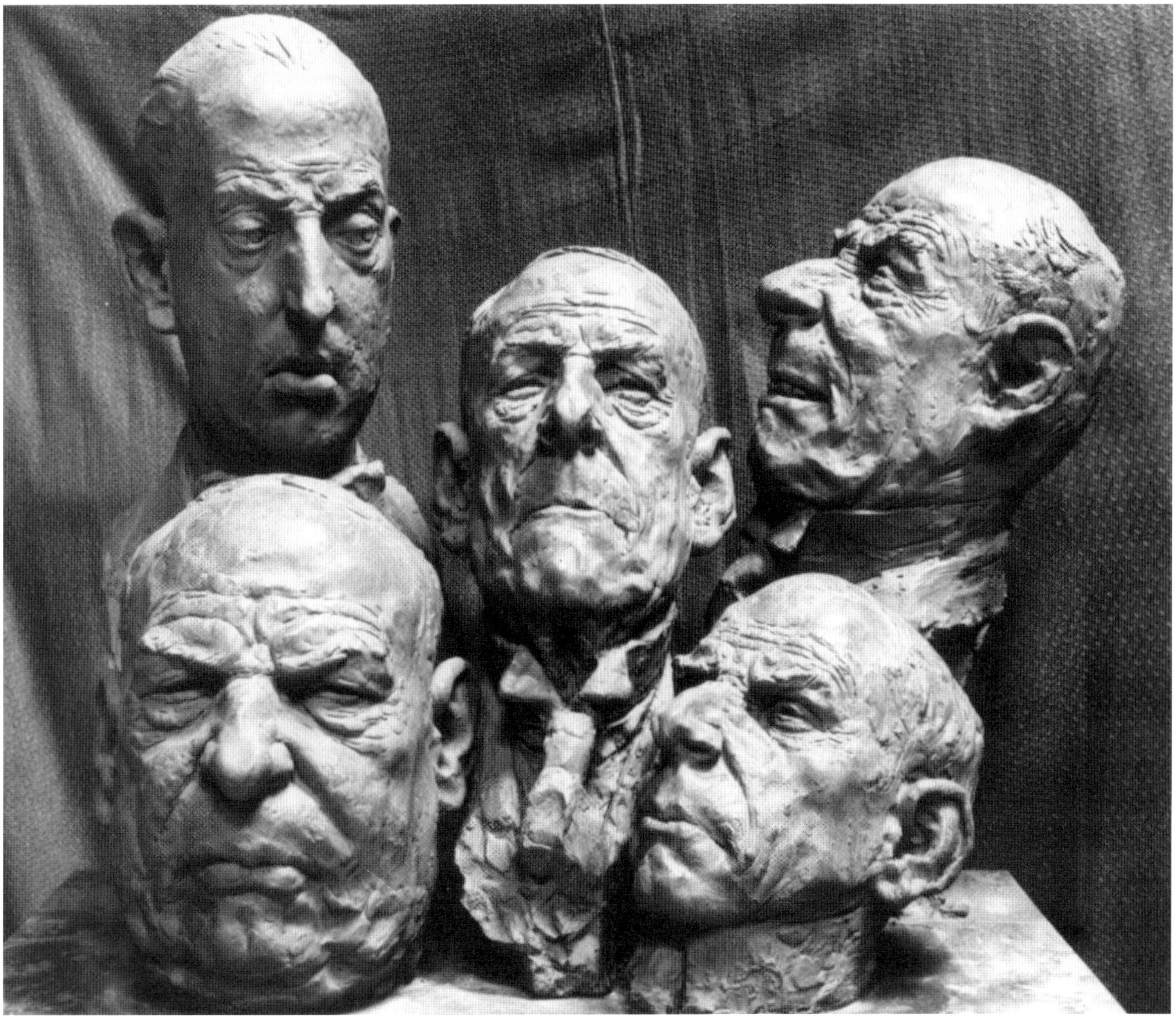

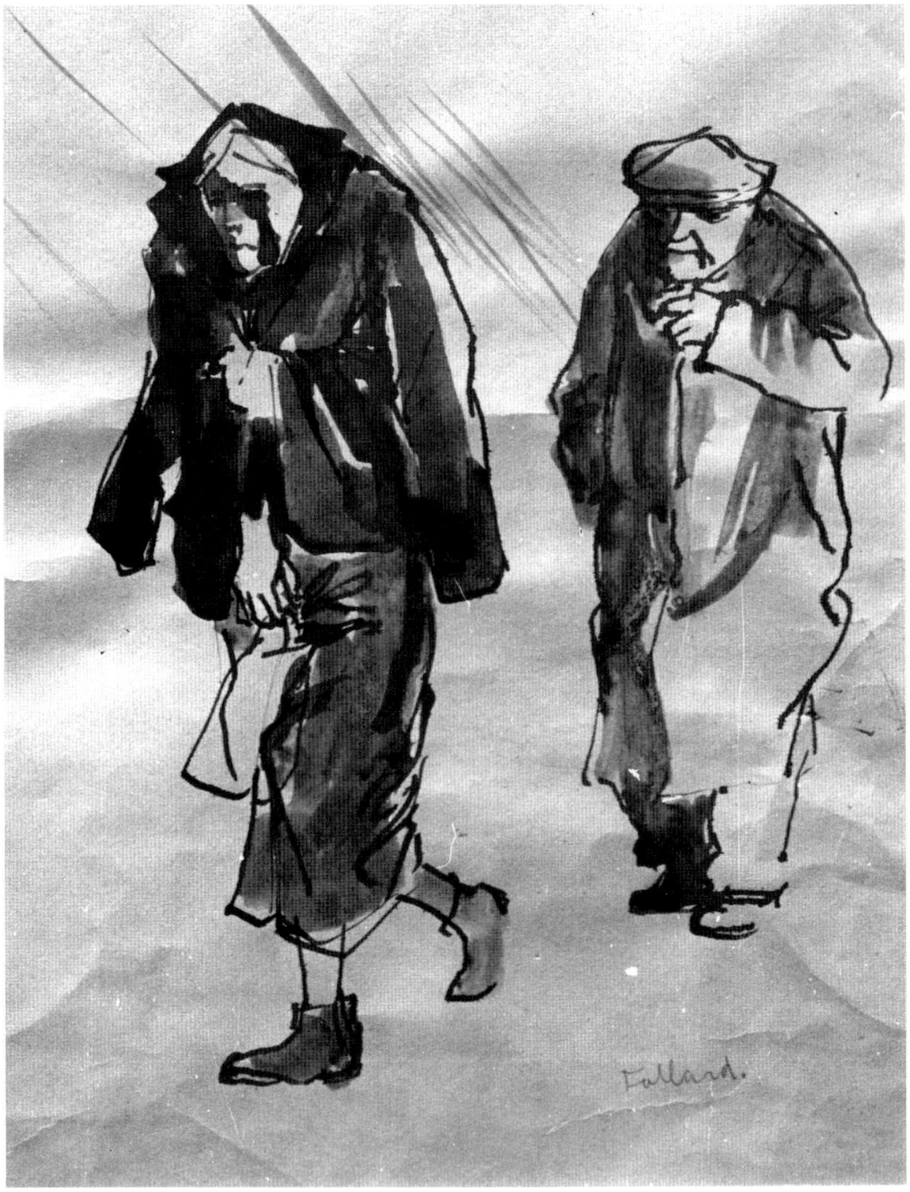

Plate 31
Two figures undated
Pen-and-wash on paper
This drawing was shown in the *Looking Forward* exhibition at South London Gallery in 1956.
Private collection

Many of Fullard's works of the 1950s *were* large, raw and angry: they were certainly not the kind of work which might have been included in the series of exhibitions *Sculpture for the Home*, instigated by Frank Dobson in 1948, and, indeed, were rarely shown in other Arts Council exhibitions of the 1950s. Fullard shared more than just social relationships with artists such as Greaves and Smith, whose broad concerns, at that time, were with the details of everyday life, domestic surroundings and the grim realities of industrial areas such as Sheffield.[14] Fullard's drawings and sculpture from the earlier years of the decade drew on traditions of realism: *Politicians*, since destroyed, is a satirical comment in realist style, recalling Daumier's caricature heads; his entries for the Football Association's 90th anniversary exhibition held in 1953, are other early examples. There is also his preoccupation with the ordinary worker, so prevalent in the drawings he did in Sheffield, which continued into his work in the 1950s. One of Fullard's earliest showings at a West End gallery was a drawing, *Miners in the shower bath*, in the Leicester Galleries 1956 exhibition, *Young Artists of Fame and Promise*.

OVERLEAF
Plate 34 (Cat.23)
Head of a worker 1956
Ciment fondu
33.2 x 22.2 x 23 cm

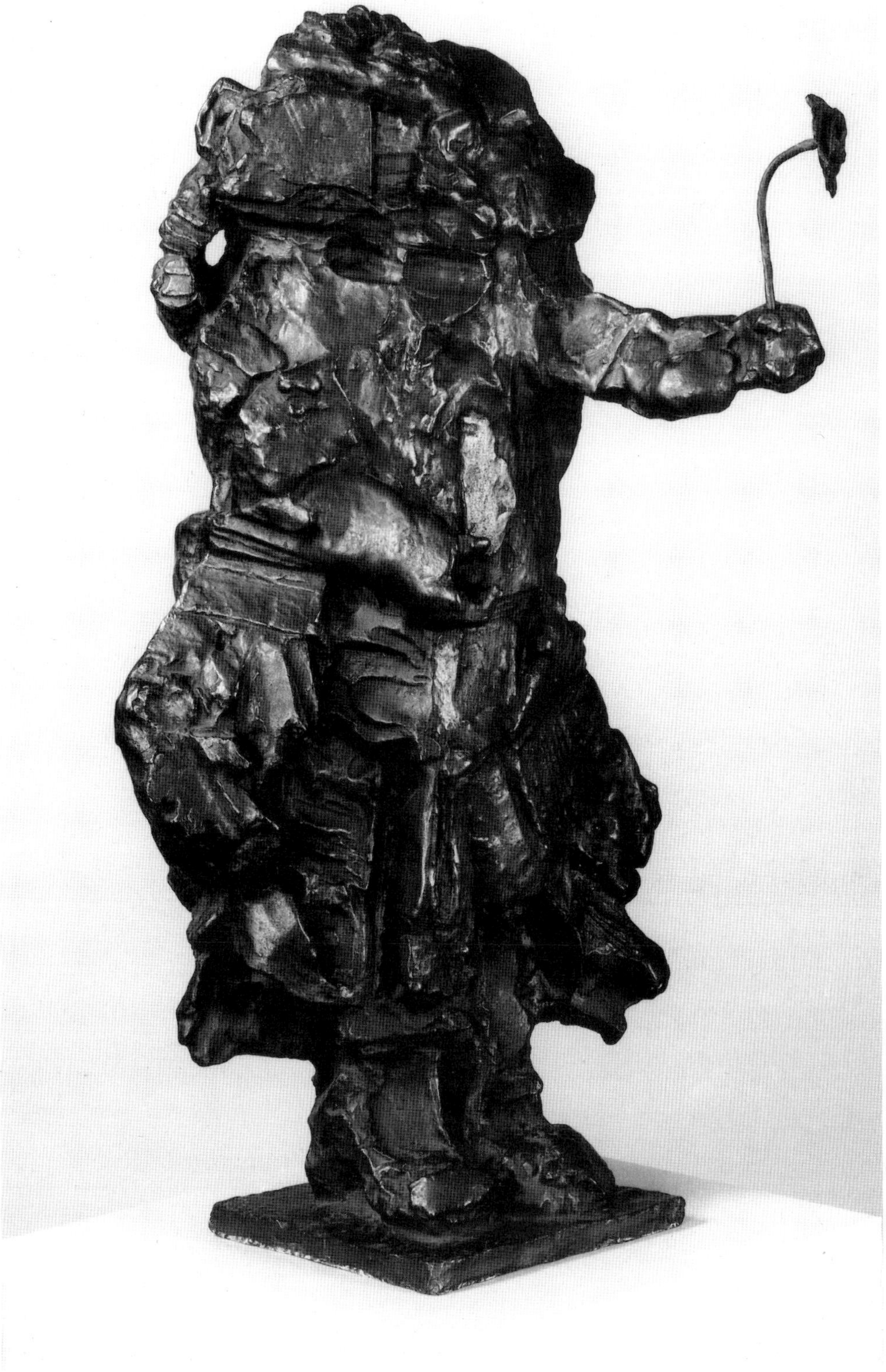

Plate 32 (Cat.29)
Infant with flower 1958
Bronze
76.2 x 42 x 38 cm

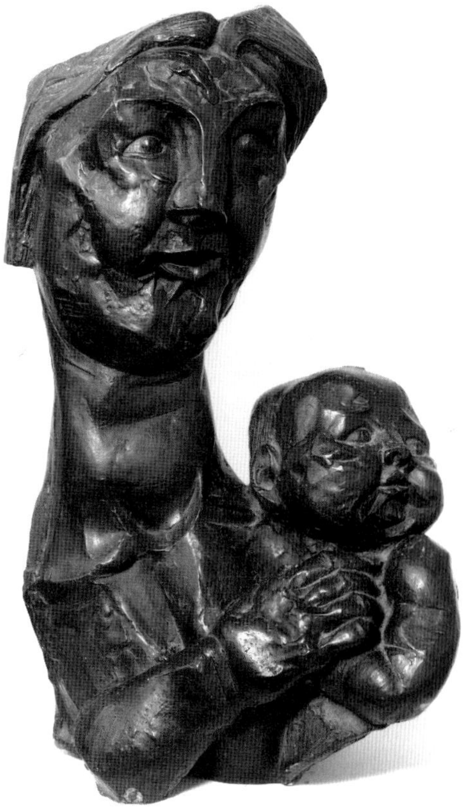

Plate 33 (Cat.20)
Mother and child 1956
Bronze
67.3 x 37 x 28 cm

Berger's choice of 'proletarian' as descriptor is significant but Fullard's subjects were, as has already been stressed, 'ordinary' people, usually working-class, occasionally specifically 'workers'. However, more significantly, in Berger's view, these artists had acquired a reputation as the 'famously unacceptable' because of their assocation with 'Social Realism' – a subject, Berger implied, which met with near universal distaste and derision.

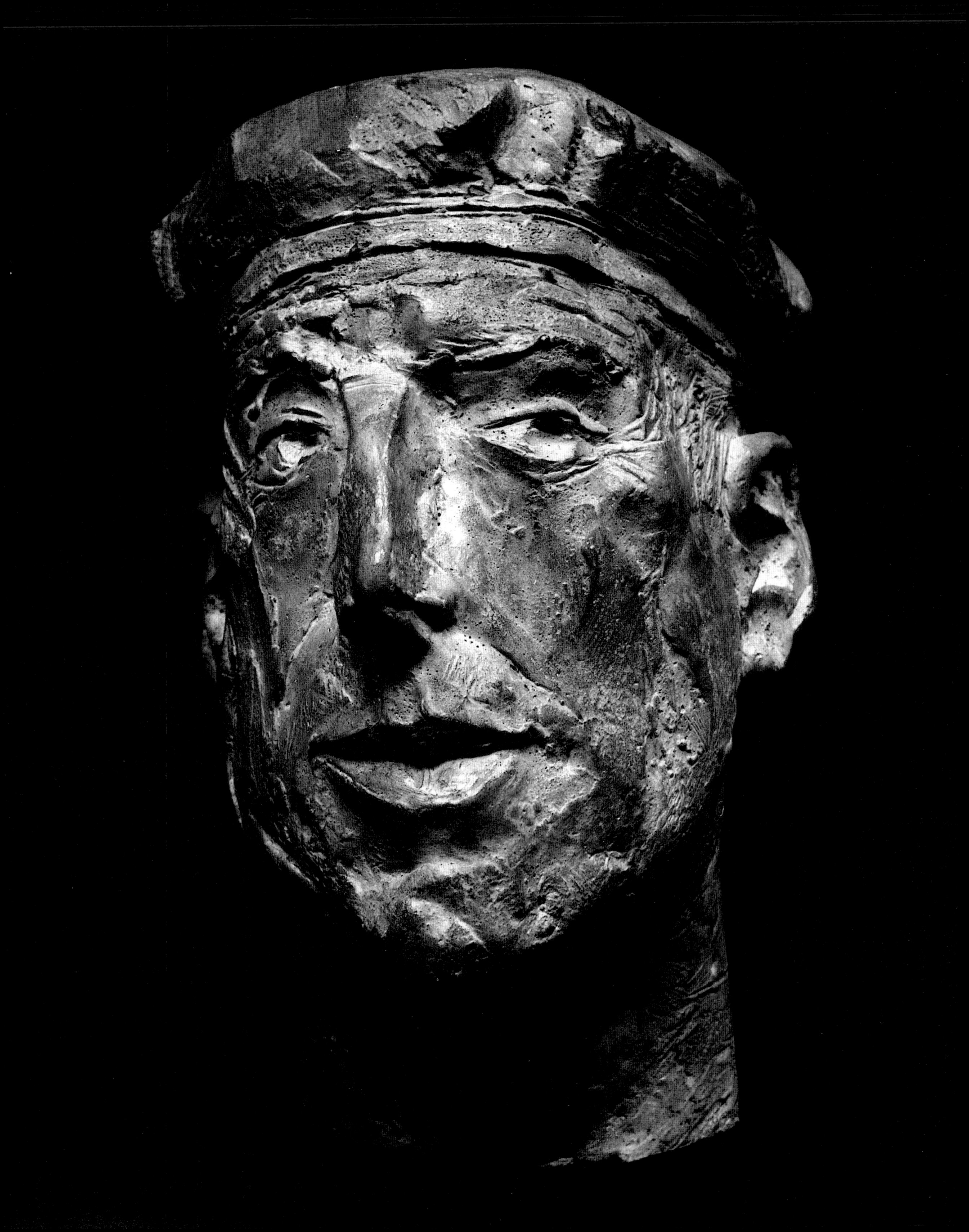

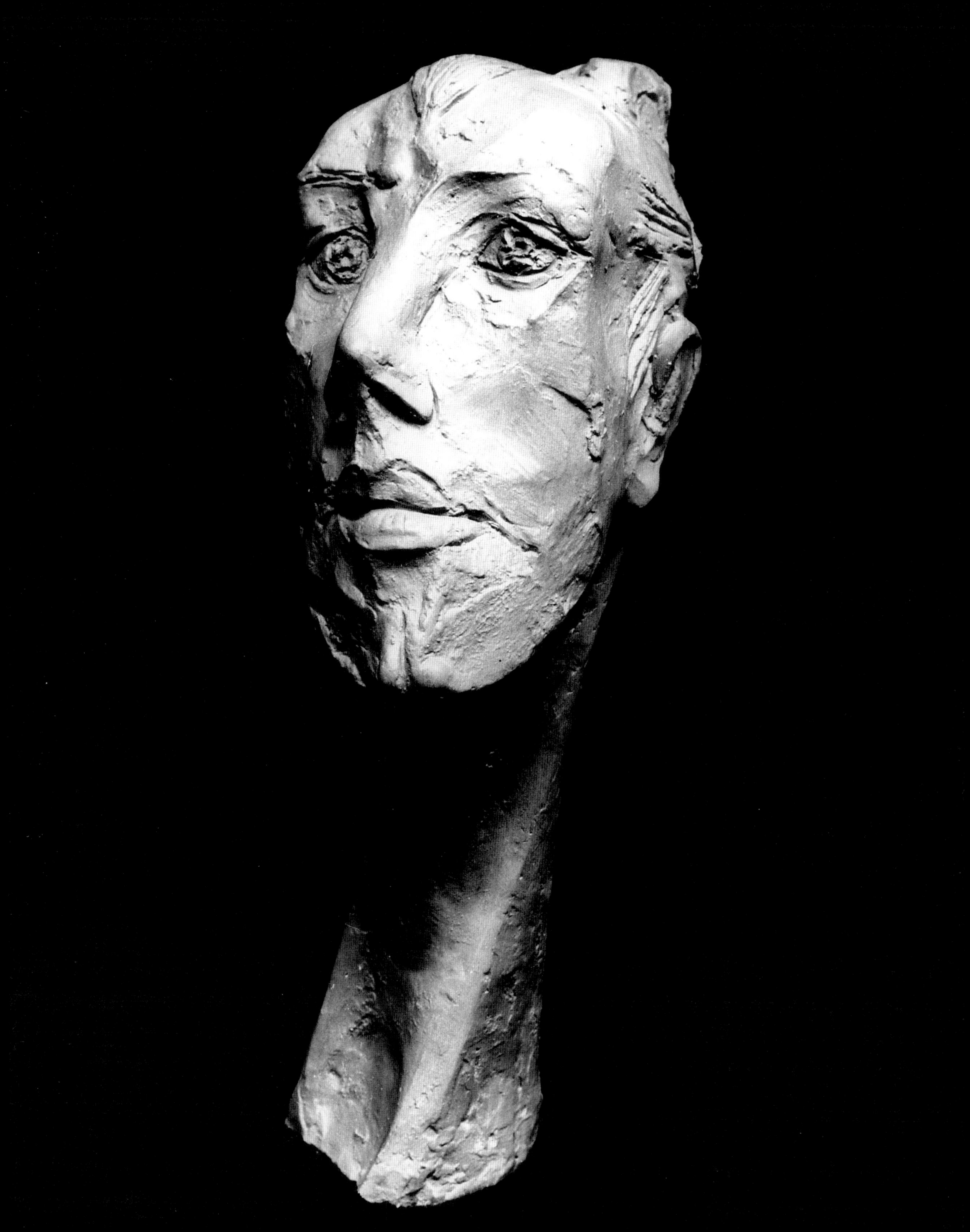

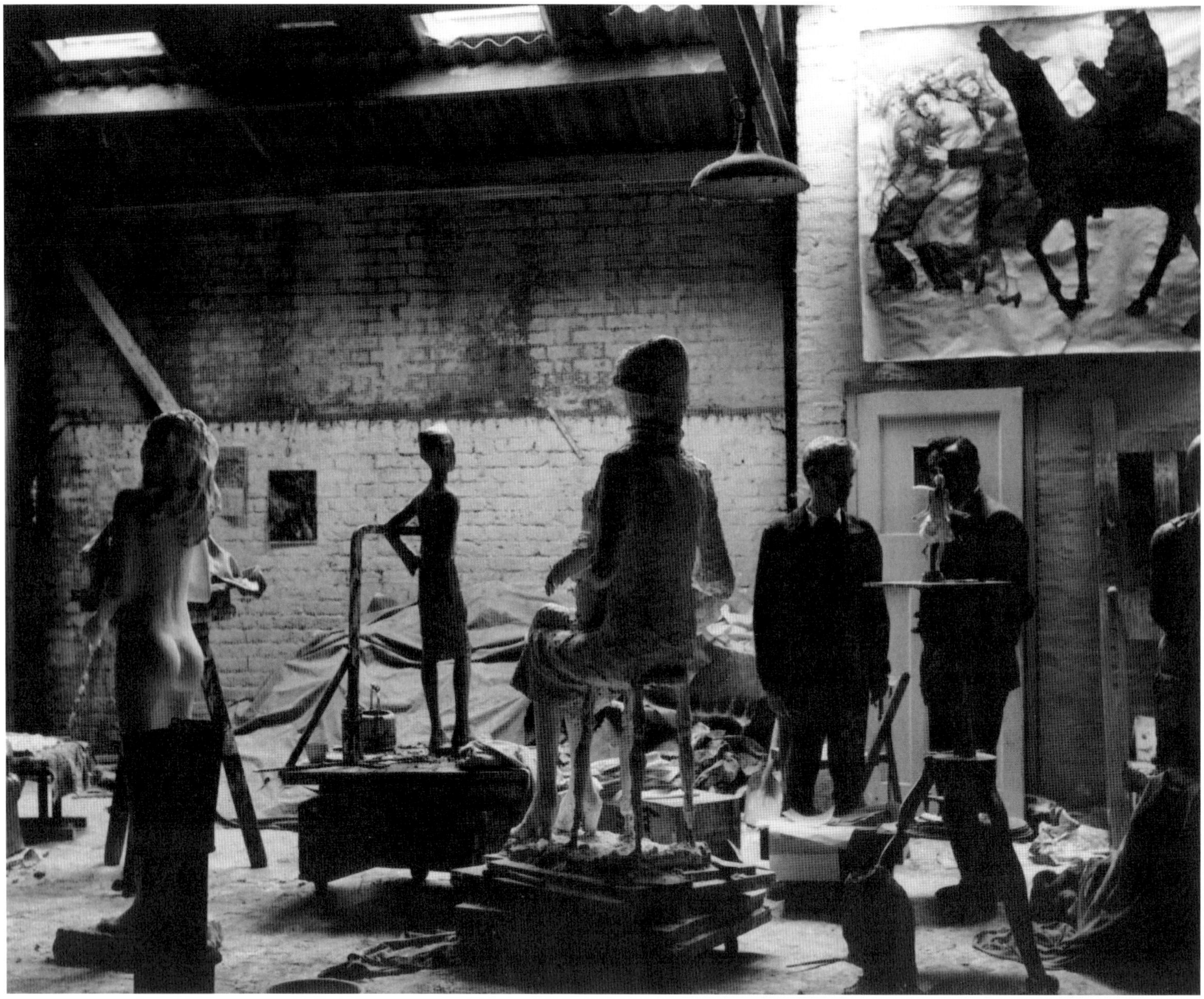

Plate 36
Fullard with Frank Monaco at Fawcett Yard *c.*1956

A 'social' form of realism, distinct from the 'figurative tradition' of the Academy, and related to political radicalism, had been firmly established well before the war.[15] However, Andrei Zhdanov's declaration at the Soviet Writers Congress in 1934, that 'Socialist Realism' was the only appropriate approach for social revolutionaries particularly inspired and expanded the debate in Britain.[16] The question of which form of art was the most revolutionary – abstract or realist – was debated in Artists International Association publications, and elsewhere, by Francis Klingender, Herbert Read and others.[17] Indeed, pre-war debate was largely dominated by the quest for a politically progressive art with the whole question viewed rather narrowly as a formal problem with formal solutions – and the 'Left' tended to argue, often vociferously though by no means exclusively, for a realism of style and content.

However, the political climate of the post-war scene provided an entirely different setting for any discussion of realism. The immediate post-war years offered little prospect of reconciliation, stability or peace and the inter-

PREVIOUS PAGE
Plate 35 (Cat.18)
Head 1956
Plaster
45.7 cm (height)

national political scene rapidly deteriorated. In 1960, a *New Statesman* editorial looked back on the decade as the 'Jittery Fifties'. The Second World War had barely ended when the Cold War began: an era which plunged humanity, in Eric Hobsbawm's view, 'into what can reasonably be regarded as a Third World War'. The de-facto division of war-ravaged Europe ossified into a permanent armed polarisation between the capitalist and the Soviet camps. 'Entire generations grew up under the shadow of global nuclear battles which, it was widely believed, could break out at any moment, and devastate humanity.'[18]

In such a situation, all aspects of cultural life became partisan, including art. The Soviet Union denounced the abstract art of the West as 'decadent'. The Soviet model glorified labour in a visual language which was often heroically realistic and utterly without irony.[19] Importantly, anyone associated with 'realism' in the West, risked being linked with the Soviet camp.

Stories of conspiracies, plots and witch hunts are well-known. The atmosphere was such that Berger felt it necessary to pre-empt his attackers, by commenting in the catalogue to his first *Looking Forward* exhibition that there was no such thing as a 'realist conspiracy'. A letter sent out to potential host galleries by the Art Exhibition Bureau rebutted any suggestion that Berger's comments were out of place: 'The word "Realism" now occurs in almost every article written about contemporary art. It is a word which is misunderstood, disliked and vigorously championed ...'[20]

Berger launched his appeal for a new 'social realist' art, brazenly criticising newly venerated figures such as Moore, recipient of the International Prize at Venice in 1948, and Hepworth, who had shown at Venice the following year. Reviewing a Hepworth exhibition in 1954, Berger commented: 'What is this evasion of real content, this retreat into an abstract world or a world so generalised that all identity and therefore all conflict and therefore all vitality disappears? As an artist Miss Hepworth hasn't the conviction to face up to the real consequences of the crisis in which we live ...'[21]

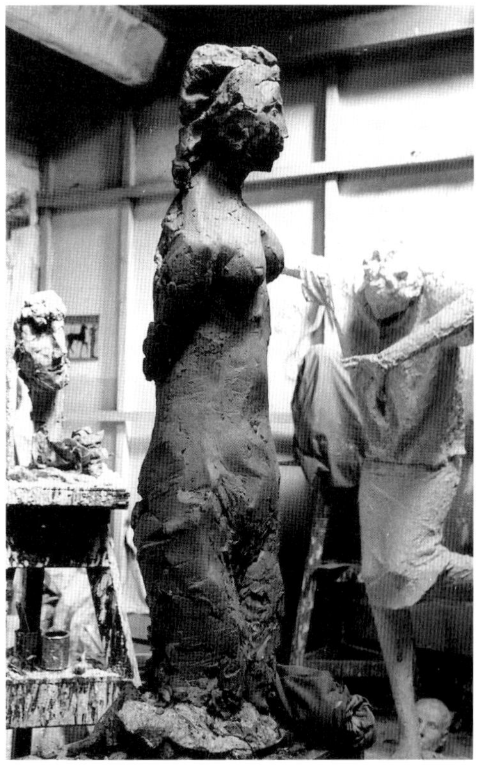

Plate 37
Work in progress at Fullard's Fawcett Yard studio. In the background is the clay *Torso* 1956 (Cat.17).

Berger's comments in the *New Statesman* about 'conviction' and 'crisis' were deliberately provocative: the role of the artist in post-war society was of widespread contemporary interest and was not a marginal issue. Sartre's polemical essay 'What is Literature?', first published in 1947, had addressed the role of the 'committed writer' and re-kindled the controversy about the idea of the 'engaged artist' among the intelligentsia. However, the issue was not confined to esoteric circles. The accessibility of art – both stylistically and physically – was an important concern in the 'new democratic Britain'. The role of the artist, and perhaps more publicly the sculptor, interested, for example, the editor and readers of *Studio* and local authorities seeking artworks for new housing projects.

Fullard's work of the 1950s was perceived by Berger as that of someone who was, in a very broad sense, a 'social realist', a 'humanist' and an artist of conviction and commitment. Fullard's own political allegiances were deeply rooted in his personal social background. Although he never rejoined the Communist Party after his war-service, there is much evidence of where his political sympathies lay and some connections were maintained. His writing, correspondence and other testimony, shows that he retained a strong sense of

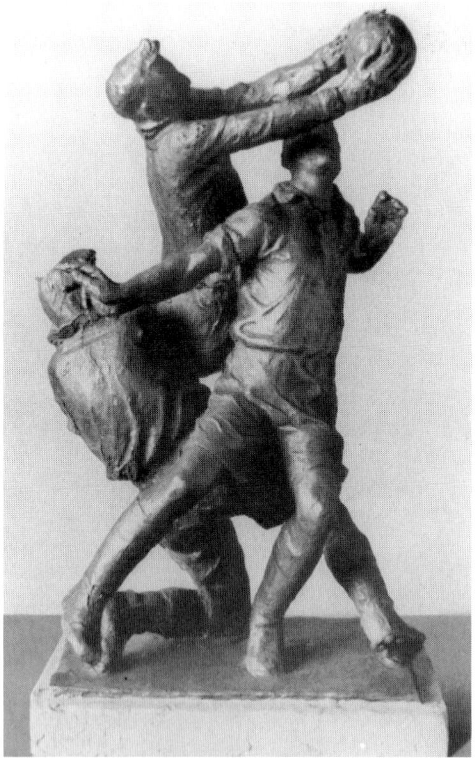

Plate 38 (Cat.12)
Goalmouth 1953
Plaster
Dimensions unknown

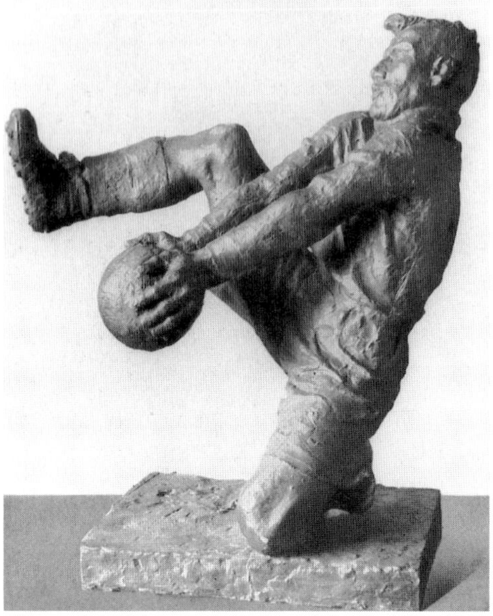

Plate 39 (Cat.11)
Goalkeeper 1953
Plaster
Dimensions unknown

personal radicalism and social commitment. Apart from his involvement with Berger in the 1950s, he showed work at the New Left's Partisan Café. He also had some links with the British Communist Party Artists' Group and with a little-known journal, with which Berger was also involved, *Realism*, circulated in 1955 and 1956.[22]

The kind of realism with which Berger associated Fullard has to be given careful consideration. Realism was a crucial issue in the 1950s – but the concept was ambiguous and has come under scrutiny more recently.[23] Berger's attempts to define social realism in the *New Statesman*, and elsewhere, were frequently vague, didactic and contradictory. Nevertheless, Berger was emphatic in distancing himself from Muscovite 'photographic naturalism' and was highly critical of Soviet cultural policy. He, and others involved with the British Communist Party Artists' Group journal *Realism*, recognised the shortcomings of Soviet-style orthodoxy and criticised it openly. 'We, who have become sick of Socialist Realism in subject matter, a so-called pictorial art, lacking in formal excitement and organisation, illustrative and passionless ...'[24]

For Berger, realism did not necessarily involve observing and reproducing actual lived experience. Neither did it involve the manipulation of 'stock' images or subjects. Realism did not even rule out an element of abstraction. Crucially important, for Berger, was the potential of an artist to see and convey specific universal aspects of experience and the human condition. On Fullard and the other young 'social realists', he commented: 'They are realists because ... in their selection of what they choose to describe about one case, they try to discover those facts which are typical of many others ...'.[25]

In 1990, Christine Lindey argued that prejudice in favour of modernism has not only hidden the diversity of art in the twentieth century but has also restricted an understanding of realism.[26] Cries of 'reaction', on the one hand, or 'revolution', on the other, have stereotyped it as merely representational and equated it with Soviet uniformity. Realism can have breadth. The dissident Russian poet Yevgeny Yevtushenko wrote in 1963 that he loved all art but of all the 'isms' – unexpectedly – realism was art at its most essential.

> But realism as I understand it has hundreds and thousands of facets and it need not be representational. I see as realism whatever is genuinely begotten by life and moves the human spirit, even if there are no images of people, houses or trees....[27]

Social commitment, political conscience, an ability to communicate universal aspects of human experience, an exploration of the human condition – these were the qualities of 'social realism' for Berger. Further, the debate about the kind of art which could embody these qualities was part of a wider European discussion about the social responsibility of the artist in post-war society. The model was Italian realism – an amalgam of modernist styles, figurative and historical humanist traditions and a distinct resistance to the Soviet line. These characteristics were epitomised, for Berger and others, in the work of the Italian Realist Renato Guttuso and in the work of sculptors Ossip Zadkine, Peter Peri and George Fullard.[28]

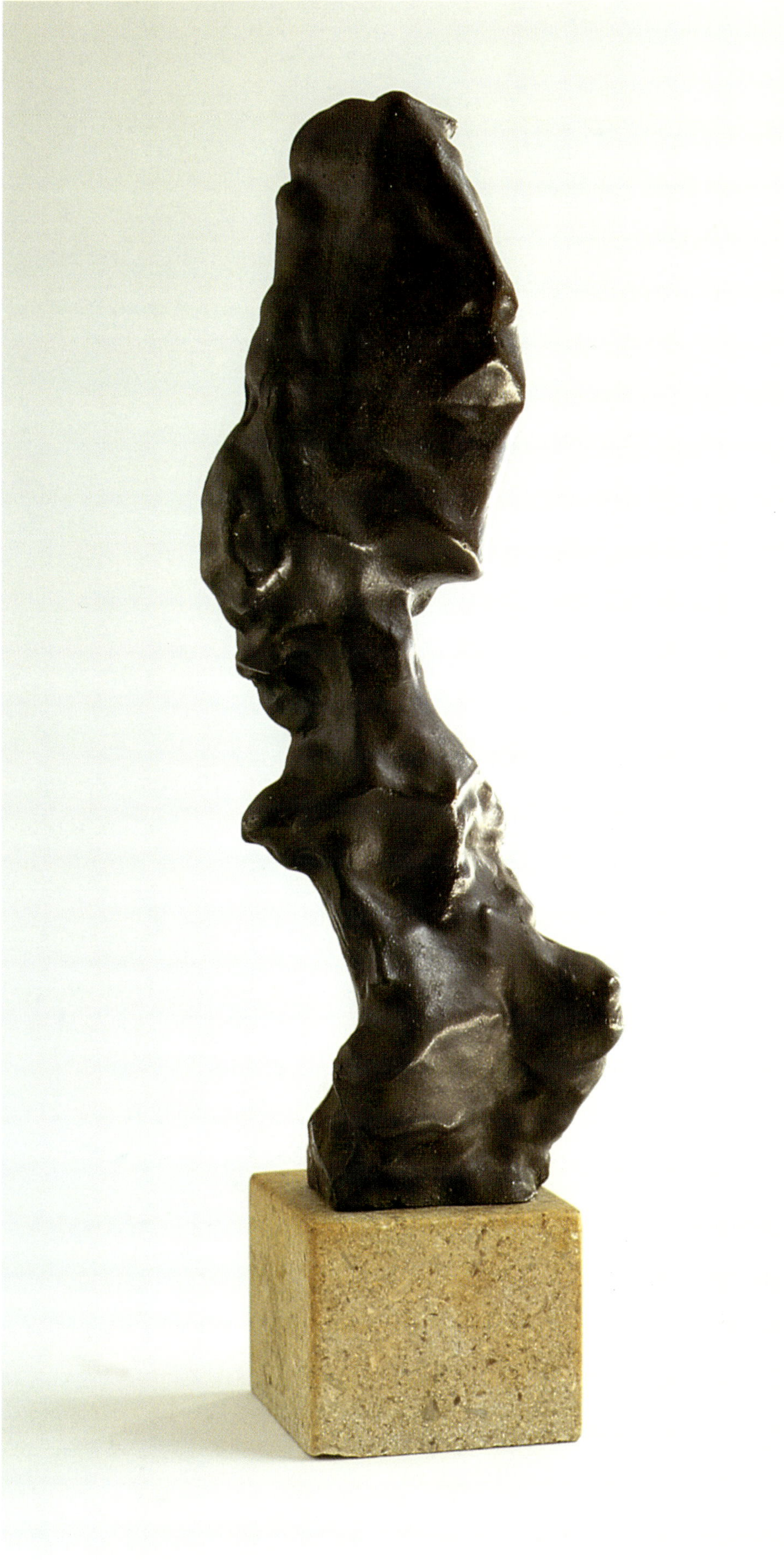

Plate 40 (Cat.46)
Head 1960
Bronze (edition of two)
26 x 9.5 x 5 cm

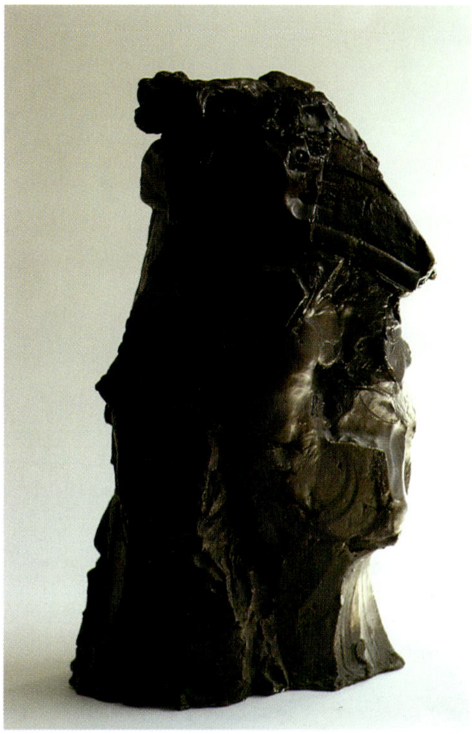

Plate 41 (Cat.43)
Head 1960
Bronze
66 x 32 x 30 cm

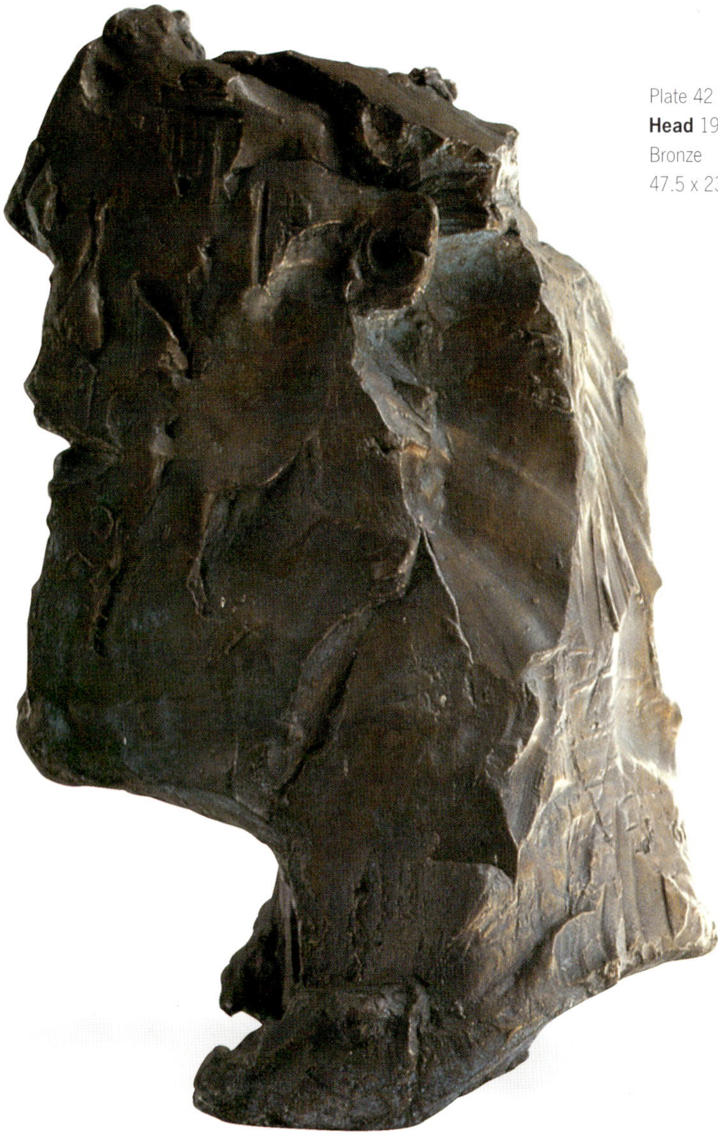

Plate 42 (Cat.50)
Head 1961
Bronze
47.5 x 23.7 x 33 cm

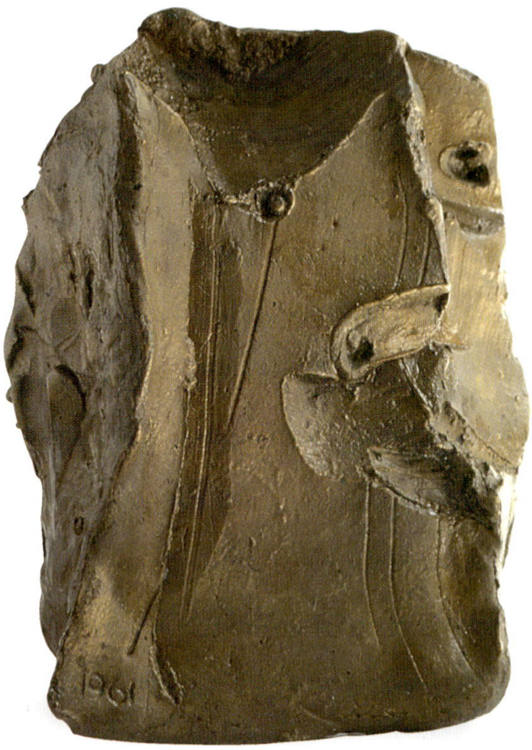

Plate 44 (Cat.52)
Head 1961
Bronze
24.2 x 19 x 10.2 cm

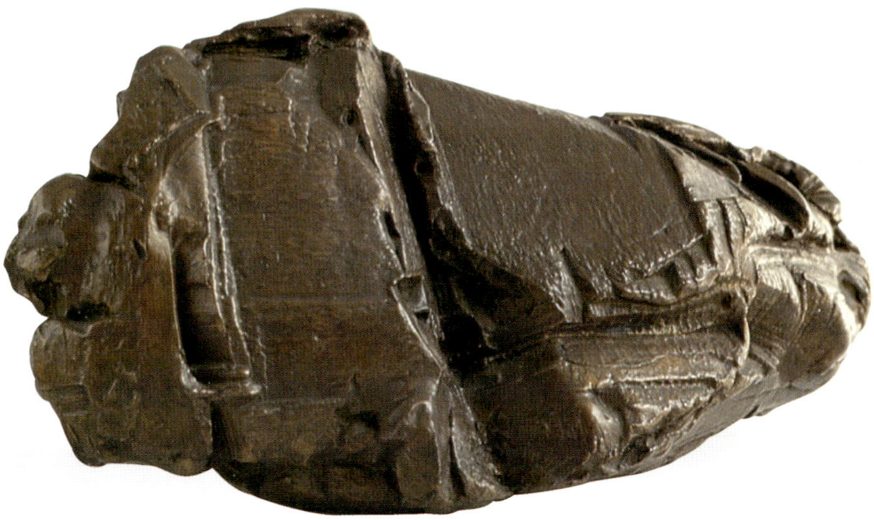

Plate 43 (Cat.51)
Head 1961
Bronze
20.3 x 40.4 x 16.5 cm

OPPOSITE
Plate 45 (Cat.34)
Pregnant woman 1959
Wood (edition of two)
61 x 27 x 13 cm

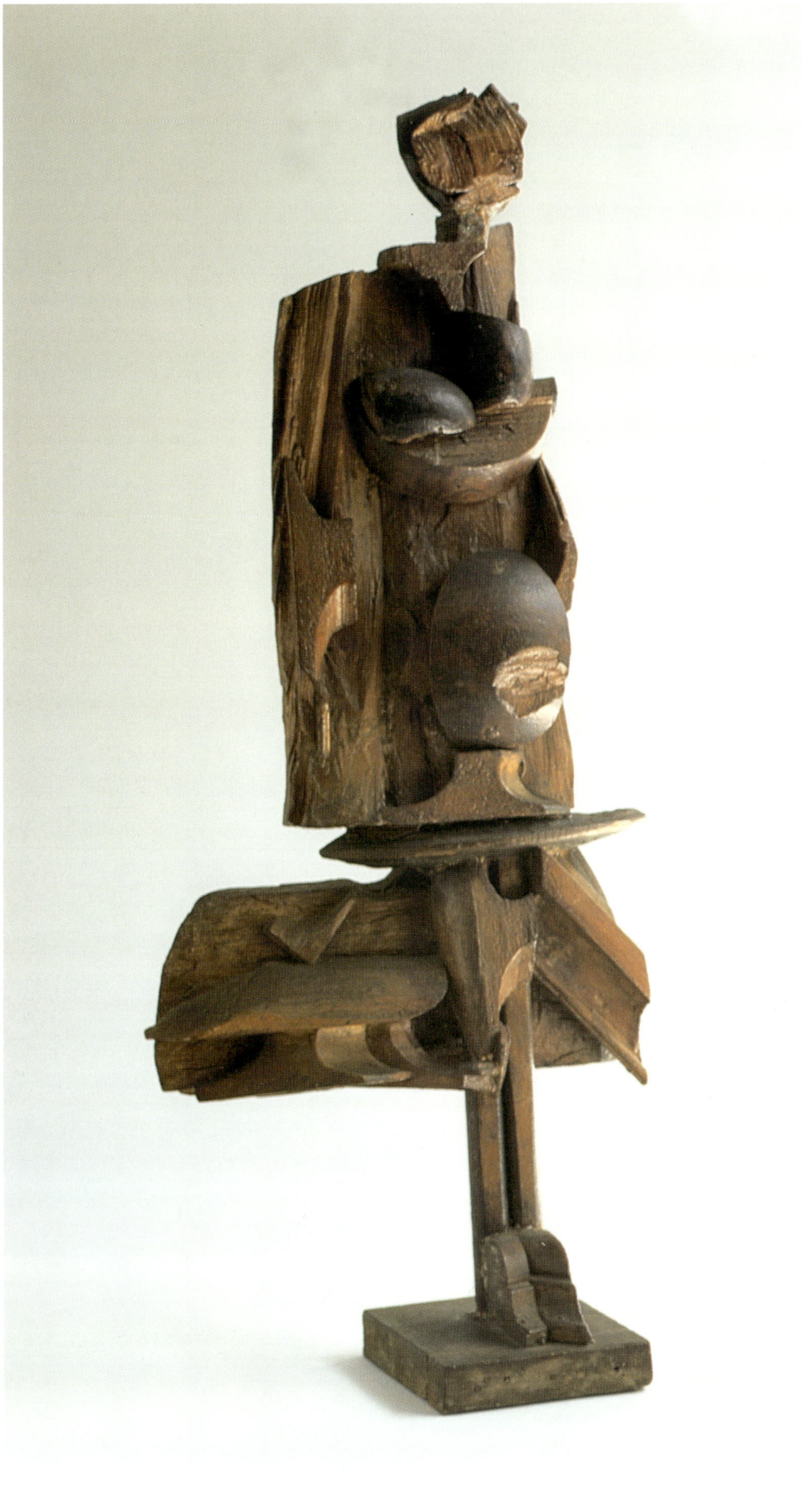

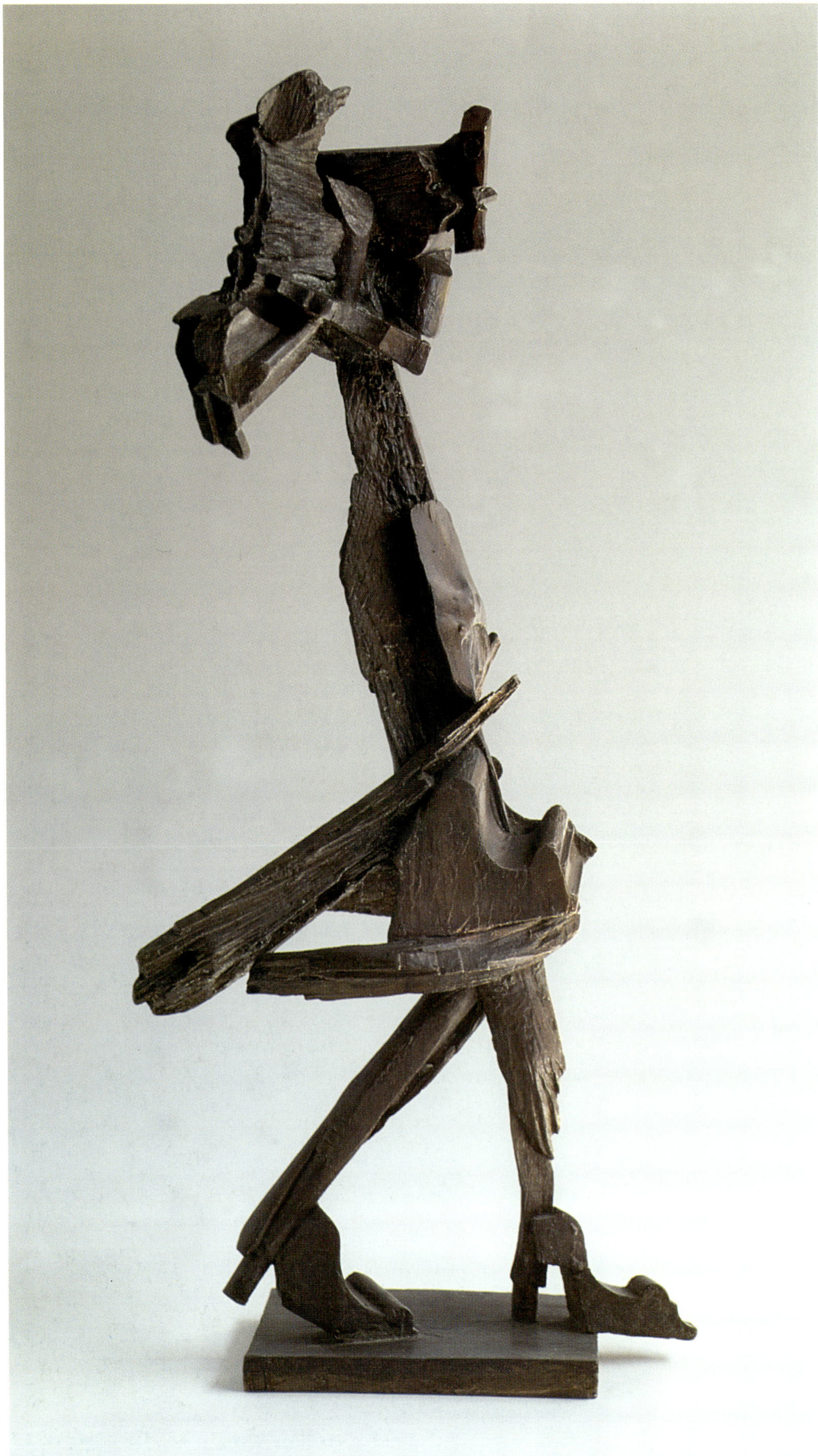

Plate 46 (Cat.35)
Striding woman and child 1959
Bronze
(edition of two)
80 x 31 x 24 cm

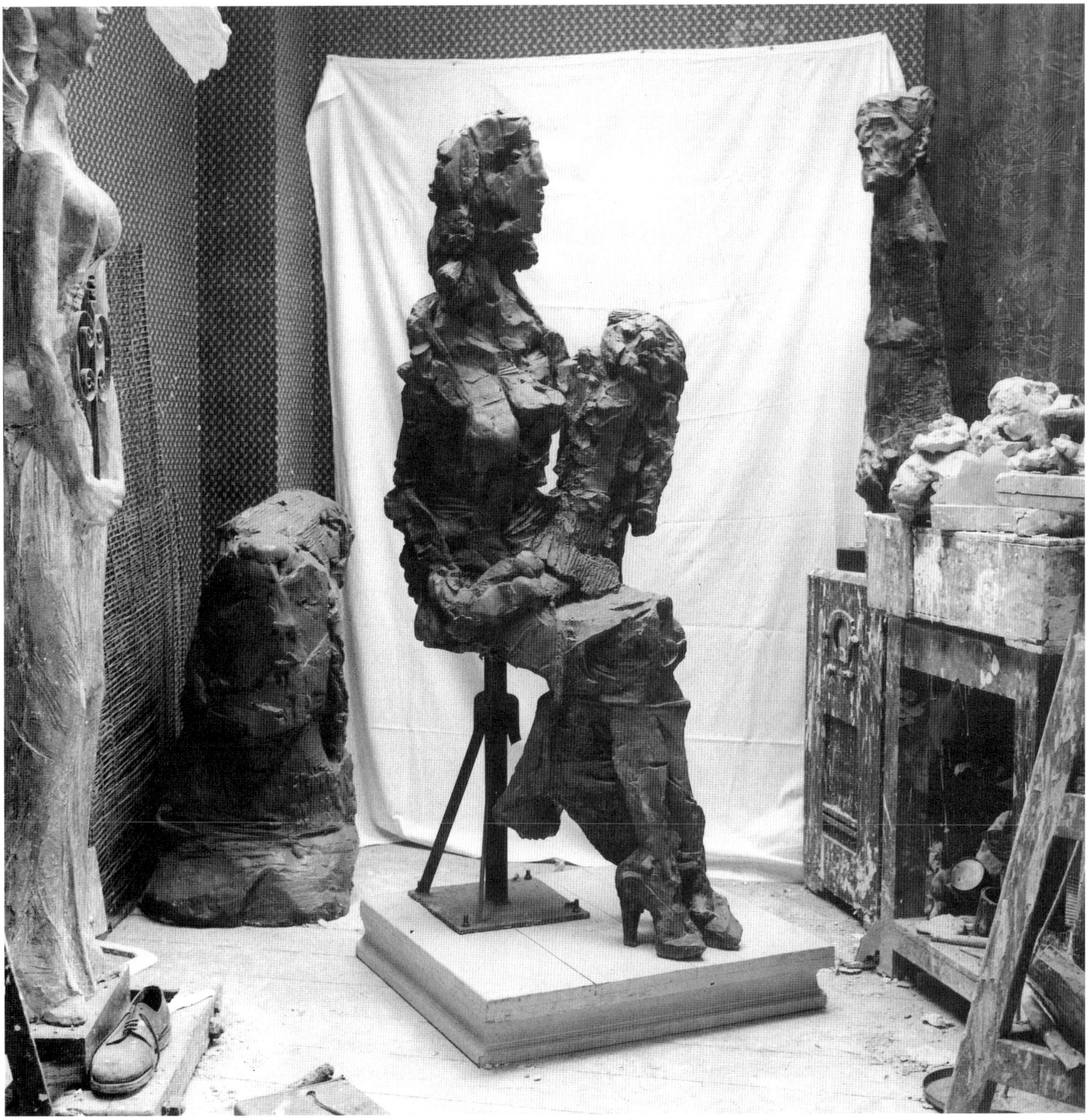

Plate 47
View of works in Fullard's Park Walk studio with *Mother and child* 1958 (Cat.31), plaster for bronze, in the centre.

Yet Fullard's work rarely had an overt political motivation. Throughout the 1950s he focused firmly on the human figure. Women are prominent, particularly mothers with young children or babies. Occasionally there is a male figure. Fullard's sculpture certainly shows a concern with the universalities of human experience. Yet these are not the bland universalities of an ahistorical liberalism. Fullard's work at this time has sociological sophistication. His individuals experience their individuality within emphatically

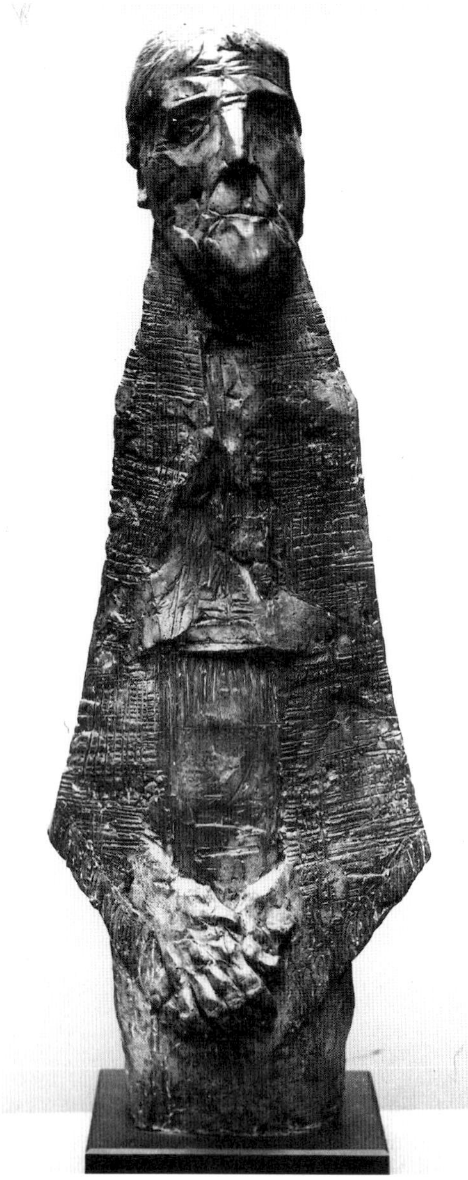

Plate 48 (Cat.25)
Old woman 1957
Ciment fondu
108.5 x 38.5 x 8.5 cm

concrete social and historical structures. Tellingly, his work was never 'realistic' in any superficial sense and he had little inclination towards re-creating individual likeness as his following comments illustrate:

> Figurative work ... recognizes the fact of art and life as parallel but separate realities, and the requirement is not for intentional resemblance to life, but for the phenomenon of coincidental significance. This is a requirement quite disconnected from that appalling appeal to public sentiment which so often disguises itself as figurative art.[29]

In the same article, Fullard stressed his sculptural interest in the 'in-significant figure'. His comment may refer to the notion of the human being belittled by the vastness of the natural and social forces impinging on it. Equally, it may be Fullard's rejection of the traditional notion of a sculpture as a monument, commemorating some celebrated figure from public or political life. It implies that monuments to the 'workers' – the exchange of one set of individuals for those of another social class – are no solution either. It emphasises, again, Fullard's concern for the unremarkable unknown figure, the ordinary person – the 'nobody'.

The stress on the human figure and the humanist view which placed man and woman at the centre of things was central to Fullard's work and ideas. 'Humanism' was, of course, strongly linked to Renaissance ideas, but it was consciously adopted as a key concept of the political left in the 1950s. In 1932, Lukács had written of the need to incorporate humanism into partisanship and later humanism became absorbed into the language of communists and sympathisers. Henry Moore has been viewed as the archetypal humanist sculptor but Julian Stallabrass has pointed out that Moore's humanism was different from that of the social realists. Moore indeed became an acceptable public figurehead for post-war Britain. Though he was certainly sympathetic to socialist causes, his particular brand of 'humanism' sat quite comfortably with his links with the modernist avant-garde and was distinct from any associations with 'social realism'.[30]

For the political left in the 1950s, and Marxists and communist sympathisers in particular, humanism was, more specifically, posed in stark contrast with despair. These polarities were explored in terms of art in Paul Hogarth's article, 'Humanism versus Despair' in *Marxist Quarterly* in 1955, where the writer claimed humanism for the realists and the political left – and allotted despair and a lack of faith in humanity to those who had abandoned figurative art and turned to abstraction or pained images of animal, bird or insect life. Emphatically referring to the anti-humanism in the work of the eight sculptors who had been hailed by the critic Herbert Read as Moore's successors at the 1952 Venice *Biennale*, Hogarth wrote,

> ... over-personalised and socially irresponsible art is encouraged as never before, isolating the artists even more from the general public ... re-armament and Cold War thinking has affected the very nature of art itself, replacing the qualities of accessibility and humanism with those of introspection and despair....[31]

Similar ideas about 'humanism' were expressed elsewhere, nowhere more succinctly than by Doris Lessing in an essay entitled 'The Small Personal Voice'. She stressed her humanist viewpoint, writing of the 'pleasurable

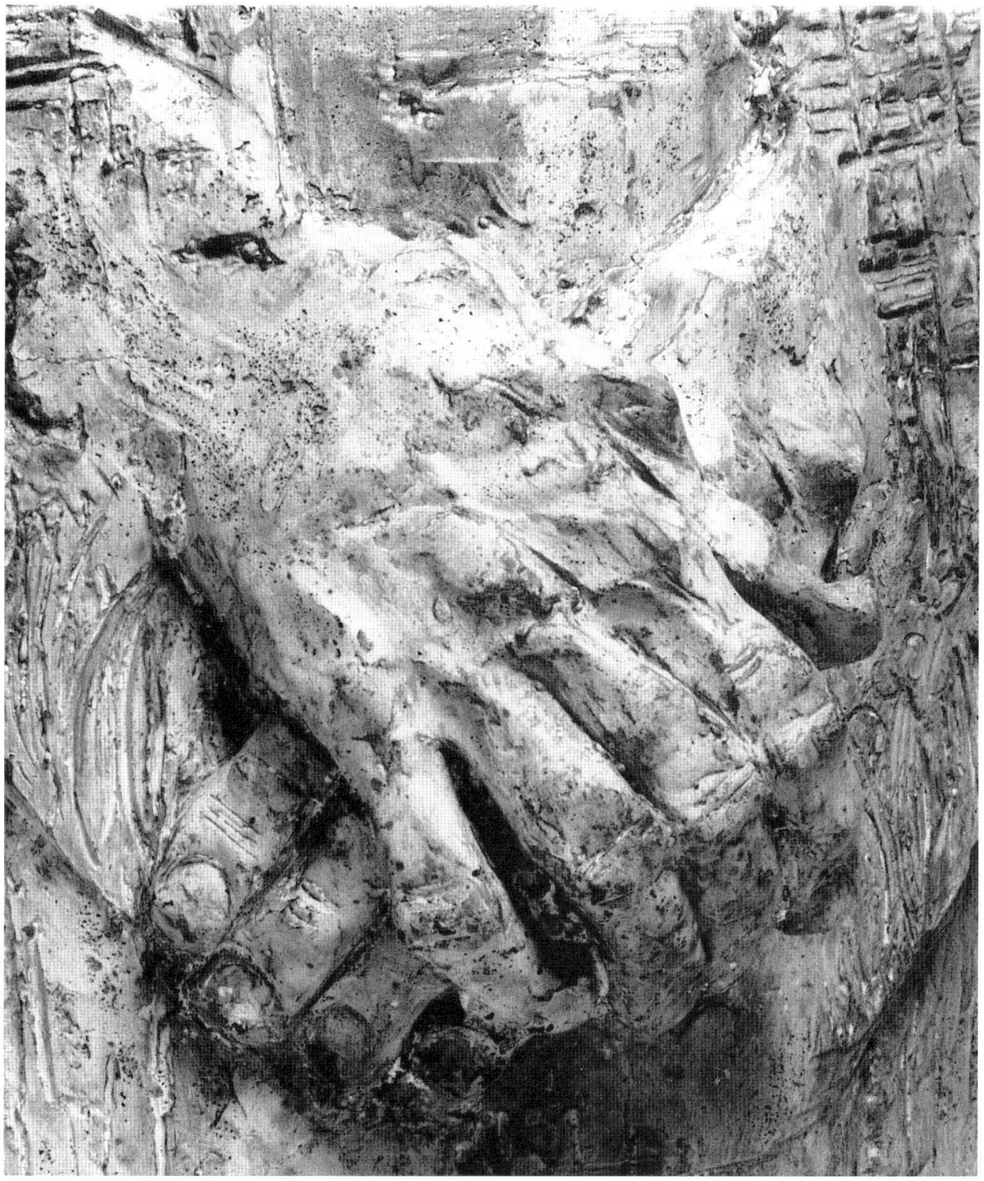

Plate 49 (Cat.25)
Old woman 1957 (detail)
Ciment fondu
108.5 x 38.5 x 8.5 cm

luxury of despair' as a betrayal. She also appealed for writers and artists to resist the demand for simple statements of political faith – as, in her opinion, they too could only lead to 'dull art'. Somewhere between the two extremes, in Lessing's view, lay the 'resting place', 'in an age of committee art, of public art, people may begin to feel again a need for the small, personal voice'.[32]

Fullard was directly involved in contemporary debate about art and culture, partly through his participation in the Geneva Club. This venture was set up in 1955 by Berger, primarily as an informal discussion forum for writers, artists, scientists and poets. The 'idea' for such a group was devised, according to one participant, at Fullard's Fawcett Yard studio. The club had been inspired by the temporary thaw in East-West relations at the Geneva summit conference and also by news of Ilya Ehrenberg's influential novel *The Thaw*, published in the Soviet Union in 1955. Initially, the members met in a restaurant but an anecdote suggests that the 'impoverished artists section' persuaded them to move to the Argyll public house, near Oxford Circus. Regulars included Fullard, his wife as 'secretary', Edward Middleditch, Jack

Smith, Derrick Greaves, Leslie Duxbury, Peter de Francia, John Willett, Randall Swingler, Michael Ayrton, Paul Hogarth, Evelyn Antal, E. P. Thompson and Peter Peri. Various people gave papers: Derek Kartun spoke about the 'Paris scene', Doris Lessing talked on African literature, Christopher Logue gave poetry readings. The informal atmosphere was, however, sometimes an uneasy mix of socialising and politics. Lessing's hindsight in a recent autobiographical work is sharply cynical:

> [Berger had] invited a great many different kinds of people, to break down those incestuously defined barriers. Everyone was there. The place was full, it buzzed, it jumped, it vibrated. What a good idea we all thought, how clever of John to have thought of it, and of course there must be many more such occasions. And then John called us to order and made a speech. It was a good cause of some kind, political. At once it was observed that the painters, having exchanged looks, were making for the door. They went first, as people remarked, 'They always did have good sense'.[33]

Views about art and politics were diverse but the members or invitees, initially at least, shared a political radicalism. Inevitably, the consensus could not withstand the international crises of 1956. The Suez crisis threatened to plunge Britain into another war. More importantly, the crushing of the Hungarian rebellion directly provoked widespread disaffection within the Communist Party and many individuals resigned. The Geneva group broke up at the end of 1956 with a rather chaotic final meeting. Nevertheless, this short-lived loose cultural group represented one attempt to bypass, on the one hand, the dictates of Soviet policy, and on the other, the apolitical wringing of hands.[34]

The international political events of 1956 were accompanied by something of a 'cultural shift' on the domestic front. For Robert Hewison, it marked a new trend which lionised and individualised a frustrated working class, and culminated in the brief triumph of the 'Angry Young Men'.[35] This 'cultural shift' was also reflected in the brief success of some of the very artists Berger had championed as 'famously unacceptable' just a year earlier – painters Greaves, Middleditch, Smith and Bratby, dubbed the 'Kitchen Sink' painters on their showing at the Venice *Biennale* in the same year.[36]

Surprisingly, the events of 1956 did not prevent Fullard's first major show of sculpture from travelling to the Pushkin Museum of Fine Arts in Moscow on the invitation of the Union of Soviet Artists in 1957. This was the *Looking at People* exhibition, the first show of contemporary British art to be seen in the Soviet Union since 1917, organised by sculptor Betty Rea and Paul Hogarth. John Berger had suggested Fullard to Hogarth as a possible participant in the show, following Jacob Epstein's decision to decline an invitation to take part. Although there was a brief period of 'thaw' in political relations, the exhibition was staged at a politically sensitive time. Betty Rea had expressed her concern about the possible political implications of the show in a letter to Hogarth, in which she noted her unease about sub-titling it a 'realist exhibition' because it gave it a 'political flavour and the potential to irritate a lot of people'.[37] Fullard works shown included *Skipping girl* 1955, *Mother and child* 1956, *Head of a worker* 1957, *Old woman* 1957, *Walking man* 1957 and *Running woman* 1957.

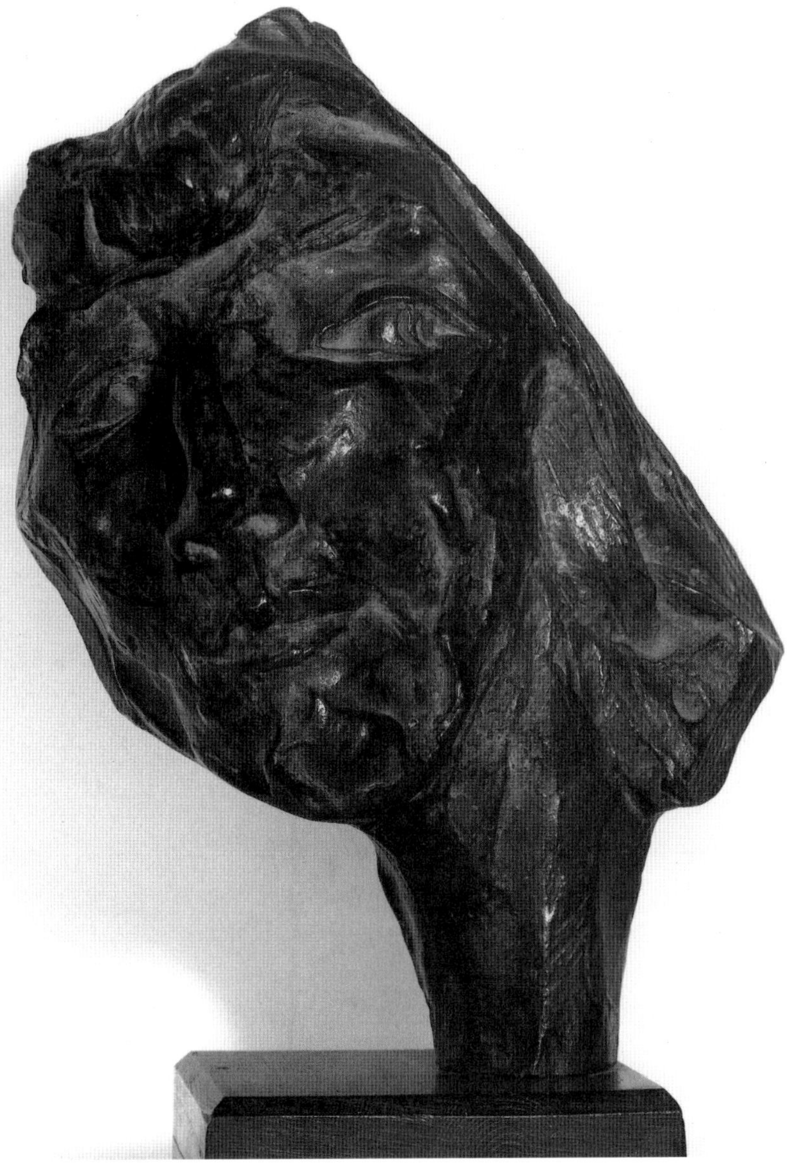

Plate 50 (Cat.22)
Glancing woman 1956
Bronze
33 x 25.5 x 12.7 cm

Around 1956, Fullard's work developed a different look. Following a couple of weeks when he had been confined to bed with influenza, he returned to his work with a renewed enthusiasm and a fresh style. One of the first pieces he made was *Glancing woman* 1956 with its angular forms and planes which owe much to Cubism. These same stylistic characteristics can be seen in the profile-like heads of his early wooden figures, such as *Woman* 1959. Their sliced flattened profiles resemble the shapes in the dark gritstone edges at Froggatt and Curbar Edge in the Peak District, an area well-trodden in the late 1930s and early 1940s by Fullard.

His work at this time also shows a growing sense of the absurd. This emerged fully in the later war assemblages but it was already present in the 1950s. There is a subversive, comic touch in the details of some pieces – especially in *Walking man* 1957 and *Angry woman* 1958. In Fullard's work, the absurd and the real converge and subvert each other, creating ambiguity and layers of meaning.

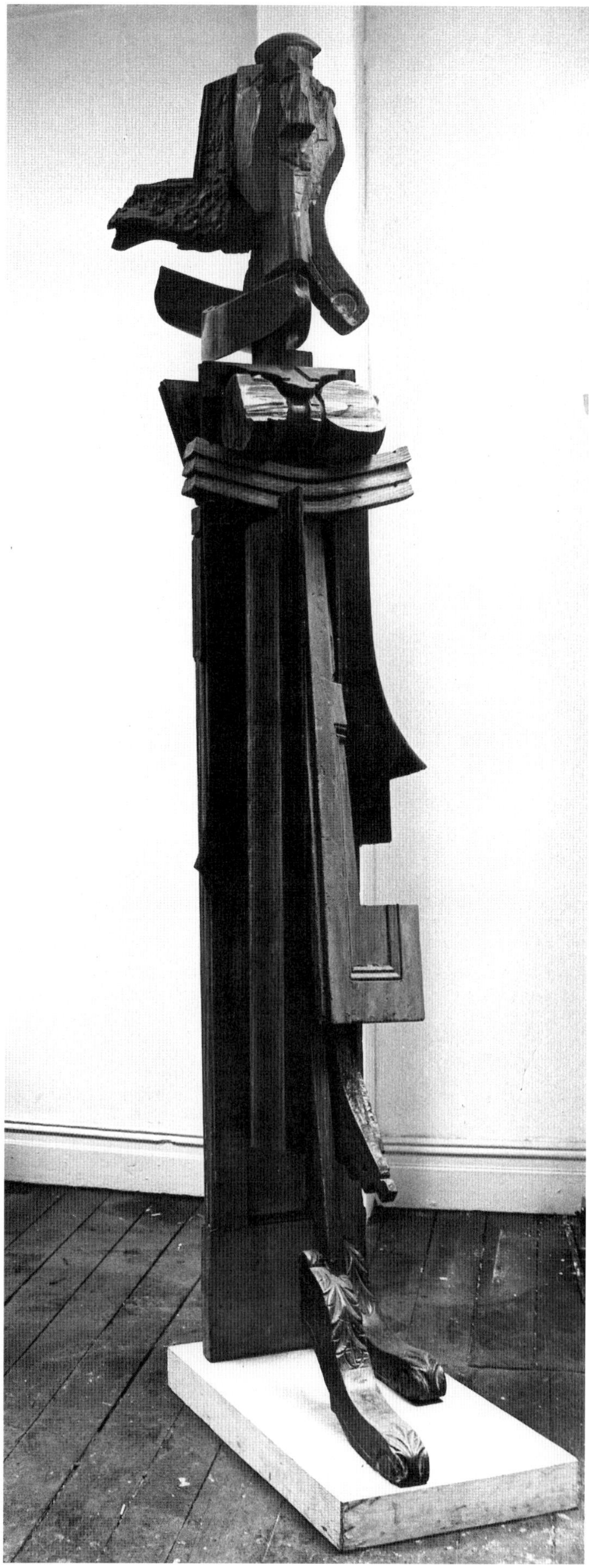

Plate 51 (Cat.38)
Woman 1959
Assemblage of various wooden items
229.2 x 43.2 x 81.3 cm

Fullard's work of the 1950s cannot be adequately understood by focusing exclusively on the artist's life and career but neither is it a simple reflection of social, cultural issues of the period. His sculpture has 'anger' but it was not the empty anger of 'Angry Young Men'. In 1957, Paul Hogarth had described Fullard as 'an angry young man on the side of man', marking a subtle but important distinction. 'Anger' may have been fashionable among a handful of literary critics of the mid-1950s but the suppressed anger in Fullard's sculpture may relate to his personal experiences as a young trooper in a tank on a battlefield in Italy.

Although the 'cold climate' of the 1950s was not conducive to a sculptor with realist associations and communist sympathies, after the Moscow exhibition Fullard's prospects began to improve. Berger's support and the Moscow show may have contributed, although no work was sold and there was little positive critical interest other than from politically sympathetic sources. In 1957, Fullard secured a regular part-time teaching post at St Albans School of Art, which enabled him to work on his own ideas without constant financial problems. He began to show his sculpture in group exhibitions and won the Junior Prize at the *1st John Moores Liverpool Exhibition*.

The end of the 1950s was a period of political and cultural transition. Looking back, Jack Smith views the end of the decade as a period of transition for many artists and feels that Fullard 'shed' a lot of his previous ideas and with that came a liberation; '... a new freedom to make objects as he wanted them to be irrespective of the past ... I think he realised, like most of us, that art has a life of its own which may occasionally mirror reality...'.[38]

However, there were certain continuities which stayed with Fullard throughout his life and these were to do with a political awareness. Whilst, in 1958, Berger had stressed the unusually 'personal' nature of Fullard's work, there is no doubt that the artist retained a strong political sense of duty and responsibility in relation to his role as a sculptor in society. There is a paradox here. Political commitment poses a dilemma for artists and writers who have to make a choice between pursuing an individual path and satisfying a collective conscience. Among others, Doris Lessing wrote about this dilemma in the 1950s. The possibilities of reconciling individual responsibility with organised society were central questions for Camus and Sartre. Fittingly, Berger had also described Fullard as a 'true existentialist', recognising him as an artist who felt a strong need to act in 'good faith'. In a notebook, Fullard wrote about the seriousness of being an artist and the need to act as a witness to the 'secret history of our times'. Fullard managed to bring together a strong sense of personal integrity with a commitment to communicate something of human value too – reconciling the 'private' artist with 'public' responsibility.[39]

The Cold War had brought both problems and opportunities for Fullard. By the end of the 1950s, his work was gaining a reputation beyond the confines of the political 'Left', he had secured a steady income, he had made his first sales and had his first solo exhibition. There were shifts of emphasis in his life and in his work but there was also a strong element of continuity. Fullard remained resolute on a number of issues: the central importance of 'real' human experience to art and his firm belief in the pursuit of integrity as an artist.

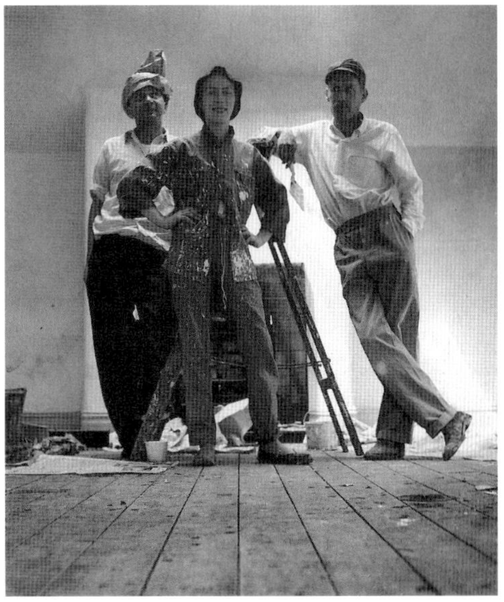

Plate 52
From left to right: friend and photographer Frank Monaco, Irena and George Fullard in May 1960.

NOTES

1. J. Berger, 'George Fullard', *The New Statesman*, 6 September 1958, Vol.56, No.1434, p.274.

2. J. Berger, 'Social Realism and the Young', *The New Statesman and Nation*, 30 July 1955, Vol.50, No.1273, pp.133-4.

3. The first open-air show in 1948 in Battersea Park, jointly organised by London County Council and the Arts Council, attracted 170,000 visitors. See R. Calvocoressi, 'Public Sculpture in the 1950s' in S. Nairne and N. Serota (eds), *British Sculpture in the Twentieth Century*, Whitechapel Art Gallery, London 1981, pp.139-41.

4. The British sculptors were Robert Adams, Kenneth Armitage, Reg Butler, Lynn Chadwick, Geoffrey Clarke, Bernard Meadows, Eduardo Paolozzi and William Turnbull.

5. Calvocoressi, op.cit. at note 3.

6. M. Frayn, 'Festival of Britain' in M. Sissons and P. French (eds), *The Age of Austerity*, London 1963, p.323.

7. Author's correspondence with Irena Fullard 1995-8 and Leslie Duxbury 29 March 1996 and interview with Ernest Adsetts November 1997; also see *Sheffield Star*, 23 February 1951.

8. J. Spalding (ed.), *The Forgotten Fifties*, exh. cat. Graves Art Gallery, Sheffield 1984, p.15. I am also grateful to sculptor Roy Rasmussen, for his recollections and account of the difficulties which artists faced in the 1950s. The Woodstock Gallery, which gave Fullard his first solo show in 1958, was specifically set up by Lyall Watson, Joan Knoblock and Rasmussen, to enable contemporary artists with a modern vision to show their work. Letter to the author, dated 27 March 1998, from Roy Rasmussen. Also see R. Rasmussen, *The Free Painters and Sculptors 1952-1992*, London 1992.

9. J. Bratby, 'Frustrated Painters of a Generation' in A. Brighton and L. Morris (eds), *Towards Another Picture*, Nottingham 1977, pp.18-19.

10. Fullard did briefly teach part-time at Brighton School of Art in the late 1940s; John Warren Davis and Bernard Sindall were two of his students. On the 'Buddha' project, after the film-makers had been unsuccessful in finding a commercial firm to take on the job, Fullard did it in three weeks for a fee of £100. The armature was built up with beer crates and orange boxes and the final sandpapered *papier-mâché* surface was painted gold. The film, directed by Hans M. Nieter, was released in 1956. For the project which involved the modelling of a number of horses, the sculptors hired a live horse as a model. The £850 earnt on this commission enabled Fullard to devote time to his own work for the following eighteen months. Information obtained from the author's discussions and correspondence with Frank Monaco 1995, Bernard and Jeanetta Sindall 1997, Ernest Adsetts November 1997, Leslie Duxbury 1995-7 and audio-recording of Fullard talking about his early career, made at Chelsea in the early 1970s.

11. 'Art in a Cold Climate', *Tribune*, 10 August 1956. A lot of work made in this early period was probably destroyed because of the lack of funds to cast. *Mother and child* 1958 was Fullard's first work to be cast into bronze at a foundry in Fulham. Other early castings of Fullard's work were made at the foundry of John Galizia & Son Ltd. The earliest ledger entry for Fullard, dated 8 December 1959, records the casting of a 'standing figure' at a cost of £95.

12. D. Greaves, 'Except the Kitchen Sink', *Art Review*, June 1994, Vol.XLVI, p.18.

13. Berger, op.cit. at note 2.

14. Smith, Greaves, Middleditch shared Pembroke Road at the end of the 1940s with Fullard. From 1950, the Fullards let the top floor of their residence at Stanley Studios, Park Walk, Chelsea to Jack Smith and family.

15. The radical realism of nineteenth-century sculptors Constantin Meunier and Jules Dalou particularly influenced social realists of the 1930s.

16. But it must be noted that the political 'Left' was not a homogeneous group. In the early 1920s, Trotsky was critical of a literal, narrative 'realism' and later, in exile, utterly condemned Zhdanovite ideas about art.

17. The Artists International Association showed a wide range of art but many of its formative members whether painters or sculptors, such as Betty Rea and Peter Peri, primarily worked in a figurative, realist tradition. For further information see L. Morris and R. Radford, *The Story of the Artists International Association 1933-1953*, Museum of Modern Art, Oxford 1983. More generally, see D. D. Egbert, *Social Radicalism and the Arts – A Cultural History from the French Revolution to 1968*, London 1970, which, despite being written thirty years ago, remains one of the best sources of material on art and left politics.

18. E. Hobsbawm, *The Age of Extremes*, London 1984, p.226.

19. There were, however, notable dissident sculptors. Ernst Neizvestny is one of the most interesting in this context as there are some parallels with Fullard: John Berger brought his work to the attention of the West with his book *Art and Revolution: Ernst Neizvestny and the Role of the Artist in the USSR*, Harmondsworth 1969; Neizvestny was, like Fullard, profoundly affected by his embroilment in two world wars. Neizvestny

commented 'My war ... began in early childhood and it hasn't stopped. I have always had the feeling of being in the front line.' (ibid. p.17) Coincidentally, he volunteered in 1942, aged sixteen years, was gravely wounded behind enemy lines, left for dead but, incredibly, survived. This formative experience of war informed his sculpture of the 1950s and 1960s.

20. Letter, undated presumed 1956, South London Art Gallery archive.

21. J. Berger, 'Sculptural vacuum', *New Statesman*, 17 April 1954, Vol.47, No.1206, p.498.

22. Records and correspondence of the British Communist Artists' Group show that Fullard was invited to make a sculpture for a Party Congress and was invited to join the executive committee of the new journal, *Realism*, which was a re-vamped and expanded version of a previous news-letter. The editor had also approached him about writing articles: he was, for example, asked to write a response to Pevsner's Reith lectures of 1955 about 'Englishness and Art' – lengthy notes in Fullard's 'Copie-bok' (see later for other tran-scripts) appear to be the basis of this. It was never published although the journal only ran to six copies anyhow. See records and correspondence in the National Museum of Labour History archive, Manchester.

23. For example, Deborah Cherry and Juliet Steyn explored the issue of 'realism' in the 1950s in 'The Moment of Realism 1952-1956' in *Artscribe*, June 1982, No.35, although, polarising it with 'abstraction', they concentrated on the way in which it had been 'hidden' by art history rather than differentiating between the different forms it took.

24. *Realism*, No.1, June 1955, p.3.

25. Berger, op.cit. at note 2.

26. C. Lindey, *Art in the Cold War*, London 1990.

27. Y. Yevtushenko, *A Precocious Autobiography*, (first published in English 1963) Harmondsworth 1965, p.122.

28. Guttuso was a personal friend of Derrick Greaves as they had met in the earlier 1950s in Italy. Paul Hogarth, and others, have remarked on Fullard's admiration for Guttuso's work: letter to the author, dated 22 May 1996, from Paul Hogarth. When Guttuso had a show in London in 1955, Fullard was among the guests at a special celebration party thrown by Greaves: J. Hyman, 'A "Pioneer Painter": Renato Guttuso and Realism in Britain' in *Guttuso*, exh. cat. White-chapel Art Gallery, London 1996, p.47. Steve Hurst, who taught at Chelsea from 1971, has remarked that Fullard often talked about the influence on his work of post-war communist artists such as Picasso but, especially, André Fougeron: letter to the author, 21 October 1996.

29. George Fullard, 'Sculpture and Survival', *The Painter and Sculptor*, summer 1959, Vol.2, No.2, p.9.

30. J. Stallabrass, 'The Mother and Child Theme in the Work of Henry Moore' in *Henry Moore – Mother and Child*, Henry Moore Foundation 1992, p.17.

31. Hogarth is referring to Herbert Read's, now infamous, comments that the work of these sculptors embodied the anxiety of the age – the 'geometry of fear'. P. Hogarth, 'Humanism and Despair in British Art Today', in *Marxist Quarterly*, January 1955, Vol.2, No.1, p.37.

32. Doris Lessing's essay was published in 1957 in *Declaration*, a collection of oppositional 'credos' commissioned by Tom Maschler from all the important young writers of the day, including Colin Wilson, John Osborne, Lindsay Anderson and John Wain. Notably, 'anti-humanism' was a theme taken up by Stuart Holroyd in his essay.

33. D. Lessing, *Walking in the Shade*, London 1997, p.201.

34. John Warren Davis, another regular Geneva Club attender and close friend of Fullard's, has described it as 'a very politically oriented (Marxist) drinking club'. He has also noted that, although Fullard was sympathetic to Marxism, he had 'great difficulty in reconciling social-realist art with his views of the artist as free-spirit'. Letter to the author, dated 27 August 1997, from John Warren Davis. I am grateful to former members of the 'club' for their recollections including Irena Fullard, John Willett, Peter de Francia, John Berger, Paul Hogarth, Derrick Greaves, Leslie Duxbury and also to Andy Croft for sight of his research material.

35. See R. Hewison, *In Anger – Culture in the Cold War 1945-60*, London 1981, pp.148-85.

36. In 1956, as part of the selection committee for the *Biennale*, Herbert Read visited Fawcett Yard, the studio shared by Greaves and Fullard. Greaves describes Read's party 'picking a careful way through studio detritus and muck and rubble and plaster'. (See op.cit. at note 12.)

37. *Looking at People* first showed in 1955 at the Whitworth Art Gallery, Manchester and featured work by the organisers, Betty Rea, Paul Hogarth and Carel Weight. The 1957 show added work by Derrick Greaves, Ruskin Spear, Alistair Grant, Edward Ardizzone and Fullard. See Paul Hogarth papers, archive of Royal Academy of Arts, London and also Paul Hogarth, *Cold War Reports 1947-67*, exh. cat. Norfolk Institute of Art and Design, 1989.

38. Letter to the author, dated 12 July 1995, from Jack Smith.

39. See later '**Transcripts of writings by George Fullard**'.

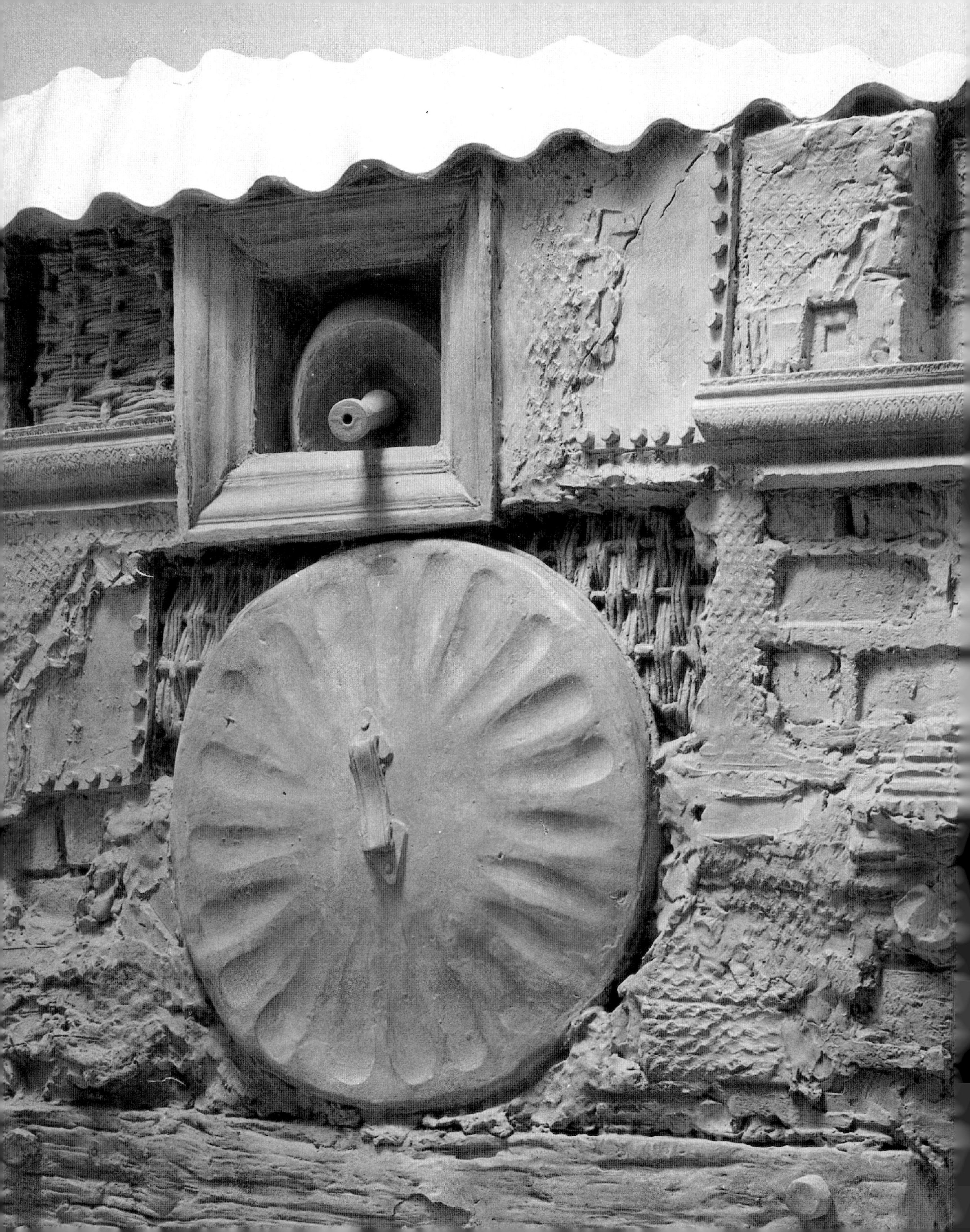

4

Assemblage and war 1959-64

Plate 53 (Cat.58)
War game 1962 (detail)
Ciment fondu
148 x 146 x 71 cm

The period from about 1959 to the end of 1964 was probably the most productive of Fullard's whole career. In these years he made and exhibited the works considered by many to have been his most important and successful: the assembled wooden figures and the war series. The year of 1961 was a turning-point for Fullard, as Gallery One staged a major solo show featuring his recent assemblages. Also, in this year he made the first of a series of sculptures which dealt with war. This subject preoccupied Fullard for the following three years and culminated in a spectacular exhibition of all the war pieces at the prestigious Marlborough New London Gallery in 1964. In the early 1960s, his work featured in Arts Council tours, London County Council open-air exhibitions and in various group shows, including ones at the South London, Portal and Brook Street Galleries in London. Edward Lucie-Smith, the resident art critic for *The Listener*, selected Fullard's *Head* 1961 for his Critic's Choice show at Arthur Tooth and Sons in 1962. At the Hanover Gallery in London, Fullard's assembled wooden figures were shown alongside sculpture by Arp, César, Giacometti, Ipousteguy, Nevelson and others. Erica Brausen, one of the first women art-dealers in London to advocate the showing of contemporary art and someone who 'courageously backed dark horses', raised Fullard's international profile by showing his work in an exhibition of contemporary European sculpture staged at the spacious new Gimpel-Hanover Galerie in Zurich in 1963.[1]

Through showing at the Hanover and elsewhere, Fullard's work increasingly came to the notice of critics and reviewers writing for international magazines: *Das Kunstwerk* featured an article on Fullard in 1964, *Metro* published one the following year. Further, his increasing reputation as a rising young sculptor earned him the admiration of Lawrence Gowing, Principal at Chelsea School of Art, who, in 1963, sought out Fullard to be Head of Sculpture at a time of rejuvenation and major redevelopment in art education. Fullard's 'shedding' of previous techniques and ideas may not have been total by any means but, undoubtedly, it had a considerable impact on his career in the first half of the 1960s.

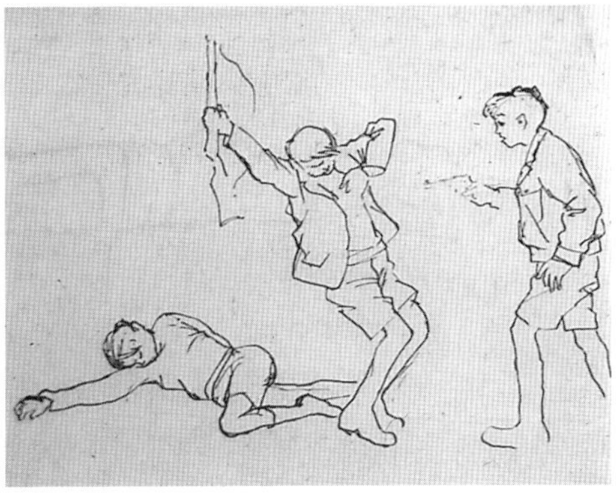

Plate 54
Boys playing at war 1960s
Ink on paper
Private collection

Survival and salvage

Old wood is ... a living chronicle. Weather-beaten, gray, it speaks to human beings in intimate ways: the great trees of vanishing forests, the fire and shelter that preserved the race over uncounted precarious centuries, or perhaps only sad fragments of childhood histories, bits of lost and broken toys.[2]

Old wooden objects and bits of furniture have a particular way of embodying human presence and past lives. Every scratch on a worn door-panel or scuffed chair-leg has a human tale. Fullard chose old wood for his first assemblages. He rescued and saved these domestic relics from the obscurity of the scrap-heap, giving the title of *Survivors* to one of his earliest pieces – perhaps an overt reference to his own 'survival' but surely echoing the preoccupation discernible in his article for *The Painter and Sculptor*, published in summer 1959, entitled 'Sculpture and survival'. Scored with childlike graffiti, these early assemblages might have been the 'sad fragments of childhood histories' or they might, tantalisingly, be the work of the artist as he purposefully evokes memories, the passing of time and grief for infant innocence. The intimate qualities of old crafted wood, which appealed so much to Fullard's artistic sensibility, were described by Harriet Janis in a comprehensive survey of collage, published in 1962. The book itself was both a reflection of and a contribution to the huge wave of interest in all aspects of collage and assemblage in the late 1950s and early 1960s.

Fullard's turn to assemblage has to be considered in the context of this collage 'revival' of the period and also as an integral part of wider cultural developments. Diane Walden's recent study of collage, the found object and assemblage ascribes collage and related activities a pivotal role in the art of the twentieth century, arguing that it has greatly expanded the language and range of art practice and provided a 'compelling history of our time'.[3] Fullard brought a distinctively individual character to his use of assemblage, exploiting the magical transformatory possibilities of ordinary objects in the self-conscious pursuit of his own particular ideas.

In 1959, Fullard began to experiment with the junk which he had been accumulating both in his Chelsea studio and also in the sculpture department at St Albans School of Art, where he taught alongside John Mills. The change of media and techniques were, however, neither as total nor as abrupt as one might assume from a cursory view of the works made. His explosive *Angry woman* of 1958 is a transitional piece which clearly shows where battens of wood have been used to shape the clay, presaging the use of assemblage. Jasia Reichardt noted this in 1965, remarking that this sculpture 'in its strong affinity with forms typical of second-hand wood, anticipated Fullard's next development'.[4] After 1959, Fullard continued to work in clay, producing a fine series of female heads in 1960-1 and four sculptures entitled *Falling woman*. Importantly, these pieces modelled in clay reflect his assemblages too. In particular, the large *Head* 1960 and the large *Falling woman* 1961, with their textured surfaces imprinted with various materials and flat objects, have a kinship with his wooden sculpture.

Fullard's exploration of assemblage may have been a result of purposeful attempts to find a new form of expression. On a more mundane level though,

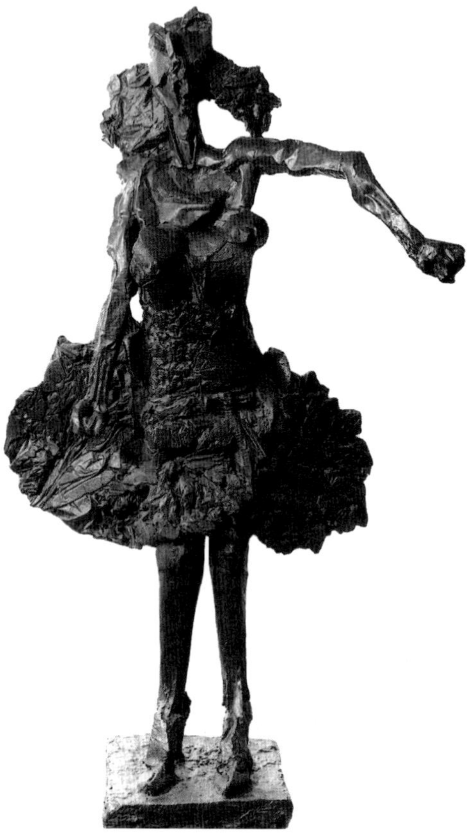

Plate 55 (Cat.30)
Angry woman 1958
Bronze
213.5 x 122 x 85 cm

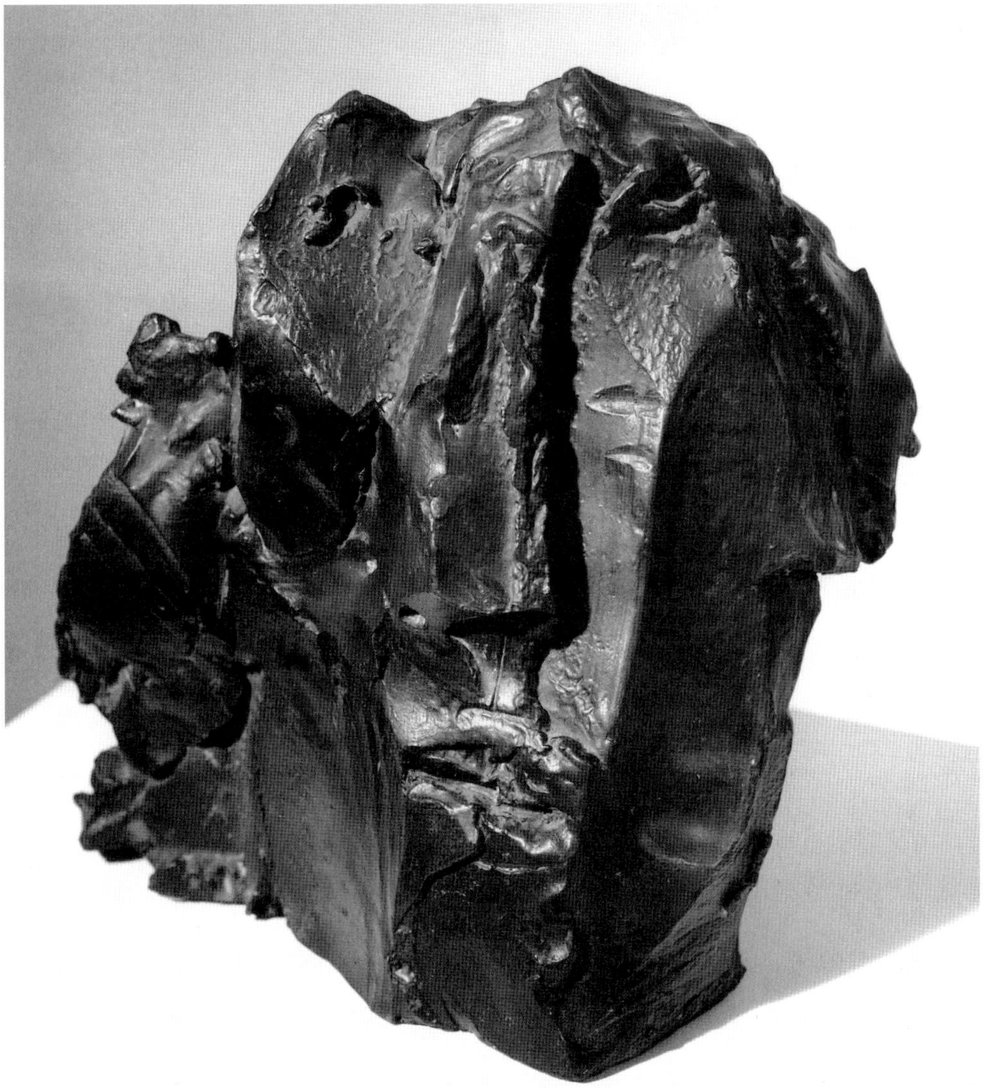

Plate 56 (Cat.44)
Head 1960
Bronze
33 x 30 x 19.5 cm

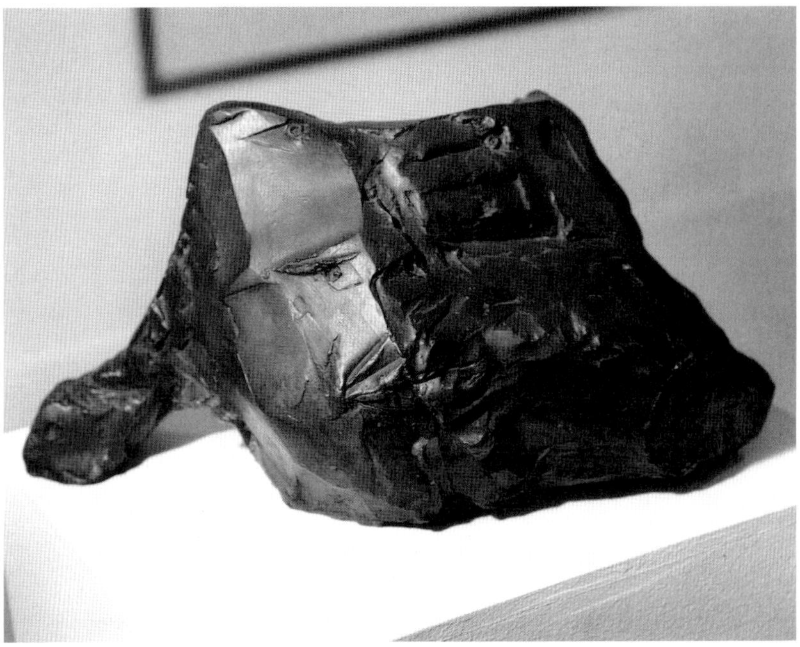

Plate 57 (Cat.45)
Head 1960
Bronze
28 x 46.5 x 23.5 cm

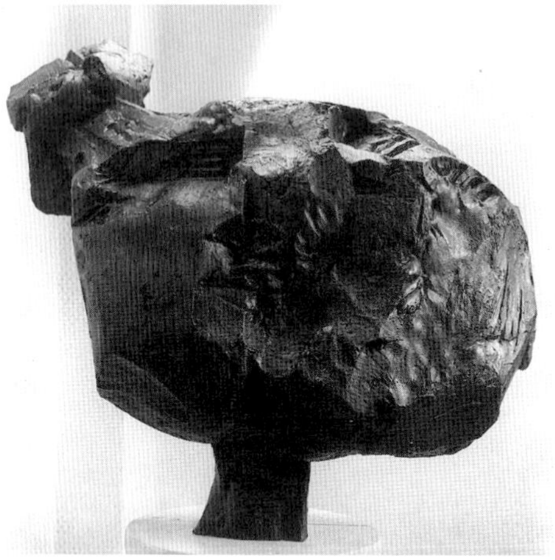

Plate 58 (Cat.42)
Head 1960
Bronze
69 x 84 x 31 cm

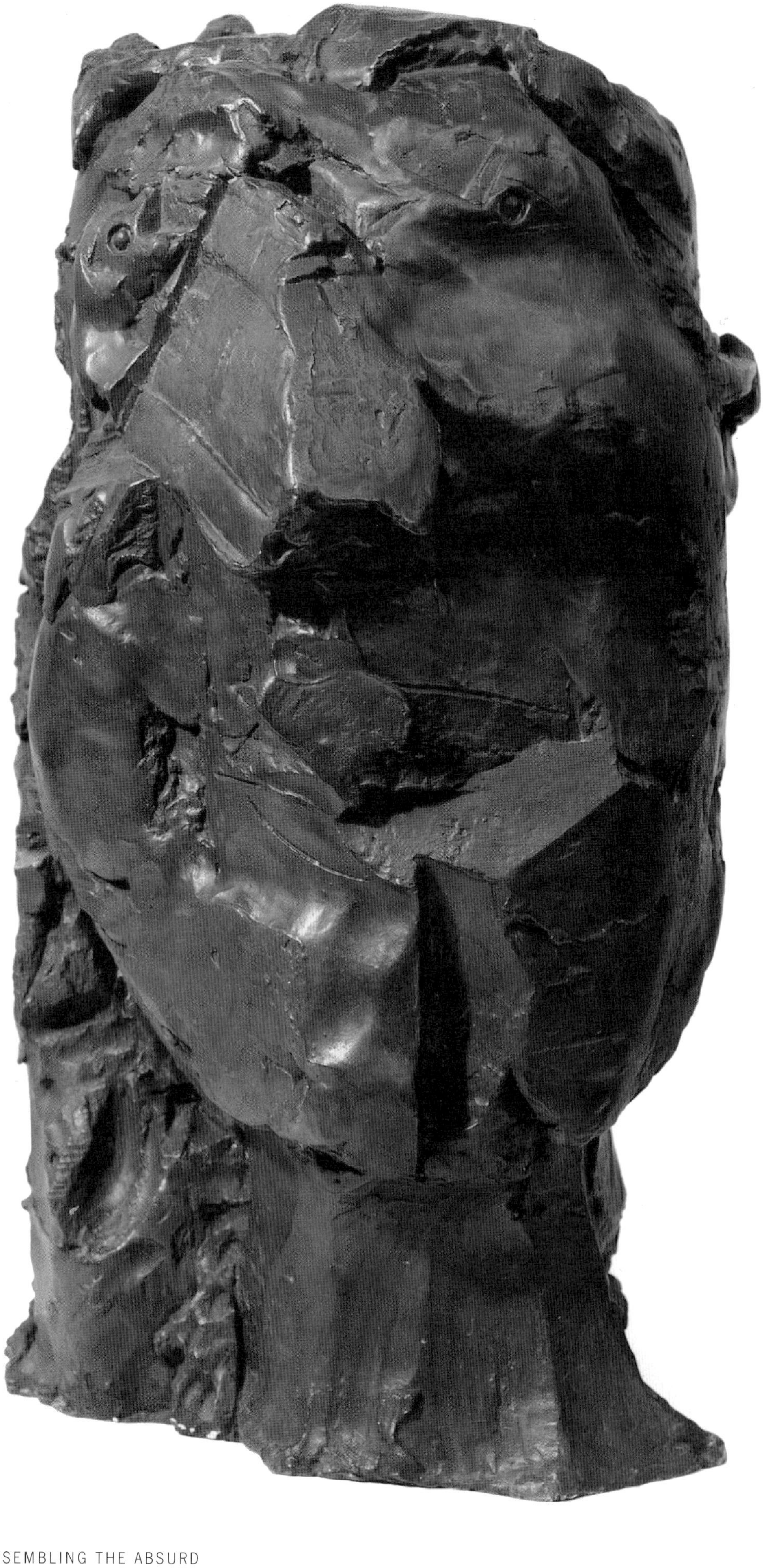

Plate 59 (Cat.43)
Head 1960
Bronze
66 x 32 x 30 cm

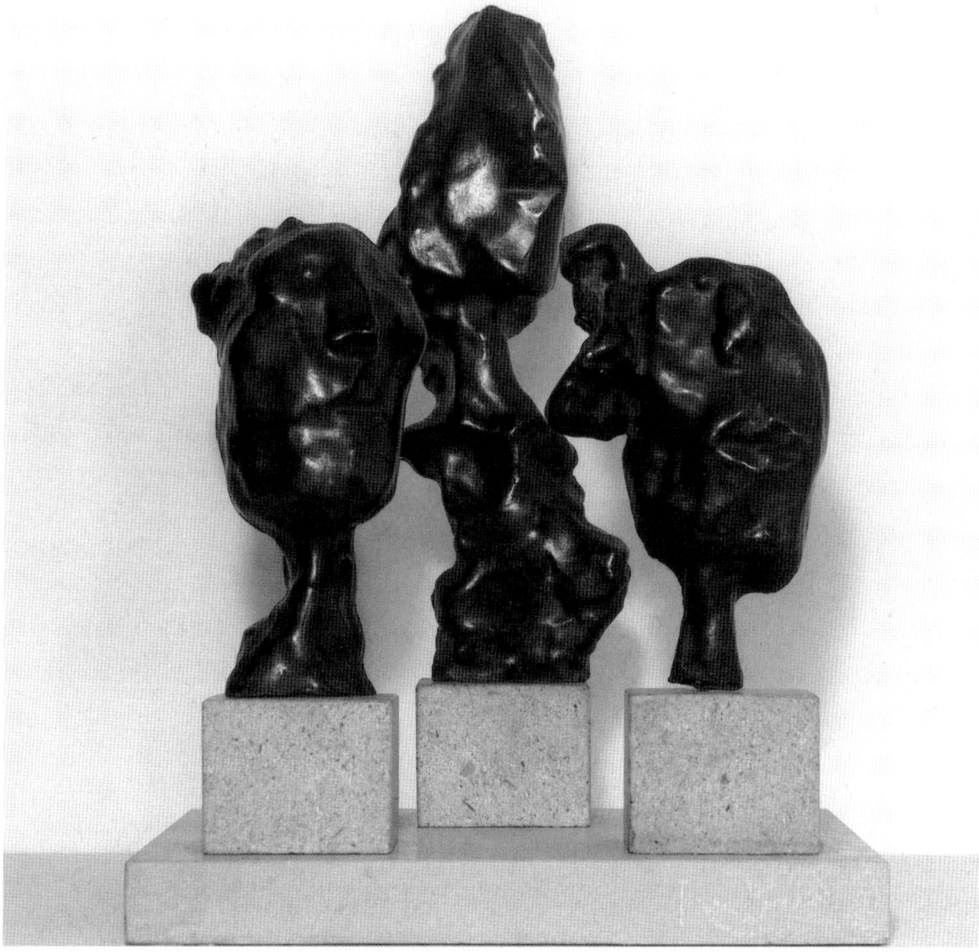

Plate 60
From left to right: *Head* 1960 (Cat.49), *Head* 1960 (Cat.46), *Head* 1960 (Cat.47).

BELOW
Plate 61 (Cat.55)
Falling woman (3) 1961
Bronze
42 cm (length)

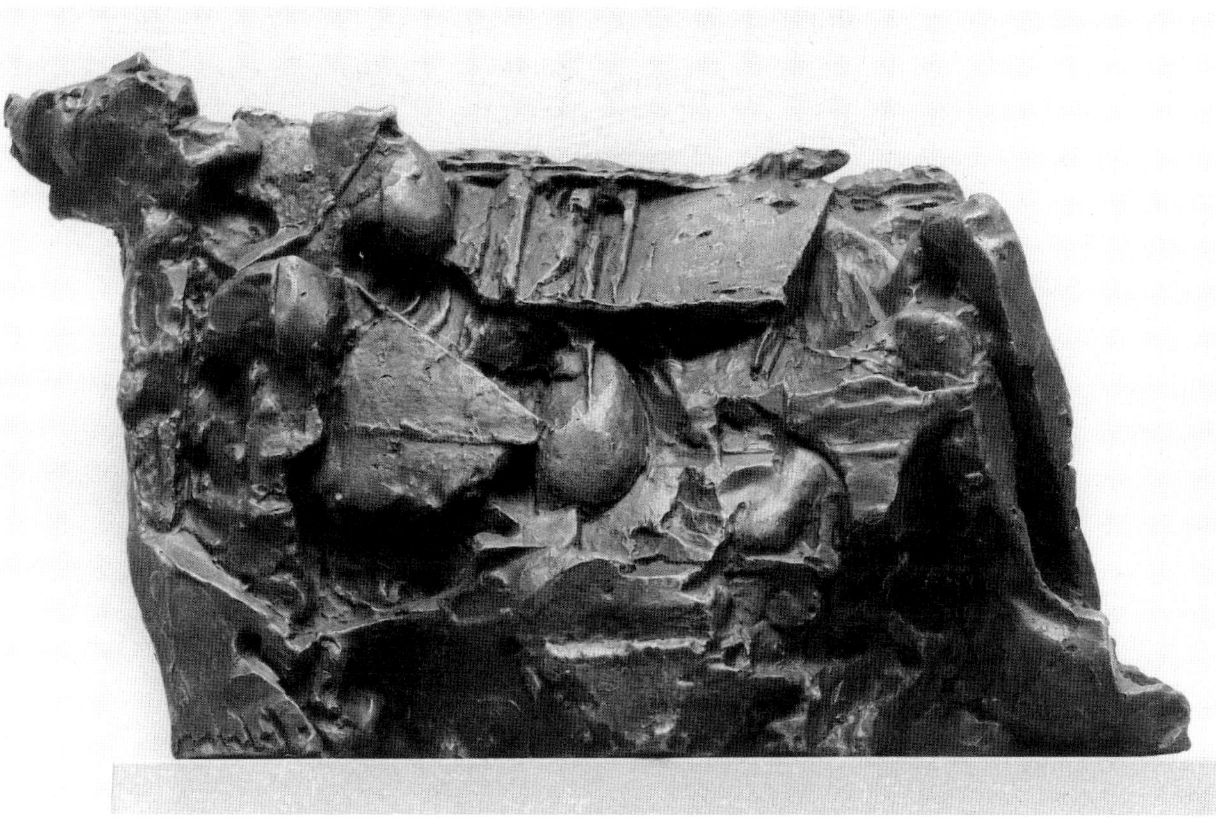

financial considerations probably contributed – the continuing post-war clear-up of bomb-sites and slum properties offered an unusual treasure trove. Greaves, who had moved to rural Buckinghamshire by 1959, believes that Fullard, as other artists, took advantage of such sources of plentiful cheap materials. A few years later, when quizzed about his turn to assemblage, Fullard recalled it as a 'chance' discovery:

> Fullard had been collecting bits of scrap wood – doors, flooring, furniture, etc., from demolished building sites, but with no special purpose in mind. One evening in 1959, sitting in his Chelsea studio in fading light some of the flotsam took on exciting forms. He had not at that time seen assemblage by other artists or, at least, was not conscious of having seen it.[5]

In an interview in 1965, Fullard emphasised his interest in the history of the wooden objects he selected but, again, stressed the serendipitous process:

> This sort of work has no precedent – you have to invent craftsmanship. My assistants are dead – they made tables and kettles and floors for me 50 years ago to which I gave new unexpected life. My way is to sit and watch the material I have collected in a sort of hallucination state and the appropriate pieces seem to gather round the idea I have in the back of my mind and help to push it forward.[6]

Serendipitous or not, it is notable that there was a contemporaneous surge of interest in collage and assemblage – the 'collage explosion' as Lawrence Alloway called it.[7] In 1958, the Lord's Gallery in London staged the first major British public showing of the work of Kurt Schwitters, and Marcel Duchamp had a major retrospective in New York a few years later. Importantly, the collage techniques of Schwitters' and Duchamp's notion of the 'readymade' have been viewed as the strongest impulses informing the revival of the use of found objects in art at the turn of the decade. From about 1958 to 1962, 'Neo-Dada' was the term coined and used, liberally and often misleadingly, to describe the work of numerous artists, including Fullard, who worked loosely with assemblage or displayed subversive irreverence for the conventions of art.[8] Whilst Fullard may well have been aware of these developments, it is possible that, as he claimed, he had not viewed at first-hand much other assembled work, as private correspondence conveys that he had a distinct disinterest in gallery-going.[9]

In the 1960s, the historical roots of assemblage and its contemporary counterparts were explored in surveys like that of Janis and, most notably, in a major exhibition at the Museum of Modern Art in New York, *The Art of Assemblage*, held in 1961. This included work by British artists Robyn Denny, John Latham and Eduardo Paolozzi and American contemporaries Bruce Conner and Robert Rauschenberg alongside that of 'assemblers' from earlier generations – Schwitters, Picasso and Duchamp. In the catalogue accompanying the exhibition, William Seitz claimed assemblage as a 'new medium', one which not only escaped the sterilities of much abstract art, but also marked a 'revised association with the environment'. Seitz traced assemblage back to the early collages, reliefs and constructions of the Cubists, through to the anti-art of Dada and the Surrealist obsession with the 'found object'.

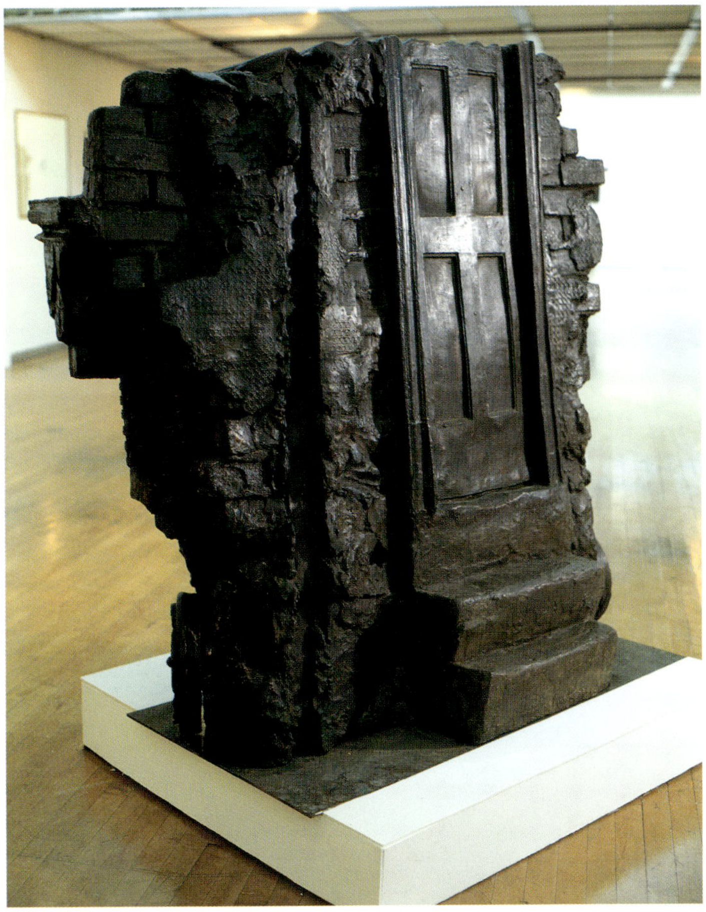

Plates 62 and 63 (Cat.58)
War game 1962
Bronze
148 x 146 x 71 cm

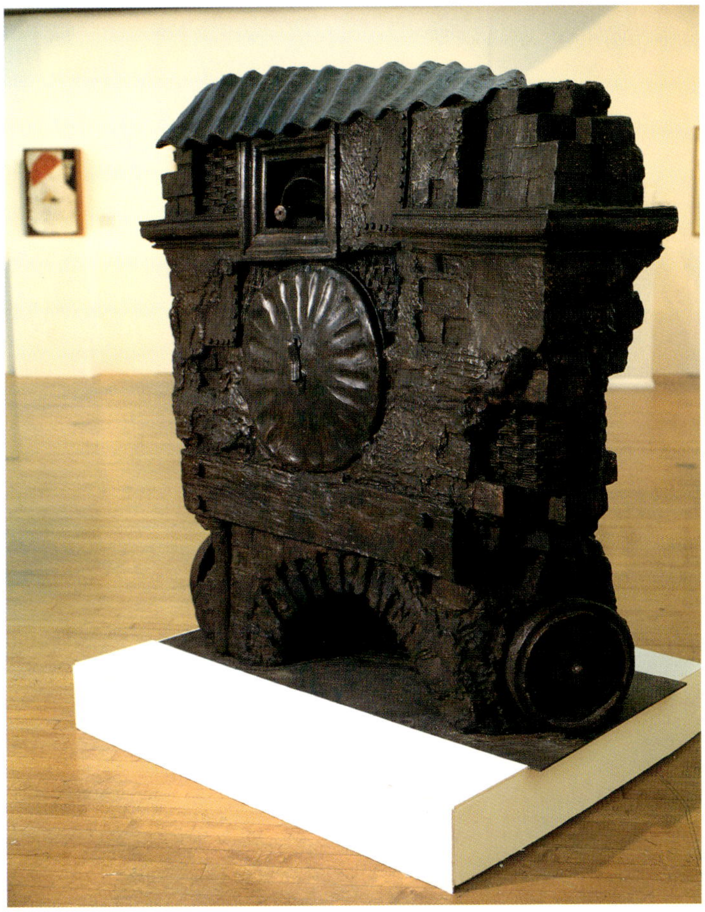

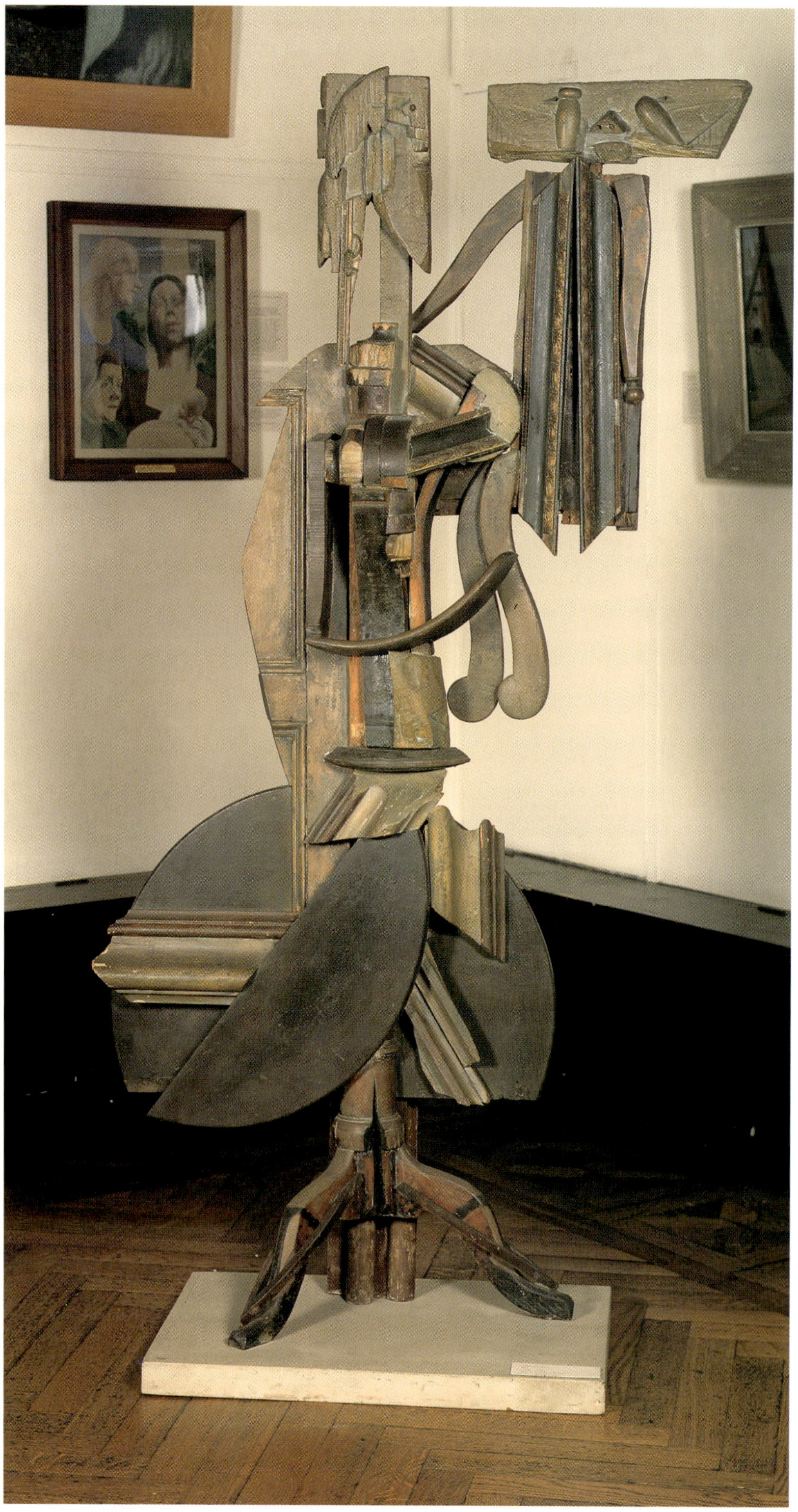

Plate 64 (Cat.37)
Mother and child 1959
Assemblage of various wooden items
195 x 110 x 49 cm

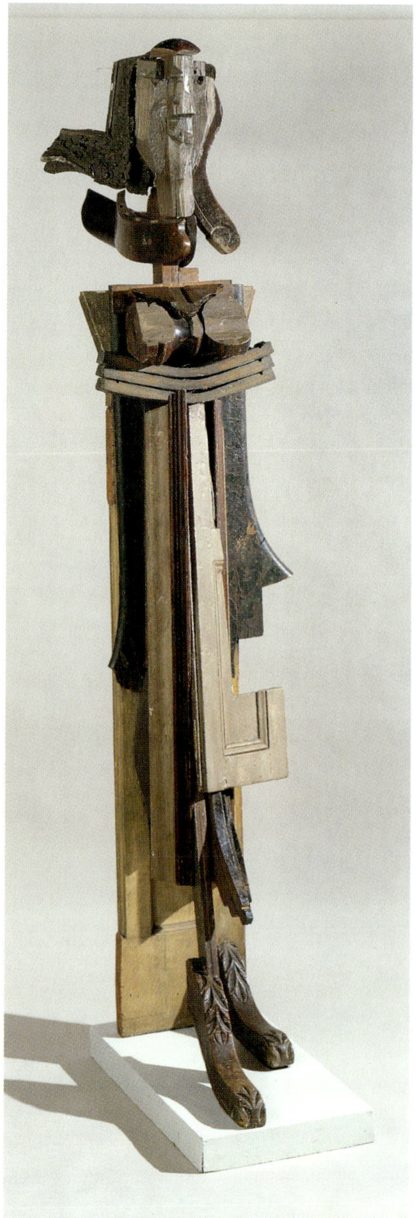

Plate 65 (Cat.38)
Woman 1959
Assemblage of various wooden items
229.2 x 43.2 x 81.3 cm

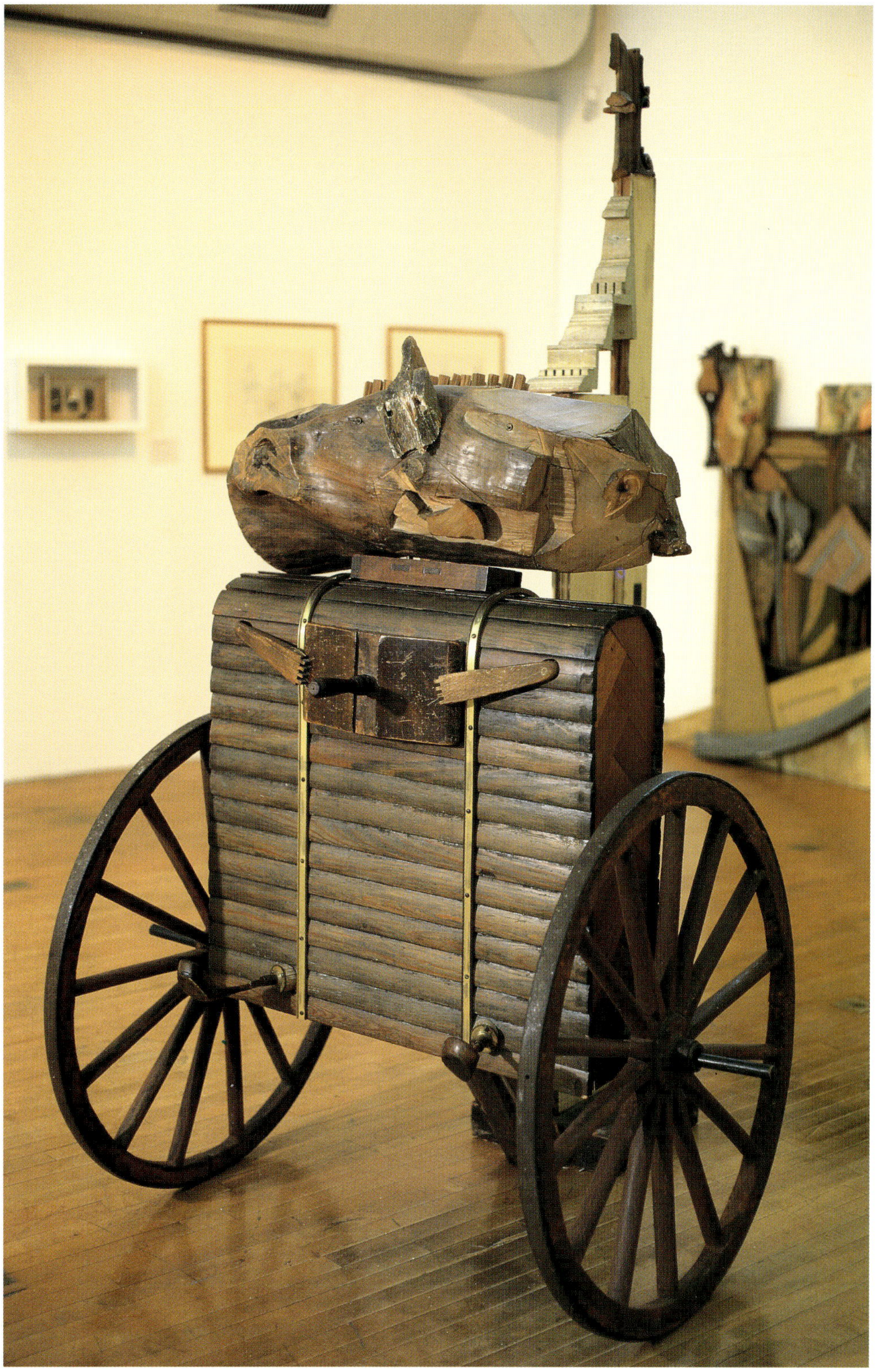

Plate 67 (Cat.59)
The infant St George 1962-3
Assemblage of wooden objects
211.5 x 115.5 x 124.5 cm

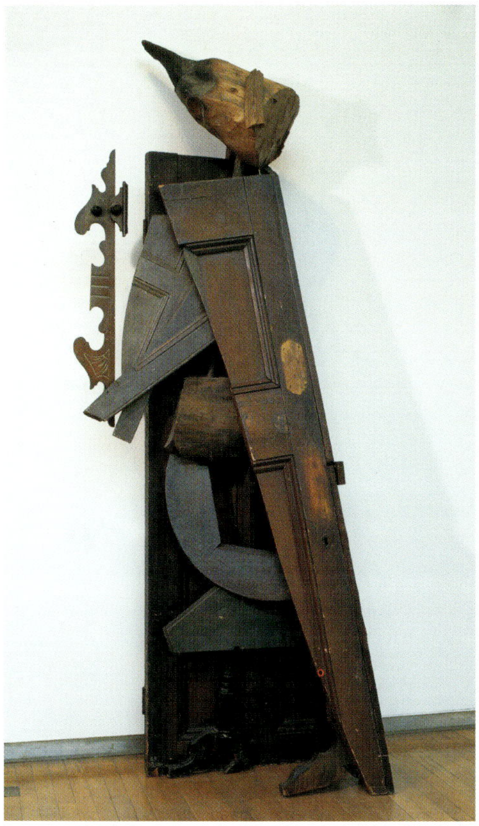

Plate 66 (Cat.39)
Woman with flowers 1959-60
Assemblage of various items
244 x 101.5 x 38.2 cm

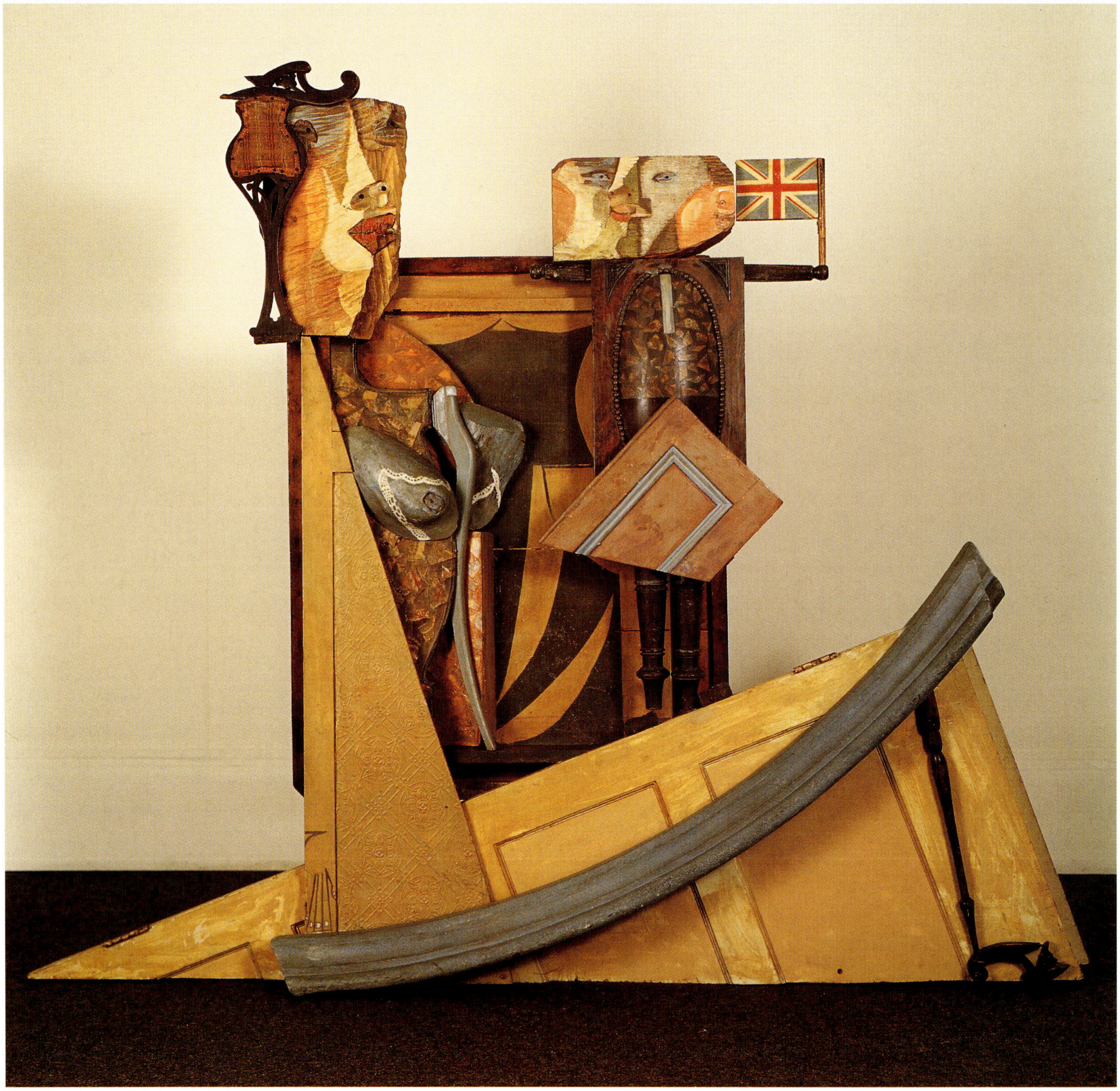

Plate 68 (Cat.40)
The patriot 1959-60
Assemblage of mainly painted wooden items
178 x 214.5 x 31.7 cm
View at the 1974 exhibition, Serpentine Gallery, London

The exhibition extensively featured the work of Jean Dubuffet, who, perhaps more than any other artist, held responsibility for taking the collage idea into new directions – using the most ignoble materials to produce works of 'fine art' – with his 'assemblages' of clinker, slag, sponge and charred wood in the mid-1950s.[10]

Contemporary interest in the technique of assemblage was not confined to the visual arts but was an aspect of broader post-war cultural developments with parallels in the fields of music, poetry and literature. Early modernist writers, such as James Joyce, had already introduced a *collagiste* approach to narrative, meaning and time but in the late 1940s and 1950s traditional constraints on form and hierarchical ideas about materials, words and musical notation were broken down even further. 'Beat' writers in America, with their 'spontaneous bob prosody', were attempting to merge life and art with their extensive use of the vernacular. John Cage's urge to absorb everyday experience into art through his experiments with sound was particularly inspired by Duchamp's 'readymades'. Improvisation and assemblage were methods which Californian artist Bruce Conner applied to a broad range of artistic activities including the collaging together of film-clips.[11]

In Britain, throughout the 1950s and during his involvement with the Independent Group, Eduardo Paolozzi had been exploring collage with an extensive range of popular materials, from sci-fi comics to advertisements. Besides basing much of his sculpture and graphics work on the principles of collage and assemblage, he also made Burroughs-like 'cut-ups' of poetry and a series of short films made up of quotations and snatched images.[12] All these developments reject prior elitist notions of 'high' and 'low' art and, like assemblage, encourage the idea that no material, language or objects need be considered 'unacceptable'.

For Fullard, the assemblage techniques of Picasso, an innovative sculptor with a limitless capacity for transforming ordinary objects, were probably the most direct influence on his own work. Although, generally, Picasso's sculpture was rarely exhibited until much later, Fullard may have seen the Picasso exhibition at Marlborough Fine Art in 1955, which showed ten bronzes cast from assembled objects, including *Pregnant woman* 1950, *Goat's skull and bottle* 1951-2 and *Ape with young* 1952. However, Fullard's earliest first-hand encounter with Picasso's use of assemblage is likely to have been with his group of totem-like bronzes, *The bathers* 1956, cast from offcuts of wood and old planks, shown in the Battersea Park open-air show in 1960. Picasso's irreverance for the 'nobility' of particular materials, his enduring playfulness and his ability to turn household objects, such as kitchen utensils and children's toys, into extraordinary images impressed many artists, including Fullard.[13] The unity achieved by casting conglomerations of objects into bronze was Fullard's expressed intention for many of his early wooden figures.[14]

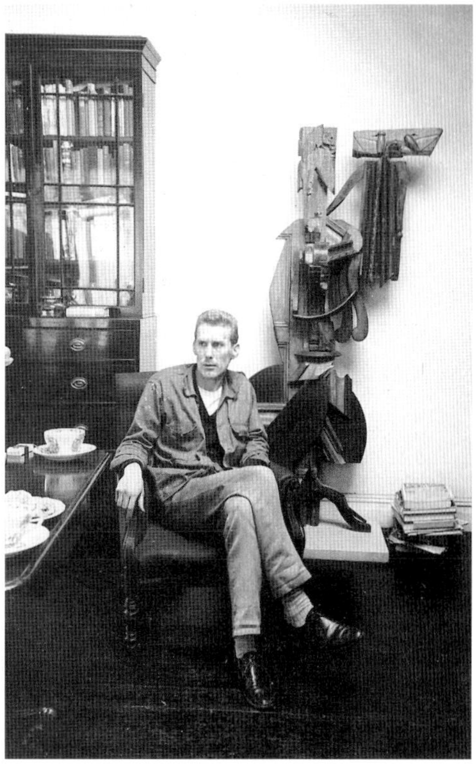

Plate 69
Fullard with *Mother and child* 1959 (Cat.37).

The magical transformatory potential of discarded domestic objects offered by the idiom of assemblage had a particular appeal to Fullard. Emphasising that sculpture was concerned with seeking the kind of effortless and intuitive inventiveness with cast-off objects that only children knew, he wrote: 'Just as the child, without effort, slips through imagination out of life to make a pepper-pot, or the heaving deck of a ship-wreck of a placid pavement, so the artist works towards the miracle of making visible that which apparently could not exist'.[15]

Like a child at play, artist-assembleurs of the 1950s rescued, recycled and redeemed debris – usually the detritus of the city. In 1955, sculptor Richard Stankiewicz remarked that for an artist in New York to use junk was as natural as for a South Sea Islander to use shells.[16] The 'junk sculptors' of the United States were exploiting their natural environment, re-packaging the industrial waste of an urban society of high-speed mass consumption: their 'junk' spoke of the present. Fullard was a city-dweller, a lover of singing, dancing, public houses, streets and the kind of brash open-ended environment offered by a city like London. His 'survivors' – his assemblages – recycled the remnants of the city. However, his interest in objects was in their human past, their investment with individual human history and memory. In his study of the city, Walter Benjamin had identified the *chiffonnier* – the rag-picker – as the 'quintessential figure who "excavates and remembers"', sifting the discarded, despised, throw-away stuff of the urban landscape and then collecting and reusing its fragments – a Baudelairean hero of the modern metropolis.[17] Fullard was, similarly, an urban archaeologist of the metropolitan wasteland, picking up fragments and retrieving, and remembering, snatches of unknown past lives. Some offer clues, like the glimpse of a worn label which reads 'The Railway Employer and Police Stores' inside *Woman with flowers*, or the chequerboard scratched onto the section of the door panel on the front of this assemblage – clues which only serve to increase the intrigue.

Fullard's early wooden assemblages of 1959, *Striding woman and child*, *Woman*, *Pregnant woman*, *Mother and child* and *Woman with flowers* 1959-60, were all made from discarded wooden objects and bits of old furniture, meticulously joined and finished.[18] An influence of Cubism is strong in these works but, most of all, they recall the lyrical, linear style of Henri Laurens or of Ossip Zadkine. The larger works have a regal presence. They tower over the viewer like primitive idols – though their modernity is given away by their elaborate comic footwear. Although some pieces may have dictated or suggested a form for the sculpture, each has been carefully selected to complete the overall image which Fullard sought to express – the head of *Woman* 1959 is especially fine with its carved profile and flying hair. Fullard re-invested the old carpentry with a renewed dignity and elegance.

Fullard's exhibition of sculpture in October 1961 at Gallery One was important because of the nature of the venue itself and also for the critical comment his sculpture attracted. The new Mayfair premises which Victor Musgrave, the proprietor, had opened in May, were reported in the press as 'expensively simple' with snow-white walls and 'Cinderella-like splendour'. Musgrave had been the first in London, at his Soho gallery, to exhibit work by Dubuffet and Yves Klein. He pioneered unusual shows by little-known European artists, many of whom worked with the idiom of collage or assemblage and were often figures associated with the extreme edge of the international avant-garde, such as Spoerri, Metzger and Koepke. On the opening of the new gallery, *The Guardian* noted that Musgrave had built up a reputation for showing 'intellectual primitives' such as Christoforou, Kemeny, Shariffe and

F. N. Souza. Fullard, who later aptly described himself as a 'fastidious primitive', had precisely the kind of idiosyncratic artistic sensibility and techniques sought by Musgrave.[19] Interestingly, Fullard's wooden assemblages have perhaps most in common with the Dutch sculptor Vic Gentils, whose figures and objects constructed from wooden mouldings and ornate picture frames had also been shown at Gallery One.[20]

The Gallery One exhibition showed nine bronzes from his series of female heads made in 1960-1, four 'falling women' pieces and seven works of assemblage. Unlike the Woodstock show of 1958, which had received little comment in the art press other than Berger's, the exhibition, and the assemblages in particular, attracted the attention of critics and other gallery-owners. Edward Lucie-Smith expressed uncertainty, finding the works of *trouvé* wood 'rather trivial', but there were many other appreciative reviews: a commentator in *The Times* noted that the work was 'full of promise and potentiality'; John Russell attributed the large falling women with 'genuine monumentality'; the *Observer*'s reviewer felt that the bric-à-brac assemblages combined 'dignity and tenderness'; another critic described Fullard as a serious artist 'whose achievement promises even greater achievement to come'.[21] Jasia Reichardt, for *Apollo*, was especially impressed with the show, finding it a revelation, full of wonder and surprise: 'To the artist there is a contradiction between the figure and a chunk of wood, between a systematic approach and an emotional end. From this disparity Fullard builds powerful and extraordinary images, sad and intense, musical and utterly human.'[22]

The idea that London was the cultural capital of the world in the 1960s, and the contribution and influence of Pop Art, has acquired mythic proportion.[23] Much of the work of artists associated with Pop drew on the collage-assemblage currency and involved the appropriation and juxtaposition of images from historical and contemporary sources. The emergence and identification of Pop at the beginning of the 1960s has some bearing on Fullard's work and on one sculpture in particular – *The patriot*, dated 1959-60. This painted assemblage continues the mother and child theme but is also a bizarre representation of Britannia 'ruling the waves', with a flag-waving infant on her knee. The subversive use of the Union Jack is of considerable significance. It became iconic in Pop Art but Fullard's use of it here probably represents one of the earliest appearances of the British flag in an artwork of this kind.[24] Further, a nostalgia for Edwardiana was a pervasive and persistent strain in 1960s popular culture, and particularly in fields of design, and *The patriot* has a distinct element of this too.

Finally, this particular sculpture also occupies an important place in Fullard's œuvre as a whole – it is a transitional work which reflects persistent themes and techniques but it also looks forward to a period of sculpture-making which was overtly political. In viewing *The patriot* we need to remember that in 1942 Fullard had enlisted primarily as an anti-fascist communist, from a family embroiled in left-wing politics and internationalism. There can be no doubt that, in this sculpture, Fullard's Union Jack – a potent symbol of imperialism – is hoisted with irony.[25]

Lucie-Smith had warned that the repeated construction of images of women and children from pieces of old wood had the potential to become mere whimsy. In one single work, *The patriot*, Fullard re-butted that criticism and paved the way to his next series of sculptures which dealt directly and powerfully with war.

Infant infantries and monstrous machines – the war series

... Below there sprawls Cassino,
hiding its rubble carcase
underneath a winding sheet of smoke,
and in among the ruined maze
the infantry play hide-and-seek ...

Alan White[26]

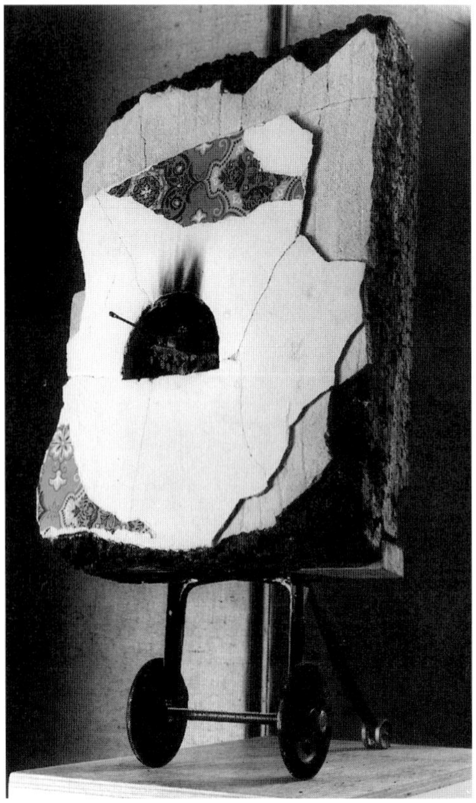

Plate 70 (Cat.67)
The third war dream 1964
Assemblage of various objects
63.5 x 32 cm

In the autumn of 1959, Anthony Caro, an exact contemporary of Fullard's, returned from a visit to the United States where he had been deeply influenced by contemporary developments in American abstract and color-field painting, and radically changed his approach to sculpture. His innovatory abstract welded and bolted metal constructions had a characteristic appearance of weightlessness. The impact of Caro's work and its influence on the subsequent development of British sculpture has been emphasised to such an extent that it has, at times, obscured the diversity of work produced by others. Importantly, Lynn Cooke identified an 'anonymity' about Caro's sculpture of this time – the individual hand of the artist had been eliminated. Caro's disciples laid even more emphasis on sculpture being 'devoid of all illusionistic, literary or subjective references'.[27] In contrast, Fullard consciously chose to make his work *more* personal and idiosyncratic to the extent that he declared that he was 'sculpting his auto-biography'. For Fullard, the 'making of a private poetry' was not only valid but valuable.[28] With his absurdist war assemblages, Fullard rejected contemporary preoccupations with an aesthetic concerned with form and objectivity – the Greenbergian formalist project – and focused primarily on his own experiences and ideas, producing a quixotic sculptural memoir.

Fullard's sculptures about war need to be viewed and placed historically within the genre of war art. In 1945 Eric Newton, surveying the record of war provided by British 'War Artists', commented '... war-art is as old as war, and war is as old as art'.[29] The enormity of the Great War, however, had entirely transformed the way in which war was viewed in the artistic and literary imagination. Wilfred Owen's ironic employment of *Dulce et decorum est pro patria mori* would have been unthinkable before 1914. In his study of the literary legacy of the First World War, Paul Fussell has compiled an index to the changed language of two generations and contrasts the 'high' feudal language of pre-war arcadian innocence with post-war directness and irony.[30]

Painters like Paul Nash and C. R. W. Nevinson had challenged an idealised

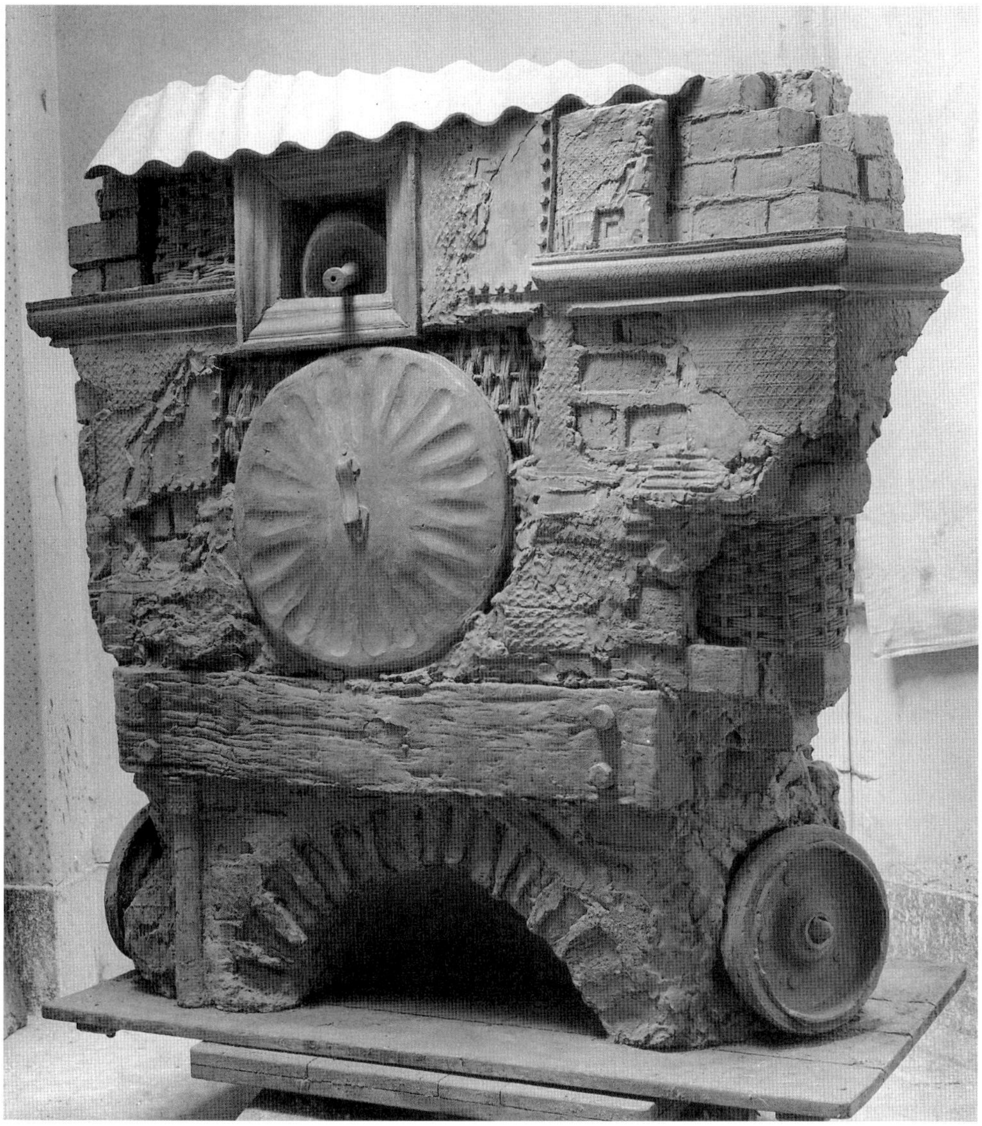

Plate 71 (Cat.58)
War game 1962
Ciment fondu
148 x 146 x 71 cm

image of warfare and had shown 'a bitter truth' – the desolate, horrific and mechanistic nature of trench warfare.[31] The sculptural legacy of the First World War, however, rarely reflects the kind of transformation which Fussell identified in literature. Charles Sargeant Jagger refused to glorify war and his figures have a gritty authenticity.[32] But the plethora of memorials to the dead of the First World War largely deploy the old language of symbolic and allegorical clichés. Richard Cork has pointed out that, with one or two exceptions, sculpted memorials were 'decorous to a fault' and in their anxiety to avoid upsetting the bereaved, they failed to convey the scale of the tragedy.[33] Admittedly these monuments were inhibited by their 'public' nature. Even so, they offered little critical or ironical comment on the nature or value of that war.

After the Holocaust, the Dresden bombings and Hiroshima, the exploration of war and the notion of commemoration have posed dilemmas for artists.[34] The immediate aftermath of the war – the anxiety of the nuclear age and the tensions of the Cold War – were conveyed in the 1950s by the spiky forms and massive figures of Germaine Richier. They were also reflected in the work of British sculptors Bernard Meadows and Lynn Chadwick. In the mid-1960s,

OPPOSITE
Plate 72 (Cat.9)
Dead Christ 1951
Mixture of cement and metal powder
208.3 cm (height)

escalating military action in Vietnam generated a highly politicised climate and provoked American artists to respond with, for example, the images of charred flesh and mangled bodies in Duane Hanson's *Vietnam scene* 1969. Ed Keinholz's *Portable war memorial* of 1968 provided one of the most satirical commemorations of that war.

However, despite being the most chronicled war in history, few sculptors have explored or concerned themselves directly with the nature of the 1939-45 conflict.[35] As such, Fullard's work was unusual and singular. Recognising the redundancy of the received rhetorical framework for describing war, he understood that the only valid language was one which explored absurdity. The recycled symbols of classical mythology and medieval chivalry were no longer appropriate but neither was any form of realism which relied on documentary depiction. Instead, Fullard's assemblages explored the inherently ridiculous nature of war, the situation where normality was always fouled up, where simply being in the wrong place at the wrong time could account for the difference between being alive or dead.[36]

It is significant that Fullard expressed a special affinity with the work of Samuel Beckett, the quintessential absurdist: '... not only does he strike a true echo in oneself, but because his whole approach is ... something at last which is new in the best and real sense, and one so far away from "modern" literature ...'.[37]

In the same letter to John Warren Davis in 1958, Fullard noted, in particular, that his reading of *Molloy* had deeply affected his ideas about making sculpture, spurring him to further explore his own 'dark' side. In *Molloy*, Beckett is preoccupied with the absurd nature of being, focusing on life's bizarre and inconsequential details whilst showing, above all, a concern for the permanently alienated state of humanity.[38] The comic incidents, macabre events and meaningless anecdotes of Beckett's spiritual hinterland have both poignancy and 'darkness' and there are direct parallels with Fullard's idiosyncratic sculptures.

Importantly, although Fullard recognised the discredited clichés of war, he did not discard them. Instead, in his exploration of the absurd, he exploited them with parody and irony. Irony, indeed, has been identified as a fundamental constituent element of all war: 'Every war is ironic because every war is worse than expected. Every war constitutes an irony of situation because its means are so melodramatically disproportionate to its presumed ends.'[39]

Analogies with literary techniques are entirely relevant in Fullard's case. His own writings were dense and reflexive. Furthermore, he placed great emphasis on the titling of his war works. *Death or Glory* 1963-4 is a prime example of the way in which Fullard 'played' with words. The title plays on the chivalric polarities of his own regimental motto. The outrageous sculpted image, in which one can pick out the 'death's head' of the regimental badge, ironises and parodies it at the same time.[40]

The transitional nature of *The patriot* has already been discussed but before examining the war assemblages of the 1960s in depth, one work from the previous decade needs to be considered. *Dead Christ* of 1951, a life-size crucified figure, modelled in clay and cast in an experimental mixture of cement and metal powder, appears at first sight to be something of an anomaly in Fullard's

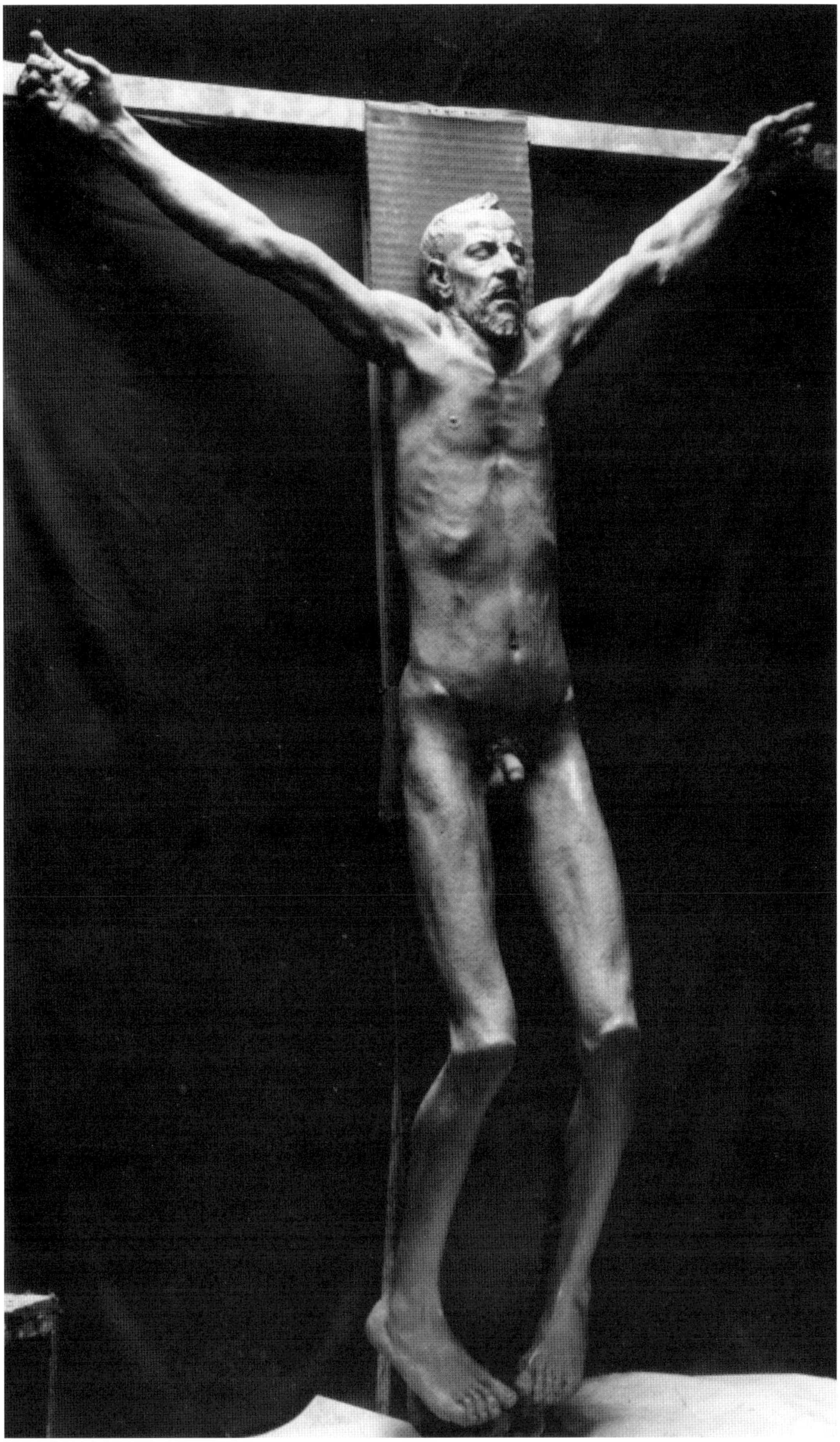

œuvre. Described as a 'militant atheist', the artist had no record of religious association or commissions.[41] *Dead Christ* is no straightforward religious work. The head bears a close resemblance to the artist's own. Is it then a paean to the secular suffering of the private soldier, an early exploration of Fullard's own calvary? The crucified figure is rich with surprising military associations. Being strapped cruciform to an immobile field gun was, apparently, a regular army punishment for indiscipline. Aptly, Fussell remarks on a further irony about this cruel practice – that troops readily embraced the image as 'quint-essentially symbolic of their own suffering and sacrifice'.[42] Fullard probably drew on an army story, which has been retold and recycled from one war to another, about a Canadian soldier who is reputed to have been crucified to death by enemy troops, his hands and feet pierced by bayonets. The anatomical facts of *Dead Christ* were probably informed by close study of the flayed guardsman in the Royal Academy's life-drawing rooms. Whatever, the inter-connections between the crucified image and Fullard's personal experience in war are inescapable in this curious effigy.[43]

Rather than modelling, however, it was the idiom of assemblage which offered Fullard the precise sculptural language to deal with the subject of war. It is significant that he preferred to call himself an 'image-maker' rather than a sculptor and others have identified him as a 'manipulator of symbols'.[44] The juxtaposition of one object with another appealed to him because it created surprising possibilities and new layers of meaning.

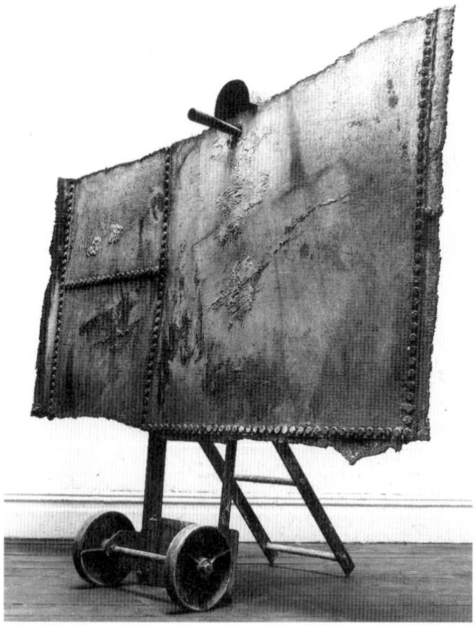

Plate 73 (Cat. 57)
War ghost 1961 (front view)
Assemblage, mainly steel
139.7 x 155 x 78.5 cm

> It is that element of the unplanned which seems to have most point for me – the conscious effort of a complex production in order to produce the unforseen. This is the basis of work – to plan and produce around a conscious 'idea' or subject really in order to permit the entry of the unexpected....[45]

Fullard's first assemblage based around the 'conscious idea' of war was *War ghost* 1961.[46] It shows Fullard's formidable facility in manipulating symbols to create a striking image: it is both battle wreck and relic, invested with memories of the dead. The idea that objects have a metaphysical significance which goes beyond their materiality was central to Fullard's work. His writings were interspersed with spectral references: notably, in 1959, Fullard had suggested that the success of a sculpture depended on the '... speed and vitality of the phantoms which precede it'.[47] In *War ghost* and other pieces, the two world wars are brought together – the ironised language of the one underlining the idiotic magnitude of the other. As we noted earlier, Fullard saw himself as part of a generation 'caught between two fires'. The 'ghosts', here, are those of the Great War as Fullard explores the ways in which that defining cataclysm has been mythologised in popular memory.[48]

War ghost, made from a piece of steel, half a soldier's helmet and a sack barrow, alludes subtly to both wars and to war in general. Resembling a military scarecrow made to ward off the enemy, it has clearly been informed by Charles Sargeant Jagger's *Royal Artillery memorial* 1921-5, a work particularly admired by Fullard. *War ghost* parodies one of the figures on the memorial – the driver with bowed head and outstretched arms – and it also echoes the recumbent figure with the tin helmet on its chest. In Fullard's *War ghost*, Tommy Atkins the ordinary private has become a ramshackle hero. In

OPPOSITE
Plate 74 (Cat.57)
War ghost 1961 (rear view)
Assemblage, mainly steel
139.7 x 155 x 78.5 cm
View at Battersea Park, London in 1963

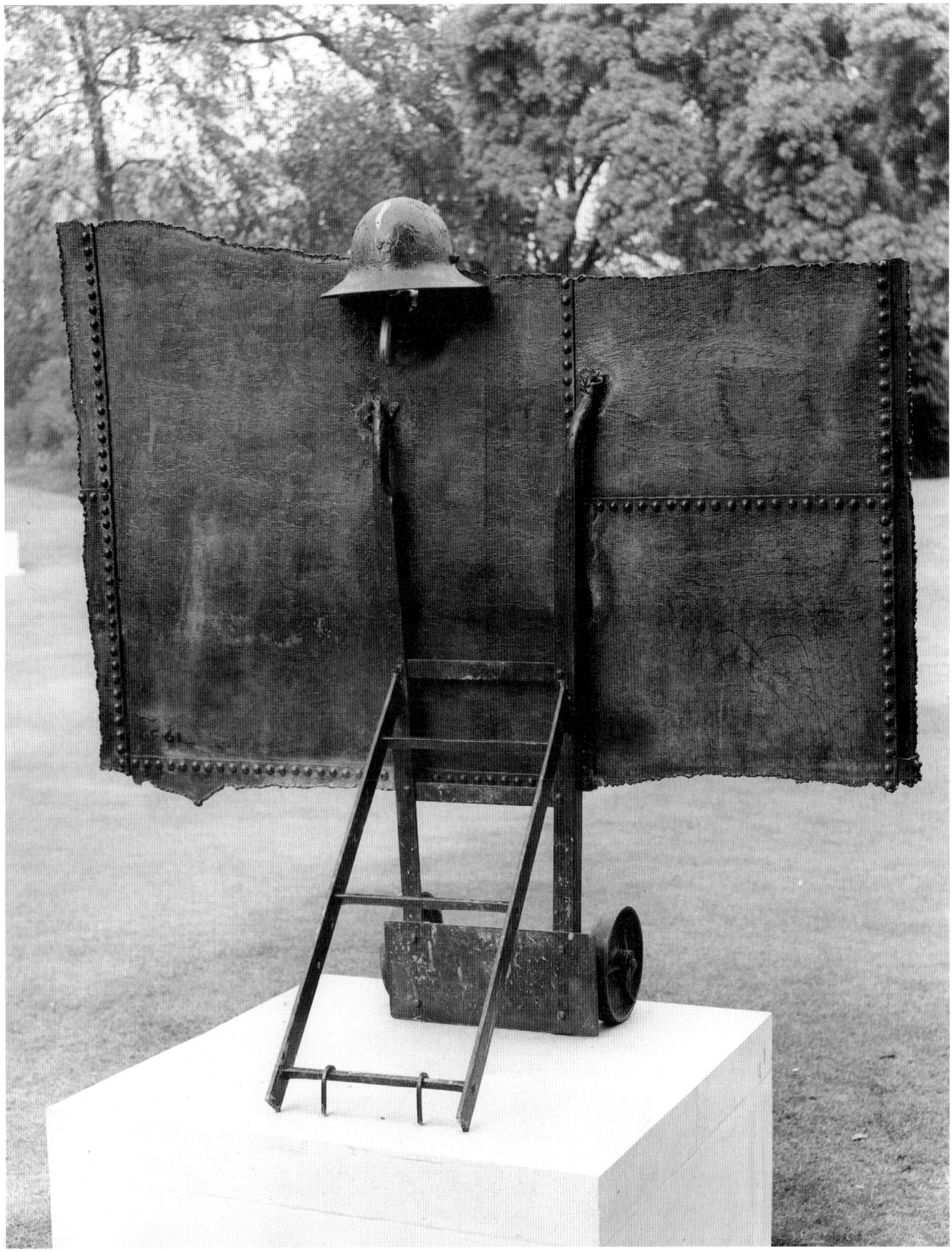

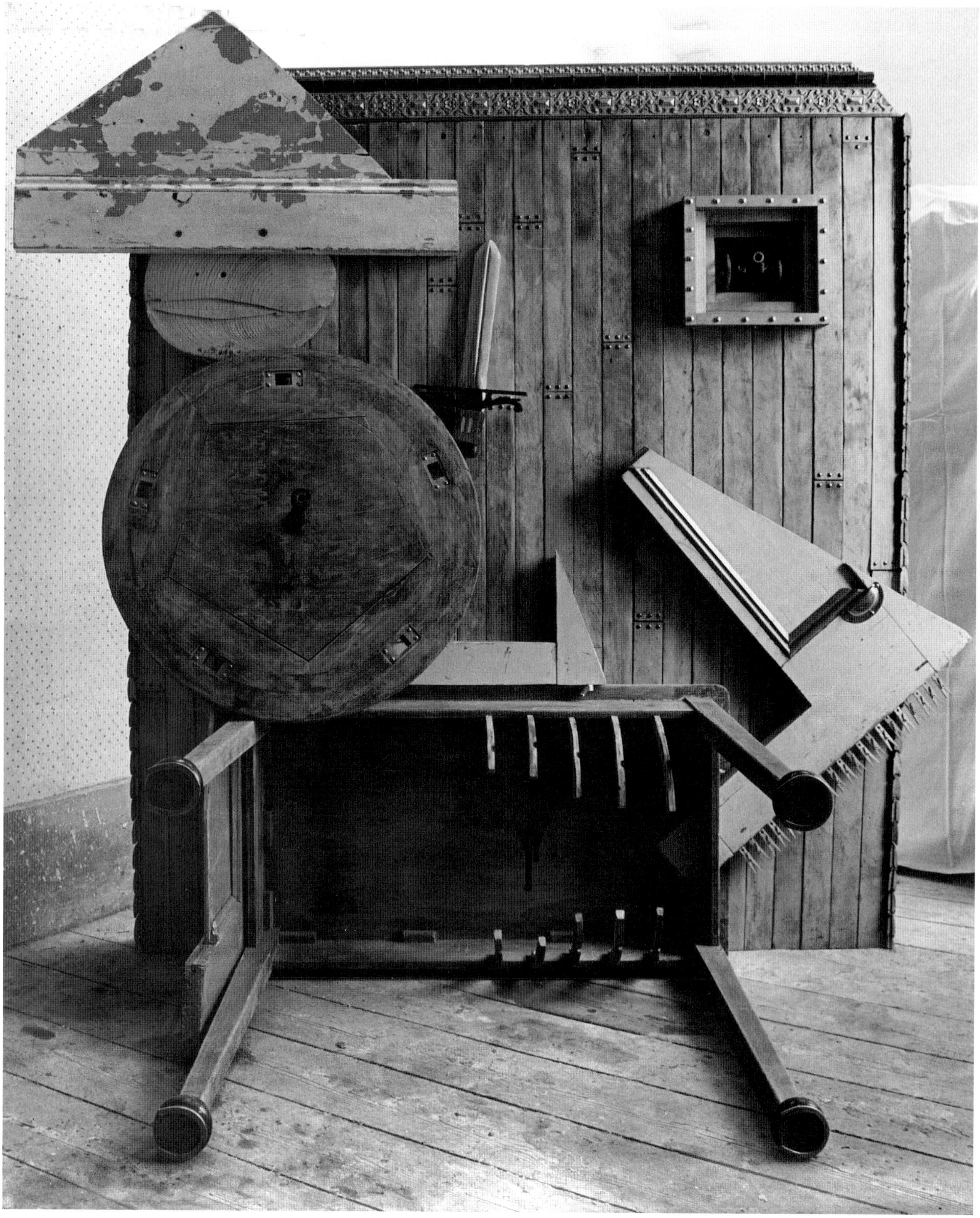

this piece, ostensibly a makeshift barricade or sniper's loophole, the skeletal detritus of Flanders mud is hideously resurrected, advancing steadily, come back to haunt and menace. One cannot help but note that only part of the helmet remains, the head has been blown away.[49]

The war works show Fullard's preoccupation with childhood – in the objects he assembled, the images he shaped and the titles he gave. Many of the assemblages incorporate Airfix kit vehicles and toy soldiers: *Fallen bastion* has a small tank; *The Cross of St George* has a miniature cannon at its base and in the apertures of the masonry chunks are two vehicles, one of which is a model of a German Tiger tank. Generally, in the war series the 'infant' takes various guises but recurs throughout: in *Mounted infant* he perches on his horse; a child brandishes a wooden sword, his table-top horse mown down in *Death or Glory*; he is the *Infant St George* being wheeled into battle; the boy with the snake-belt and paper-hat in *Captive*. Fullard's war assemblages explore a child's perception of war and this vision is reflected in his drawings of children playing at war in which boys swing plywood swords from behind dustbin-lid shields, scarves crossed over their chests like soldier's webbing. In these works, there is an equation of the state of infancy with the state of war. It is a Freudian truism that both are times of little inhibition and, sometimes, unfathomable acts of cruelty. Frederick Brill, friend and Chelsea colleague, recounted that Fullard had told him that one of the frightening things of their time was that only infants have innocence. Brill identified in these infant-soldiers Fullard's expressed wish to find that innocence, and through his work, to recover a child's vision of the world: '... these paper-hatted, pug-faced *enfants terribles* often armed with a wooden sword with which to fend off the adult world ...'.[50]

However, Fullard's work amounts to more than mere regret for a lost exalted state. *War game* confirms the general notion that war plays with human life but it also reflects Fullard's particular experience at Monte Cassino. This child's bomb-site den resembles a machine-gun nest or fortification.[51] The taking of Monte Cassino was considered, at the time, to be crucial to the Allies' advance. It famously involved the battering and bombardment of the monastery until only rubble remained. In *War game*, Fullard portrayed the incomprehensible waste of such acts by fusing the idea of 'battle' with 'games'. Similarly, the poet Alan White had written of the 'ruined maze' where the 'infantry play hide-and-seek'.

Further, *War game* satirises the Edwardian paradigm which viewed bravery in battle as an extension of the spirit of fairplay in sport. It 'plays' with this outmoded literary convention and presents a cutting comment on the equation of war and games classically espoused by Sir Henry Newbolt in the 'Vitaï Lampada'. In the face of machine-gun fire, the ranks are rallied to 'Play up! play up! And play the game!'.[52]

Fullard's sense of the 'absurd' had been implicit in the figures of the later 1950s. In *The infant St George* 1962-3, *Mounted infant* 1963, *Death or Glory* 1963-4 and *Cross of St George* 1964 it is consciously explicit. In a number of these works, Fullard ridicules the chivalric symbol of Englishness – Saint George – employed by earlier war artists to inspire troops in battle.[53] Jasia Reichardt described *The infant St George*, with its oversize head and tiny golf-club feet, as

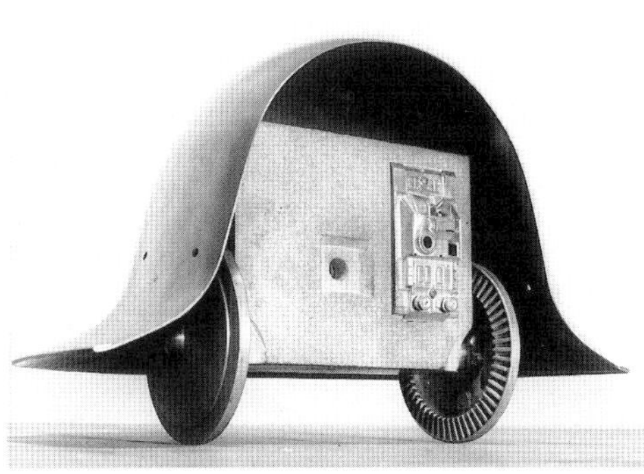

Plate 76 (Cat.62)
Fallen bastion 1964
Assemblage, including stone and steel
17.1 x 28.6 x 21.6 cm

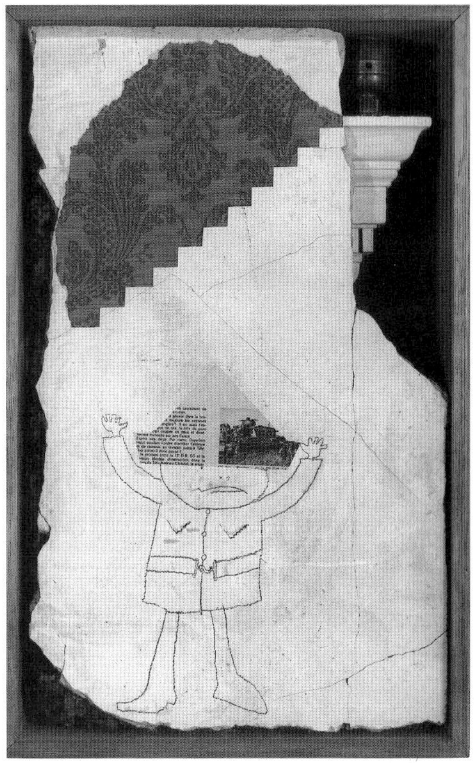

Plate 77 (Cat.68)
Captive 1964
Boxed assemblage, including a drawing
72 x 46.5 x 13.5 cm

OPPOSITE
Plate 75 (Cat.61)
Death or Glory 1963-4
Assemblage of various wooden objects
188 x 191 x 97 cm

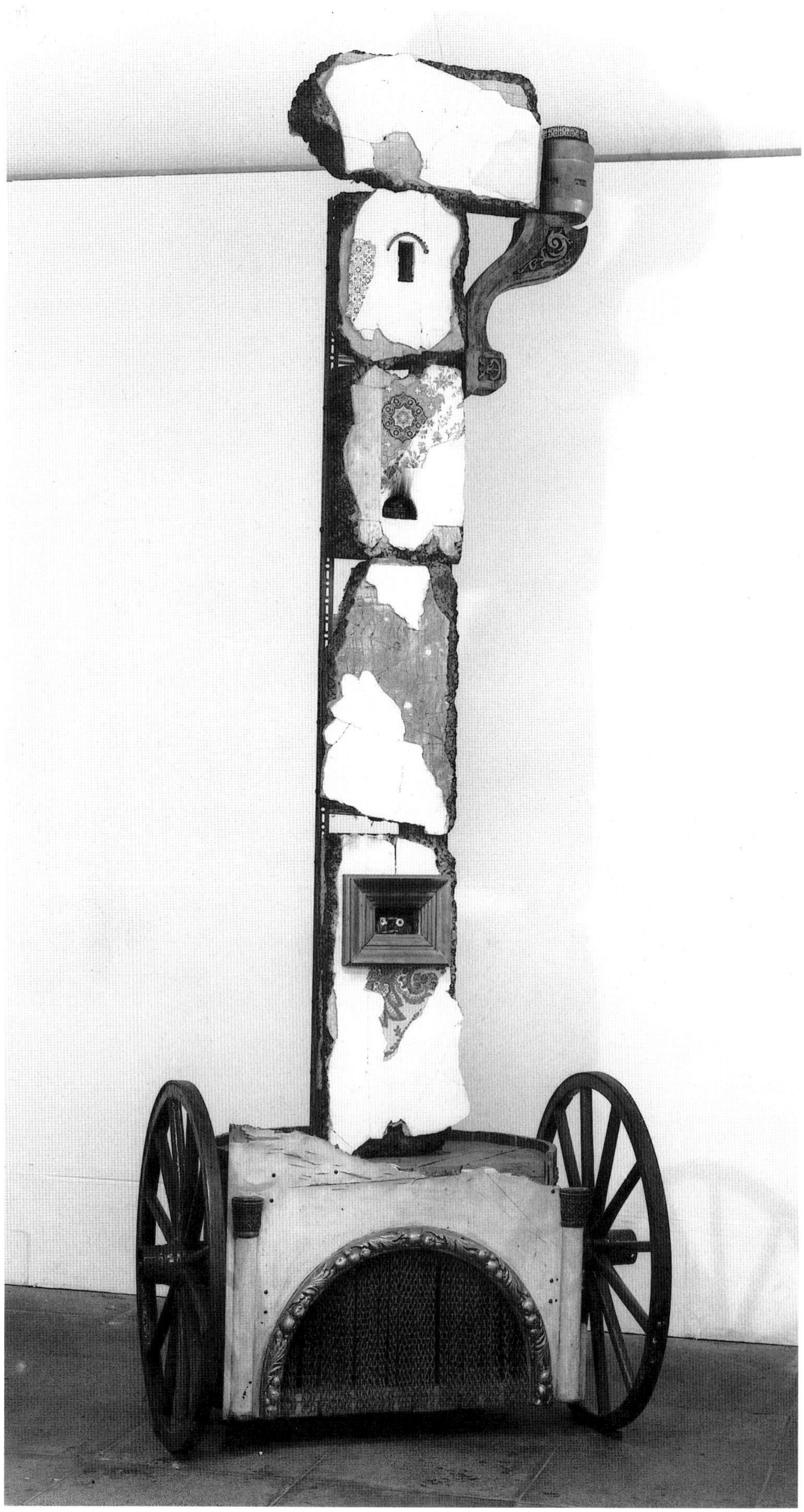

Plate 78 (Cat.63)
The Cross of St George 1964
Assemblage of various objects
298.5 x 115 x 95.4 cm

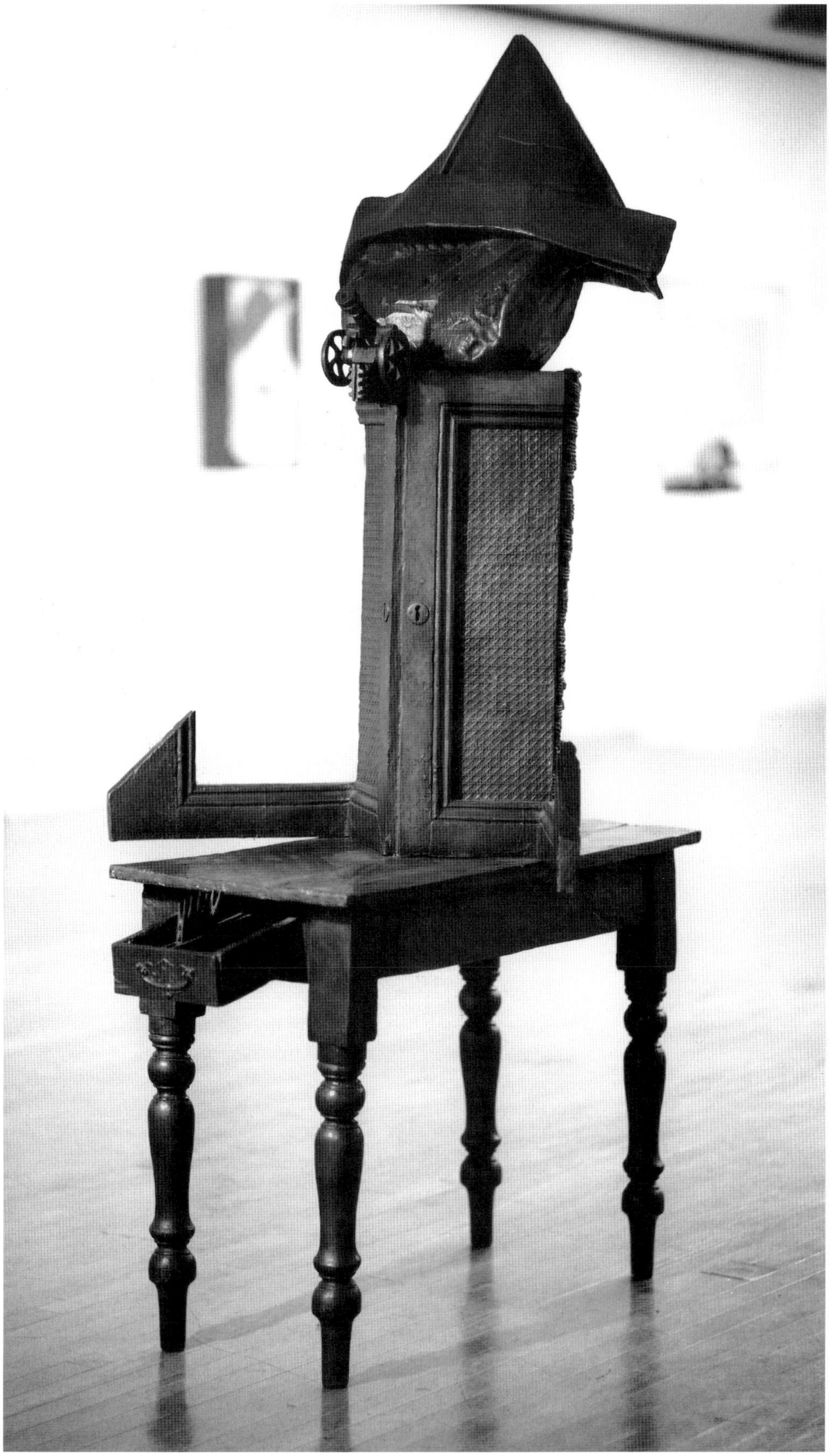

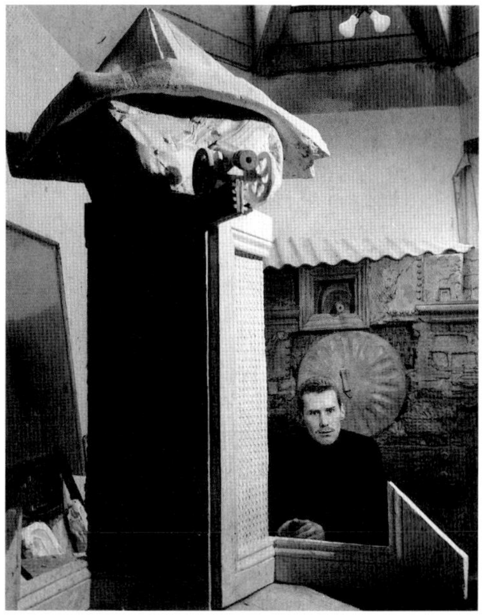

Plate 80
Fullard with *Mounted infant* 1963 (Cat.60) and the ciment fondu *War game* 1962 (Cat.58).

Plate 79 (Cat.60)
Mounted infant 1963
Bronze
195 x 91.4 x 117 cm

Fullard's 'menacing baby saint'. In her view, his 'babies' had the 'domineering quality of miniature Napoleons'.[54] This overbearing character can be seen in the towering *Cross of St George* – yet another of Fullard's war pieces that stands on wheels. It requires little imagination to envisage *War ghost*, *War game*, *The infant St George*, *The third war dream* and *Fallen bastion* mustered at attention, awaiting the advance. Like a monstrous toy box batallion – the child's war game gone mad.

With *Mounted infant* 1963, a conglomeration of domestic objects and fashioned materials cast into bronze, Fullard explored the 'darkness' and absurdity he had identified in Beckett. He also continued to sharpen the irreverent edge in his work first prompted by those satirical leftist cartoons of the 1930s. The head is crudely modelled in an almost childlike way, recalling the Art Brut of Dubuffet. However, *Mounted infant* was partly inspired by the central character in Günter Grass' novel *The Tin Drum*. Osker, the monstrous dwarf, refuses to grow up and, like Fullard's *enfants terribles*, he shuns the horrific adult world by beating his toy drum and indulging in sessions of high-pitched screaming.[55] The specific image of Osker, as an equestrian drummer with a paper helmet, may have particularly attracted Fullard but more general parallels can be drawn with the writings and ideas of Grass, who constantly used puns and 'sinister' nursery rhymes to comment on the tensions in contemporary Germany. Michael Hamburger has noted how Grass excels at 'rendering the mentality of children, with all its fantasies, cruelties, perversities, as well as its ingenuosness'.[56]

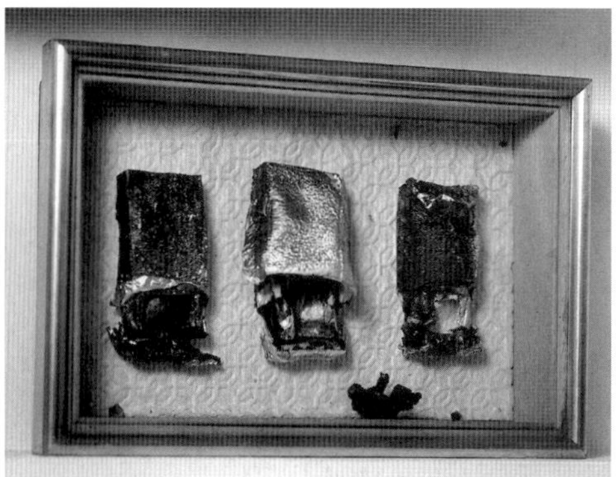

Plate 81 (Cat.65)
The first war dream 1964
Assemblage of various items
19 x 27.9 x 6.9 cm

Within the three-year period during which the war assemblages were made there is noticeable development. The year of 1964 was a prolific one for Fullard as he completed two of his largest pieces and also made five smaller works. Whilst the exploration of absurdity continued, the smaller works are definitely cathartic. They express an introversion and intimacy which is not discernible in the larger works. Despite the fact that he called them 'dreams', the smaller works have a literality, a playing out of personal experience. The cigarette boxes in *The first war dream* might represent three burnt-out tanks. A single survivor appears to have escaped but is, nevertheless, trapped behind the glass. *The second war dream* also has tiny figures which look to have been engulfed by a huge war machine. In their understatement, these works convey a matter-of-factness about the predicament of the helpless individual who is incapable of escaping not only events but memories too. The tiny soldiers in *Lost patrol* 1964 are similarly stranded in a landscape of war. But here it is inverted. The playthings are ensnared in a world-turned-upside-down.

In 1964, the Marlborough New London Gallery showed Fullard's complete series of war assemblages in a major solo exhibition. The subject of war in art was problematical for contemporaries and critical reception was mixed. Given the scale of anti-war protest at the time, and the recent showing of the Theatre Workshop's *Oh What a Lovely War!*, they were mistakenly taken by some to be the expression of a conscientious objector. Fullard's personal views on war were complex: war was an absurd act of folly but it was, for him, also an inevitable part of life and a central aspect of his own experience which he could not deny.[57] Indeed, it is precisely these contradictory tensions which enhance the war works. Fullard expressed his resentment of simplistic readings of his

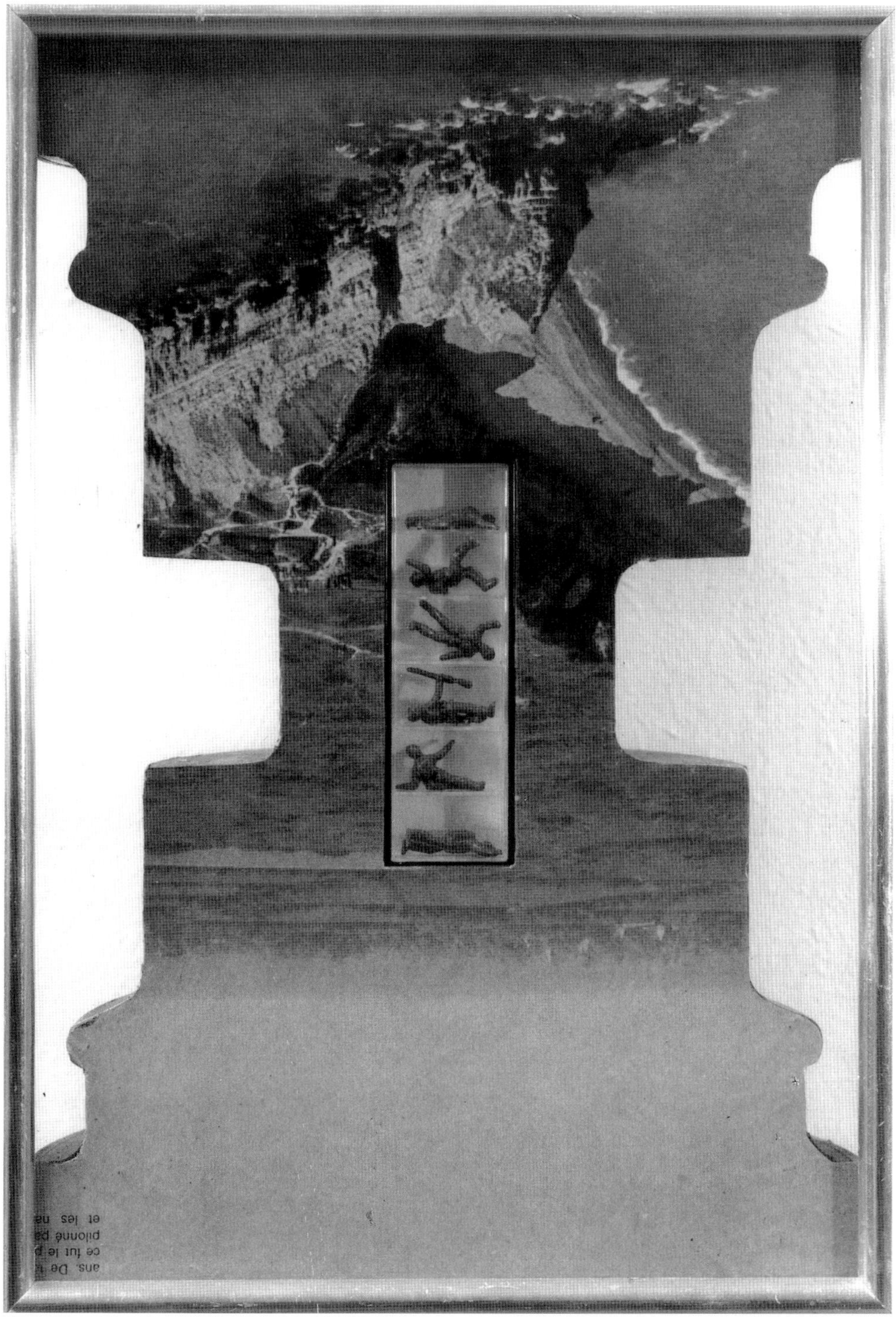

Plate 82 (Cat.64)
Lost patrol 1964
Assemblage of various items
33.6 x 24.4 x 10.8 cm

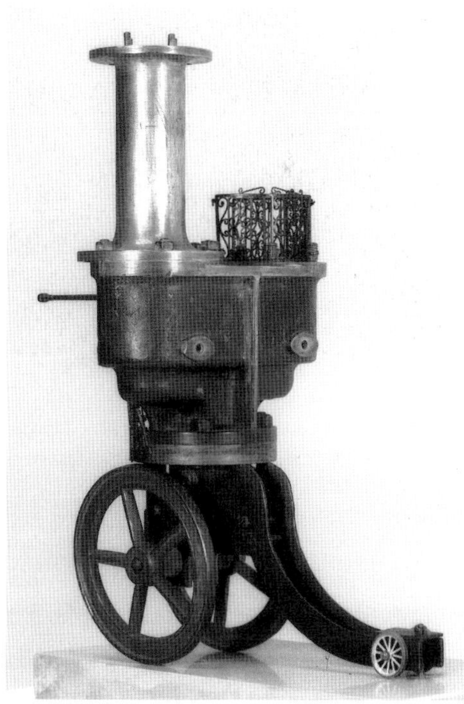

Plate 83 (Cat.66)
The second war dream 1964
Assemblage, mainly metal
26 x 14 x 22.2 cm

work in a letter to the *New Statesman* in 1964 in which he took issue with Robert Melville.[58] In addition, although a younger generation was vociferous about Vietnam and removing the nuclear threat, there was little interest in the experience of those who had suffered in the last conventional war. Undoubtedly, Fullard felt alienated from others who had not shared his experience and recognised the impossibility of bridging such a gulf of understanding.

Responses to the Marlborough show inevitably attracted negative comment about the idiom of assemblage. 'Pop' and 'junk art', with which Fullard's work had some affinities, continued to be treated with derision and, in some quarters, was considered unworthy of any association with 'fine art'. However, Nigel Gosling of the *Observer* singled out Fullard's idiom as particularly apt. He also immediately identified the essential qualities of his work, appreciating Fullard's wit without under-estimating his sophistication.

> Fullard's idiom is as sophisticated and sharp-edged as a Jonathan Miller monologue. His thoughts revolve particularly around war – not as a terrifying explosion of sadism and violence, but as a symbol of man's touchingly foolish self-inflation....[59]

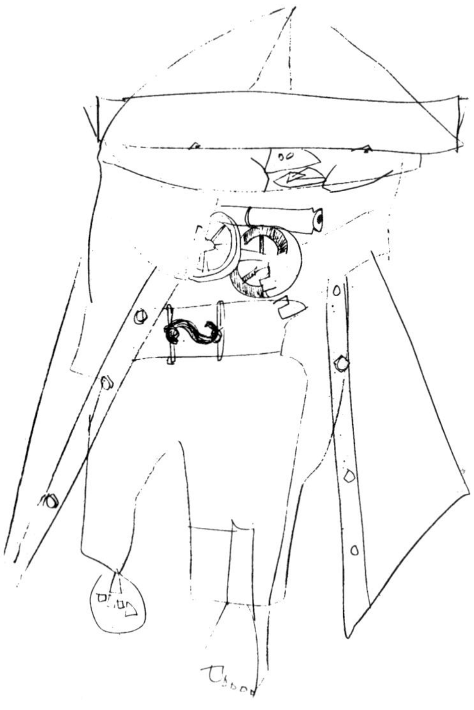

Plate 84
Untitled drawing 1963
Private collection

The genuine nightmarish quality of Fullard's infantile contraptions and the manipulation of imagery associated with the First World War was also seized upon by critics. John Russell recognised the 'dug-out, the crackpot experimental weapon, the laborious non-mechanised transport: all are metamorphosed here'.[60]

Finally, the war assemblages affronted viewers with their mockery. Gosling intimated that this might pose a 'problem' with his remark that '... jokes in sculpture are not always easy to crack ...'. A year later in an essay surveying the state of contemporary sculpture, Charles Spencer noted how few British sculptors worked with assemblage. Tellingly, he commented that 'perhaps the superficial frivolity of the medium offends our native Puritanism'.[61]

Even in the late twentieth century, the inability to respond to humour in the artistic sphere remains an issue. Noting our tendency to wince at puns, Marcel Gutwirth has observed that this may be to do with our refusal to accept that laughter can have victory over sense.[62] Being offended by jokes can be a form of self-protection against the unfathomable – perhaps it signifies a desire to evade the 'darkness' which Fullard purposefully set out to explore.

With both wit and seriousness, Fullard played masterfully with paradox. He brought out the absurdity of war in general by focusing on the traumatic but rich particularities of his own experience. Though the notion of 'sculpting one's auto-biography' might be said to reveal a conventionally romanticist project, Fullard's work was never self-indulgent or overly precious despite the private references and intimacies which it sheltered. He succeeded in synthesising the technical scope of assemblage and his own individual poetic sensibility into a sculptural language capable of expressing the sometimes necessary, but always insane, reality of war.

NOTES

1. Brausen's adventurous policy was noted in the catalogue for the sculpture exhibition which was staged for the opening of the Zurich Gallery in November 1962.

2. R. Blesh and H. Janis, *Collage – Personalities, Concepts, Techniques*, London, Philadelphia and New York 1962, p.147.

3. D. Walden, *Collage, Assemblage and the Found Object*, London 1992, pp.8-9.

4. J. Reichardt, 'George Fullard and the Menacing Baby Saint', *Metro*, 1965, No.9, pp.27-9.

5. C. S. Spencer, 'Sculptor in search of the labyrinth, George Fullard' in *Studio International*, July 1963, Vol.166, No.843, pp.8-9.

6. *Weekend Telegraph*, 19 February 1965, p.24.

7. L. Alloway in *The Listener*, 5 April 1962, Vol.LXV11, No.1723.

8. The first comprehensive retrospective of Duchamp's work was in 1963 at the Pasadena Art Museum. See S. Hapgood, *Neo-Dada – re-defining Art 1958-1962*, exh. cat. American Federation of Arts, 1995. Fullard's exhibition at Gallery One was mentioned in *Quadrum*, 1961, No.12, p.176, where Fullard is described as 'un jeune sculpteur, utilisant des matières de rebut, objets trouvés dans la bonne vieille tradition dadaiste'.

9. Private correspondence, late 1950s and early 1960s, between Fullard and John Warren Davis.

10. See W. Seitz, *The Art of Assemblage*, Museum of Modern Art, New York 1961. Dubuffet's work had featured in *Quadrum* in 1957. Keith Sutton, in *The Listener*, 26 April 1962, No.1726, noted the current 'eminence' of Dubuffet. Sutton commented that, despite his importance, his work had only rarely appeared in public galleries in Britain. Astutely, Sutton identified a 'problem' with appreciating Dubuffet – and one which has relevance to the reception of Fullard's work then and later – noting that its primitive energy and kinship with 'child art' touched on the borders of prejudice.

11. For a full discussion of various movements and developments see S. Hapgood, op.cit. at note 8. Also, J. Fineberg, *Art Since 1940*, London 1995 and *Beat Culture and the New America 1950-1965*, Whitney Museum of American Art, New York 1996.

12. C. Finch, *Image as Language – Aspects of British Art 1950-65*, Harmondsworth, 1969, pp.36-45.

13. Picasso had cast conglomerations of objects, including leaves and twigs, as early as the 1930s. The Picasso exhibition May-June 1955 at Marlborough Fine Art, Old Bond Street, London had shown sixty-three drawings and ten bronzes.

14. *Pregnant woman* 1959 was the only assemblage cast into bronze at the time. Fullard remarked that an approach to the Arts Council had been greeted by the comment that assemblages of such objects were unworthy of the 'nobility' of bronze-casting. Information as at note 9.

15. George Fullard, 'Sculpture and Survival', *The Painter and Sculptor*, summer 1959, Vol.2, No.2, p.12.

16. Stankiewicz' remark was made at 'The Club' on 8th Street, New York, March 1955 – recorded by Irving Sandler and quoted in Fineberg, op.cit. at note 11, p.186.

17. See G. Gilloch, *Myth and Metropolis, Walter Benjamin and the City*, Polity Press, Cambridge 1996, p.166.

18. *Mother and child* 1959 was originally entitled *Survivors* and was the first of Fullard's wooden figures to be exhibited – at the *2nd John Moores Liverpool Exhibition* at Liverpool in November 1959.

19. Gallery One publicised itself as 'world agents' for Souza. Musgrave favoured 'intellectual primitives' but with a strong figurative element and humanist qualities. A distinct satirical anarchic edge was also characteristic of much of the work shown at Gallery One: for example, in a catalogue for an exhibition in 1961, Souza noted 'I use aesthetics instead of knives and bullets to protest against stuffed shirts and hypocrites'. In 1959, Enrico Baj, who used a bewildering array of materials including Lego and Meccano to create his collages, included a poem by E. L. T. Mesenz – a cutting ode to the 'artistic bourgeoisie' which included the lines '... And the stylistic corpses who look at you with despicable grins. From their respectable transparent and geometrical coffin....' At Gallery One's *Festival of Misfits* in 1962, Daniel Spoerri lived in the window of the gallery. Information from the Tate Gallery archive of Victor Musgrave and Gallery One, Ref.TGA 8714.

20. On the instructions of Fullard, Musgrave made enquiries about Gruppe 58 based at Hessenhuis, Antwerp as Fullard wanted more information about the group of painters and sculptors which had been founded by Gentils. Correspondence also notes that Gallery One would be sending two of Fullard's wooden assemblages to Antwerp. Information from op.cit. at note 19, Gen Corres TGA 8714.3.4.

21. E. Lucie-Smith in *New Statesman*, 13 October 1961, p.530; *The Times*, October 1961; J. Russell in *Sunday Times*, 22 October 1961; N. Wallis in the *Observer*, 16 July 1961; G. Butcher in *The Guardian*, 3 October 1961.

22. J. Reichardt, *Apollo*, October 1961, No.75, p.124.

23. A contribution to the attempt to deconstruct the 'perceived ascendancy' of Pop Art was made by the Barbican Art Gallery in 1993 with *The*

Sixties Art Scene in London exhibition. In the accompanying book, John Hoole, curator, challenged this view, which he argued had been perpetuated by the Royal Academy exhibition in 1991, by stressing the diversity of art practice in the 1960s and bringing back into view much 'overlooked' art. However, Fullard's work was a significant omission and featured in neither exhibition nor catalogue. D. Mellor, *The Sixties Art Scene in London*, Barbican Art Gallery, London 1993, preface (Hoole) and p.120.

24. Jasper Johns had, of course, made irreverent art out of the flag of the United States of America much earlier. In Britain, Geoffrey Reeve, textile student at the Royal College of Art, has been attributed with the earliest subversive use of the Union Jack which he employed as a design on sunglasses before transferring the design onto cloth in 1960 – for which he was threatened with expulsion. Significantly, Fullard taught part-time in the Sculpture School at the RCA from 1960-1. In the 1970s, David Brown, of the Tate Gallery, considered *The patriot* to be Fullard's most important work and one of considerable significance in relation to other Pop works (author's correspondence with David Brown, March 1997). See comments on *The patriot* in the Catalogue of Sculpture. For information about the use of the Union Jack in Pop see A. Seago, *Burning the Box of Beautiful Things*, Oxford 1995, p.196.

25. Although he had 'served his country', as had his father before him, Fullard was a confirmed anti-royalist and sceptical patriot. In the late 1930s, his father had written a play about the First World War, *The Devil's Tattoo*, since lost, which had focused on the mutinying of soldiers in the trenches. It is evident from Fullard's war assemblages (notably those utilising the symbol of 'St George' – see comments in next section), his own writings and from the testimony of those who were close to him, that the character of 'Englishness' and the relationship between nationhood and art certainly continued to engage him.

26. Extract from a poem, 'Monastery Hill', by Alan White, poet and artilleryman killed at Monte Cassino in 1944, in V. Selwyn (ed.), *Poems of the Second World War*, London 1985, p.233.

27. Lynn Cooke, 'New Abstract Sculpture and its Sources' in S. Nairne and N. Serota (eds), *British Sculpture in the Twentieth Century*, Whitechapel Art Gallery, London 1981, p.175.

28. Notes by Fullard in Tate Gallery archive, TGA 752. 6.1-11.

29. E. Newton, *War Through Artists' Eyes*, London 1945, p.7.

30. P. Fussell, *The Great War and Modern Memory*, Oxford 1975, pp.21-2.

31. Remark from Paul Nash's letter to Margaret Nash, mid-November 1917, 'Feeble, articulate will be my message, but it will have *a bitter truth*, and may it burn their lousy souls'. Quoted from *Outline. An Autobiography and Other Writings*, London 1947, p.211, in R. Cork, *A Bitter Truth – Avant-Garde Art and the Great War*, New Haven and Barbican Art Gallery, London 1994, p.8.

32. See illustration and comments regarding Jagger's chillingly realistic *No Man's Land* 1919-20, a bronze relief which was commissioned by the British School at Rome in Cork, ibid. p.237.

33. Ibid. p.247.

34. The 'problems' of commemoration have been shown by the difficulties surrounding the competition and commissioning of a monument in Judenplatz, Vienna. See R. Comay, 'Memory Block – Rachel Whiteread's Proposal for a Holocaust Memorial in Vienna' in *Art and Design*, Profile No.55 'Sculpture, Contemporary Form and Theory', London 1997, pp.64-75.

35. Michael Sandle is one of the few British sculptors who has examined the place of memorials and dealt in images of the Second World War and twentieth-century war in general in his work. See N. Lynton and C. Amery, *Memorials for the Twentieth Century*, exh. cat., Tate Gallery, Liverpool 1995. For a survey of protest war art of the last 400 years, see D. J. R. Bruckner, S. Chwast and S. Heller, *Art Against War*, New York 1984 – although relatively little sculpture is included. The authors conclude that, in visual terms, 'World War II just never made it as a myth', ibid. p.90.

36. Or, to use the private's vernacular version, SNAFU – Situation Normal All Fucked Up.

37. Letter from Fullard, dated 28 July 1958, to John Warren Davis.

38. Samuel Beckett's *Molloy* was originally published in French by Les Editions de Minuit, Paris 1950, first published in English by Olympia Press, Paris 1955. It was not published in Great Britain until 1959.

39. Fussell, op.cit. at note 30, p.7.

40. The 17/21st Lancers were popularly known as the 'Death or Glory' boys.

41. Letter to the author, dated 27 September 1997, from Irena Fullard.

42. Fussell analyses this image in poetry and popular myth in some depth, op.cit. at note 30, pp.117-24.

43. Discussions and information from Irena Fullard 1995-8, and Bernard and Jeanetta Sindall 1997. The *écorché* figure of James Legg hangs in the Life Room at the Royal Academy.

44. Author's interview, July 1995, with Phyllida

Barlow, sculpture student at Chelsea School of Art when Fullard took up his full-time post as Head in 1963 and later a teaching colleague at Chelsea.

45. Notes by Fullard, dated 19 June 1966 in 'Copiebok', in private collection.

46. *War ghost* was made, with the assistance of John Mills, in an early morning rush of welding and brazing. Apparently Fullard was extremely protective and secretive about his new work and, in his haste to return it to his own studio, the drapes of cloth with which he had covered it spectacularly burst into flames. Discussion with John Mills, 1997.

47. G. Fullard, 'Sculpture and Survival', *The Painter and Sculptor*, summer 1959, Vol.2, No.2, p.9.

48. Fullard had a deep interest in the First World War: he had an extensive knowledge of various military campaigns and was an avid reader of war 'literature' such as that of Henry Williamson who had drawn on personal experiences in the First World War in his novel, *The Patriot's Progress*, first published 1930. Discussions and correspondence with Irena Fullard 1995-8 and Steve Hurst, 1996-7, who recalls meeting Williamson, with Fullard, at Chelsea Arts Club. In Hurst's view, they shared an ambivalent attitude to war. Significantly, Monte Cassino has been described by military historians as the nearest thing to trench warfare in the Second World War. See Majdalany, op.cit. and Blake, op.cit. in Street-games and remembrances.

49. Controversy surrounded the showing of this piece – the first of his war works to be exhibited – at Battersea Park in 1963. It centred around the experimental nature of the piece and its suitability for showing in the open air. Kenneth Armitage, acting as something of a 'mediator', thoroughly appreciated that Fullard was making a 'startling break' with his previous work and admired his bold stand. In an undated letter to Fullard, probably February 1963, he identified strongly with the issues which Fullard's *War ghost* had raised: 'I'm particularly interested in your rejection of the too familiar attributes of sculpture – a thing I've been wanting to work out for myself for some time now. I have grown to hate the established commercial acceptance of "bronzes", "patina", "finish", "texture" etc – the artificial preciousness of the whole sculptural image....'

The 'problem' was finally resolved and *War ghost* did appear in the show.

50. F. Brill, 'George Fullard', *Motif*, 1967, No.13, p.50.

51. Fullard had incorporated basketwork in *War game* after studying American Civil War photographs of fortifications using similar materials. Also see earlier comments about this sculpture in **Street games and remembrances.**

52. Poem quoted in Fussell, op.cit. at note 30, p.25.

53. Exemplified in *The Vision of St George over the Battlefield*, 1915, oil on canvas (Imperial War Museum, London) illustrated in Cork, op.cit. at note 31, p.76.

54. J. Reichardt, 'George Fullard and the Menacing Baby Saint', *Metro*, 1965, No.9, p.27-8.

55. G. Grass, *The Tin Drum* (first published 1959), trans. R. Manheim, London 1989.

56. M. Hamburger (intro. and trans. with C. Middleton), *Poems of Günter Grass*, Harmondsworth 1969, p.13.

57. In an interview for *Weekend Telegraph*, 19 February 1965, Fullard commented 'I'm not a conscientious objector. War is as much part of life as peace, to say it is wrong is to say life is wrong....'

58. Fullard's response to Melville was published in the *New Statesman*, 4 December 1964, Vol.LXVIII, No.1760, p.877.

59. N. Gosling, *Observer*, 16 November 1964.

60. J. Russell, *Sunday Times*, 15 November 1964.

61. C. Spencer, 'The Phenomeneon of British Sculpture', *Studio International*, March 1965, Vol.169, No.863, p.101.

62. Marcel Gutwirth, *Laughing Matter – An Essay on the Comic*, Cornell University Ithaca and London 1993, p.160.

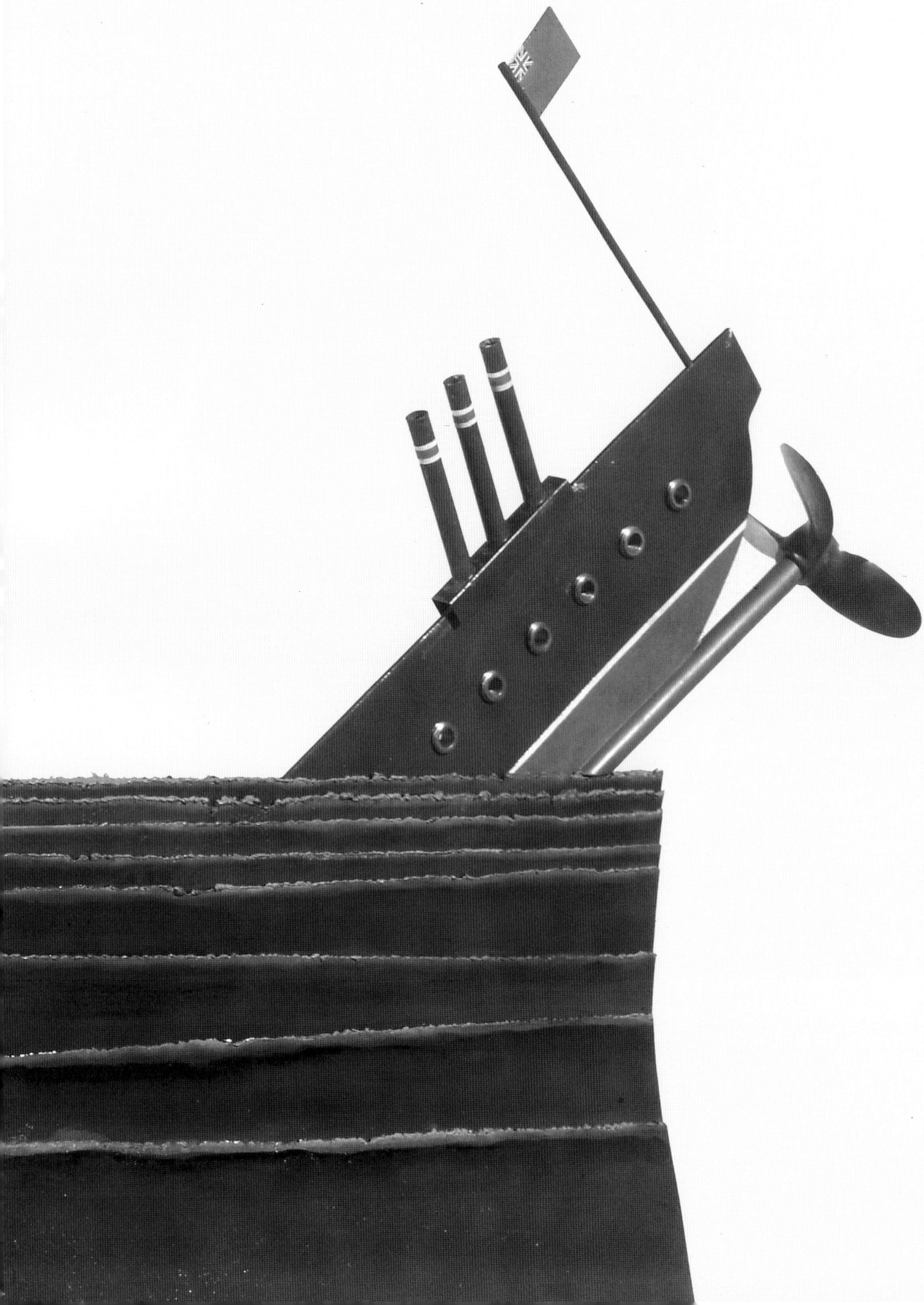

5

Plain-sailing? 1965 and after

Plate 85 (Cat.79)
Forever 1969 (detail)
Painted steel and brass
183 x 109 x 147 cm

A period of high activity had led up to his solo exhibition in 1964. In the same year, Fullard was invited to show in *Painting and Sculpture of a Decade*, an exhibition at the Tate Gallery described as the most comprehensive international survey of contemporary art since Roger Fry's *2nd Post-Impressionism* show in 1918.[1] In 1965, Fullard's work was included in the *British Sculpture in the Sixties* show, again at the Tate, and he was one of the artists featured in *Private View*, a collaborative book produced by Bryan Robertson and John Russell with photographs by Lord Snowden – a book which came to serve as a barometer of mid-1960s art. A contemporary reviewer for *Studio International* noted in October 1965 that it was 'already the "Debrett" of art – if you are not in it, you are out'.[2] In the next issue, the editor further emphasised the implications of being included for career and reputation, commenting that the prominence given to the eighty-one artists featured was likely to 'endow them with an aura that perhaps reflects their sales potential and popularity with dealers rather than superiority over artists left out'.[3] Interestingly, Fullard was featured in the final section with other young up-and-coming artists of great 'promise' who had come to the notice of the art world over the last couple of years. Evidently, by 1965 he was viewed as part of the 'phenomenon of British sculpture'.[4]

However, it appears that Fullard completed no new sculpture that year. Significantly, in 1966 he made *First voyage*, the first of a series of sculptures about the sea with which he became absorbed until his early death in 1973. After this apparently radical change of direction, he showed in relatively few exhibitions and rarely sold work. Undoubtedly, Fullard's post at Chelsea was demanding but other factors had some bearing and need to be considered: for example, the nature of the new sculpture and its relationship to earlier work and to contemporary trends and developments in sculpture within an increasingly commercialised art market. When quizzed in 1972 about why he had suddenly started to make sculpture about the sea, Fullard dismissed deeper questions by saying that, for him, themes tended to come in five-year cycles and that one theme had taken over from another.[5] It is easy to infer meaning and complexity when the imagery has been pared down to its most elemental and when the iconography of the chosen subject – the sea – is so laden with metaphorical possibilities. But, in these dreamy *tableaux*, an underlying 'darkness' disrupts their surface serenity. William Feaver described it, in 1974, as 'panic lurking'.[6] Had Fullard exorcised the 'phantoms' of his past or had he become overwhelmed by them?

Certainly in terms of subject-matter, Fullard had made a sudden abrupt departure. Apart from the intriguing piece *Valentine* 1968, an ironic intertwining of the symbolic colours of the Royal Air Force with a shape beneath it which has the form of a swastika, none of these later works have any direct references to war and share little, stylistically, with the war assemblages.[7] Instead, choosing nautical images and marine objects – steamers, sailing-boats, harbours, naval ensigns, propellers and funnels – his work related to the sea. This is an unusual subject for sculpture. In Alan Ross's view, it placed Fullard in a particularly English marine tradition in which his work showed emotional affinities with Ben Nicholson, Alfred Wallis, Edward Wadsworth, Paul Nash and Eric Ravilious.[8]

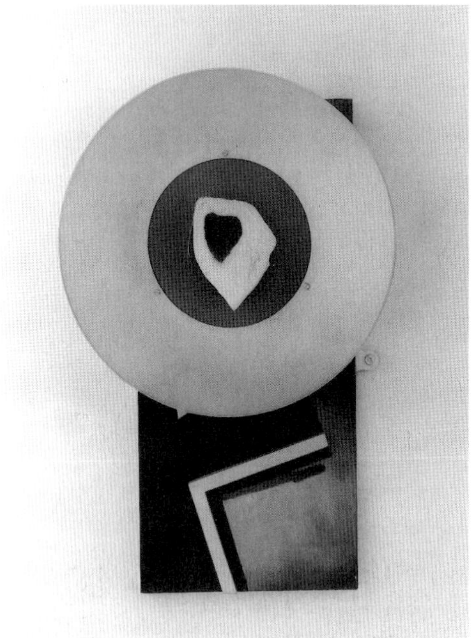

Plate 86 (Cat.76)
Valentine 1968
Mixed media
33 x 22.3 x 7.5 cm

Perhaps Fullard's interest in an English marine tradition in art had been latent. He had been particularly impressed by the paintings of Alfred Wallis which he had first encountered in the 1950s while living in Derek Hill's cottage in London. The artist's real war-time journeys across the Mediterranean may have provided an earlier source of imagery. In the mid-1960s, however, Fullard had joined Bernard Sindall and John Warren Davis on the last leg of a sea voyage which involved sailing a renovated boat back to England from Holland. The journey had been made at night and Sindall recalls Fullard being especially struck by the poetic beauty of the night sky and reflections of harbour and ship lights on the water. This experience might have generated the idea for one of the earliest of the sea works, *Night crossing* 1966.

Fullard continued to work in 'assemblage' but his sea series incorporated new materials and exploited the use of colour more than ever before. Shapes were specially cut from wood, sheet steel and aluminium and then drenched in flat hues. Works like *Voyage home* 1968, *Forever* 1969 and *Dream day* 1970-1, have strong affinities with collage and might reflect an interest in both the cut-steel figures which Picasso made in the 1960s and Matisse's paper cut-outs.[9] The curved steel seas and skies and folded 'paper' boats in Fullard's sculpture might almost be works of origami. The flat and bent shapes make the works look like sculpted pictures. Many were framed or boxed and meant to hang on the wall and this served to further underline their relation to painting, drawing and collage.

Despite the abrupt change of subject and the introduction of new techniques, there is a strong sense in which Fullard's former preoccupations remained. Most importantly, his imagery remained that of the toy cupboard and his inventiveness and vision was, again, akin to that of the infant. The three-funnelled ship is a child's schematic idea of a steamer and the spirals of smoke in *Dream day* 1970-1 and *Ebb tide* 1971 are like the scribbled pencil drawing of an infant. The boats and aeroplanes present the kind of silhouettes which a child would instantly recognise. Above all, the sea sculptures have a simplicity which Fullard had worked hard to attain. The artist's comments emphasise this: 'I believe in primary imagery – that which is clear to all

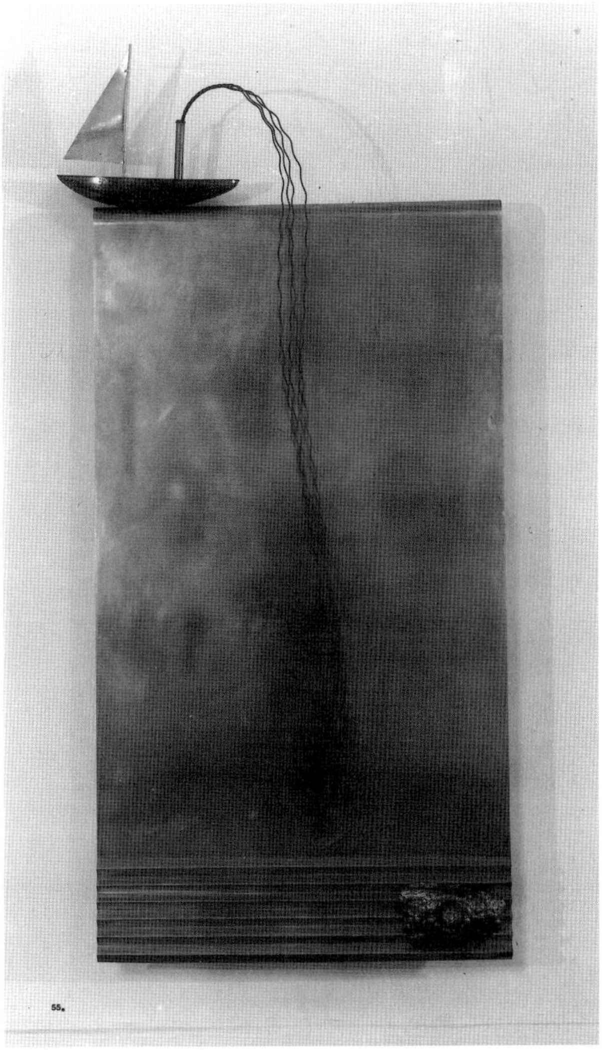

Plate 87 (Cat.82)
Ebb tide 1971
Aluminium
198 x 102 x 23 cm

Plate 88 (Cat.78)
Voyage home 1968
Mixed media
107 x 41 x 18 cm

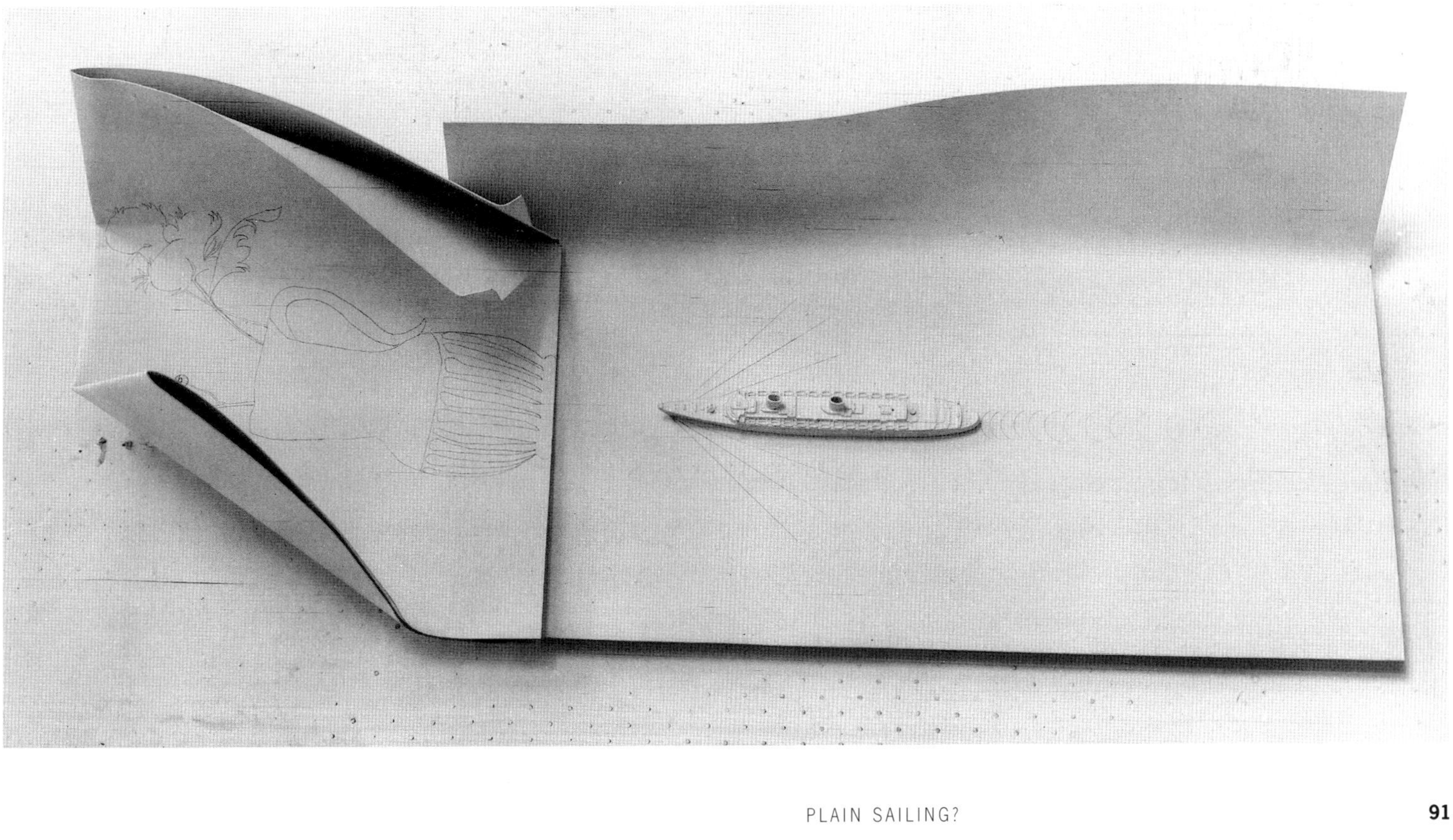

whether child or mature man. This elemental imagery which is the essence of all art is not concerned with the grandiose but often the ordinary – sometimes the trivial – even the banal.'[10]

These late works are a sculptural realisation of the artist's own paradoxical mission as a 'fastidious primitive'. Their naïvety is knowing and meticulously sophisticated. There is no mere simulated infantilism here.

Although it might seem that the artist had abandoned his autobiographical explorations after the war assemblages, this is not the case. The works continue to display the artist's preoccupation with his own boyhood memories. When asked about *Dream day* 1970-1 in 1972, Fullard remarked: 'I realised after that it was daydream back to front. One thought of a golden Saturday when one felt as if one were free to play fifty parts in one morning, to fly, to sail.'[11]

Whilst dealing in boyhood dreams, Fullard's work is not merely nostalgic. Nostalgia longs for an idealised vision of the past, a blissful arcadia that allows an avoidance of and disengagement from the present. It is essentially an escape. It is possible, though, to appropriate and consciously employ the apparatus of nostalgia as a means of emphasising and ironising the dialogic relationship between past and present, between innocence and experience. It is this dialogue which these works explore and which transcends the merely nostalgic. A full understanding of the way in which they bring together whimsicality, metaphysical puzzlement, longing and regret can only really be gained from situating the works alongside Fullard's war series. These late works are Fullard's 'songs of innocence'. In an ironic reversal of the Blakeian sequence, they follow and grow out of the dark, bizarre 'songs of experience'.

But beneath the unrippled surfaces and calm waters of these sea sculptures there is an underlying disquiet: in *Forever* 1969 the technically sophisticated steamship sinks cleanly, the fragile paper boat floats, in *Long ago* 1969 the safe harbour is, perilously, just out of reach. The idea of the 'oceanic' and sea voyages have historically provided a symbolic and metaphorical language for exploring the range of human emotional and spiritual experience. Many literary works have exploited this. Herman Melville's *Moby Dick*, for example, is a masterly exploration of the darkness of the soul and the unfathomable power of the sea. Tellingly, Fullard recounted an incident from his own childhood when he had become terrified in an outbreak of thunder. His father had made paper boats and floated them on the flood water to calm him.[12] In these last works, Fullard plays, over and over again, with the little paper helmet-cum-boat-cum-aeroplane. Consequently, it takes on even greater symbolic significance than in the war series as, here, it offers the only safe place of refuge. Whilst being mindful that this simple paper construction is also the makeshift hat of sculptors in their studios and often a child's first 'sculpture' too, it had become Fullard's emblem and had acquired a poetic significance of its own. Alan Ross succinctly remarked: 'Fullard's work is essentially the rearranging of tragedy into emblem, but the emblems have an innocent gaiety that rinses them of horror. The game and the dreams relate more to poetry than to death.'[13]

Fullard's new sculpture, then, had a reciprocal relationship with his previous work: its relationship to contemporary developments in sculpture

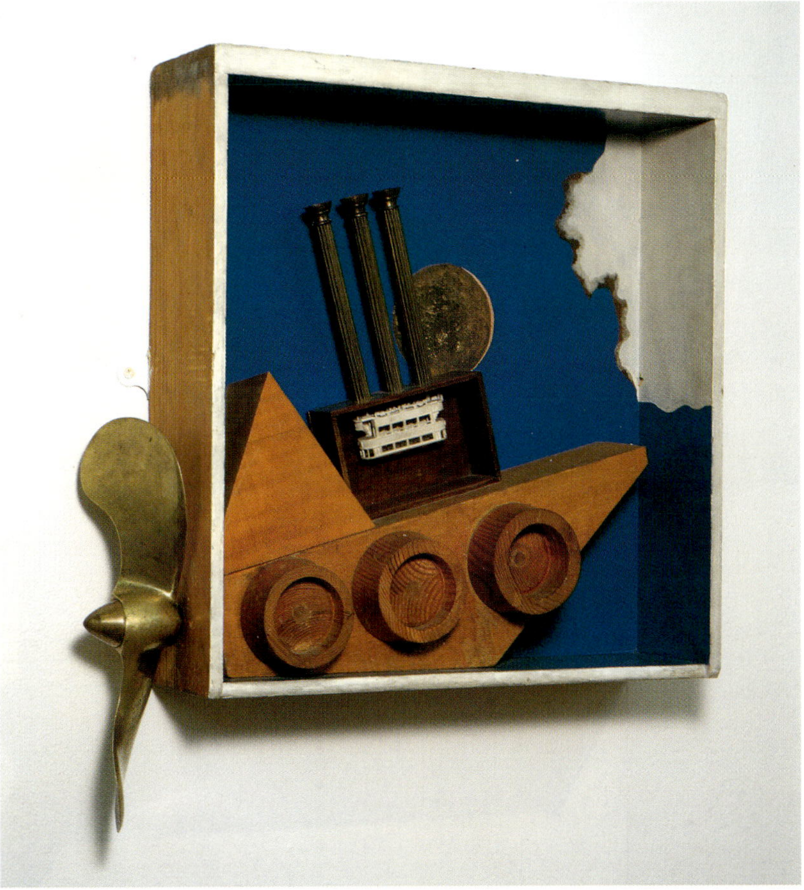

Plate 89 (Cat.69)
Night crossing 1966
Painted wood and brass
56 x 56 x 15 cm

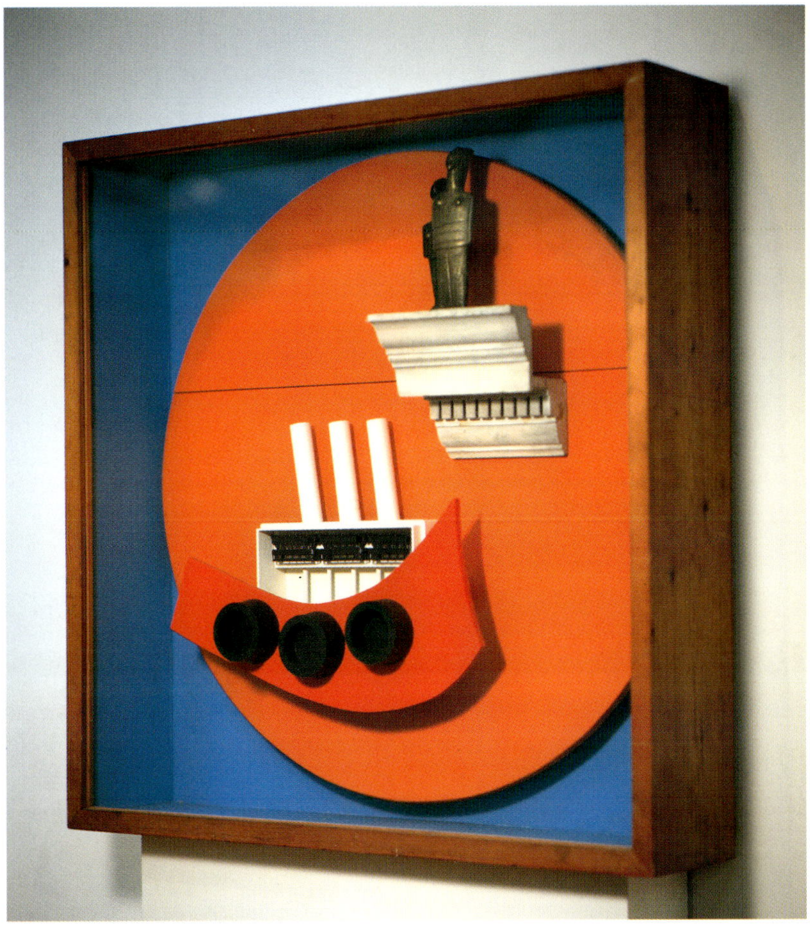

Plate 90 (Cat.70)
First voyage 1966
Painted wood and bronze
91 x 91 x 20 cm

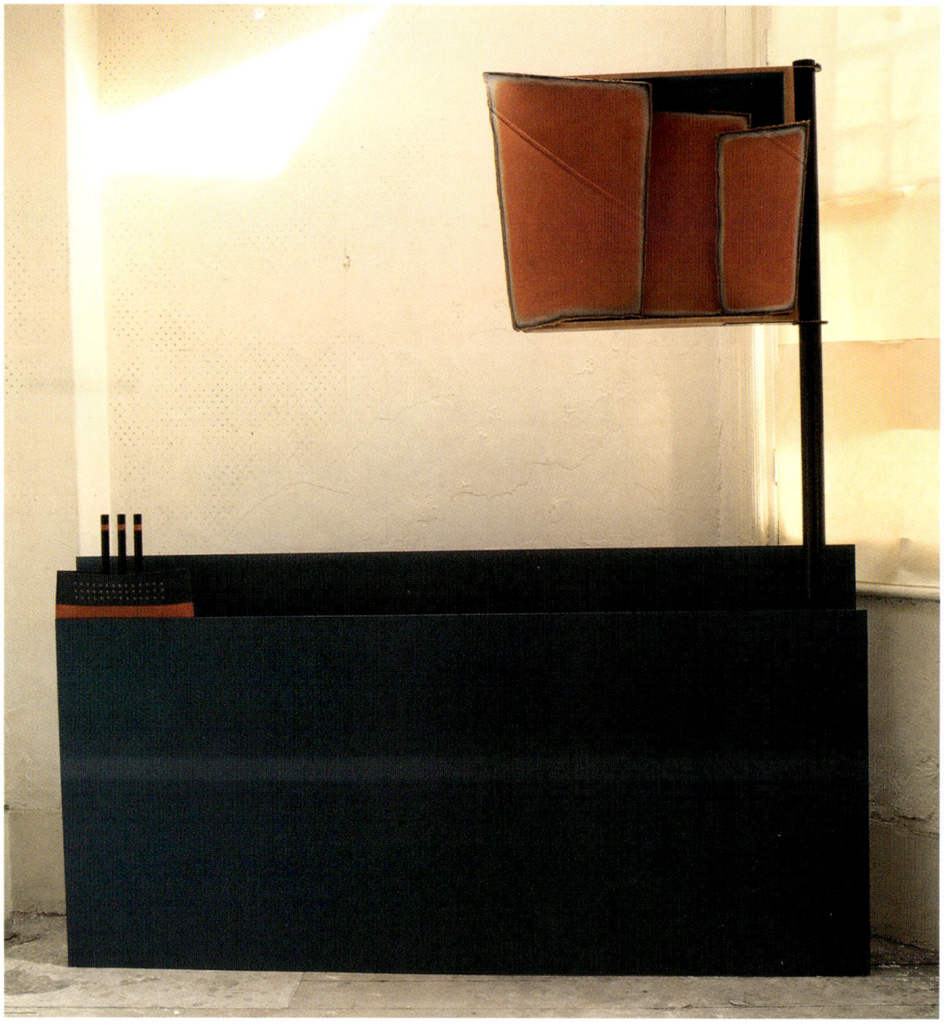

Plate 91 (Cat.73)
Near and far 1968
Painted steel
198 x 183 x 15 cm

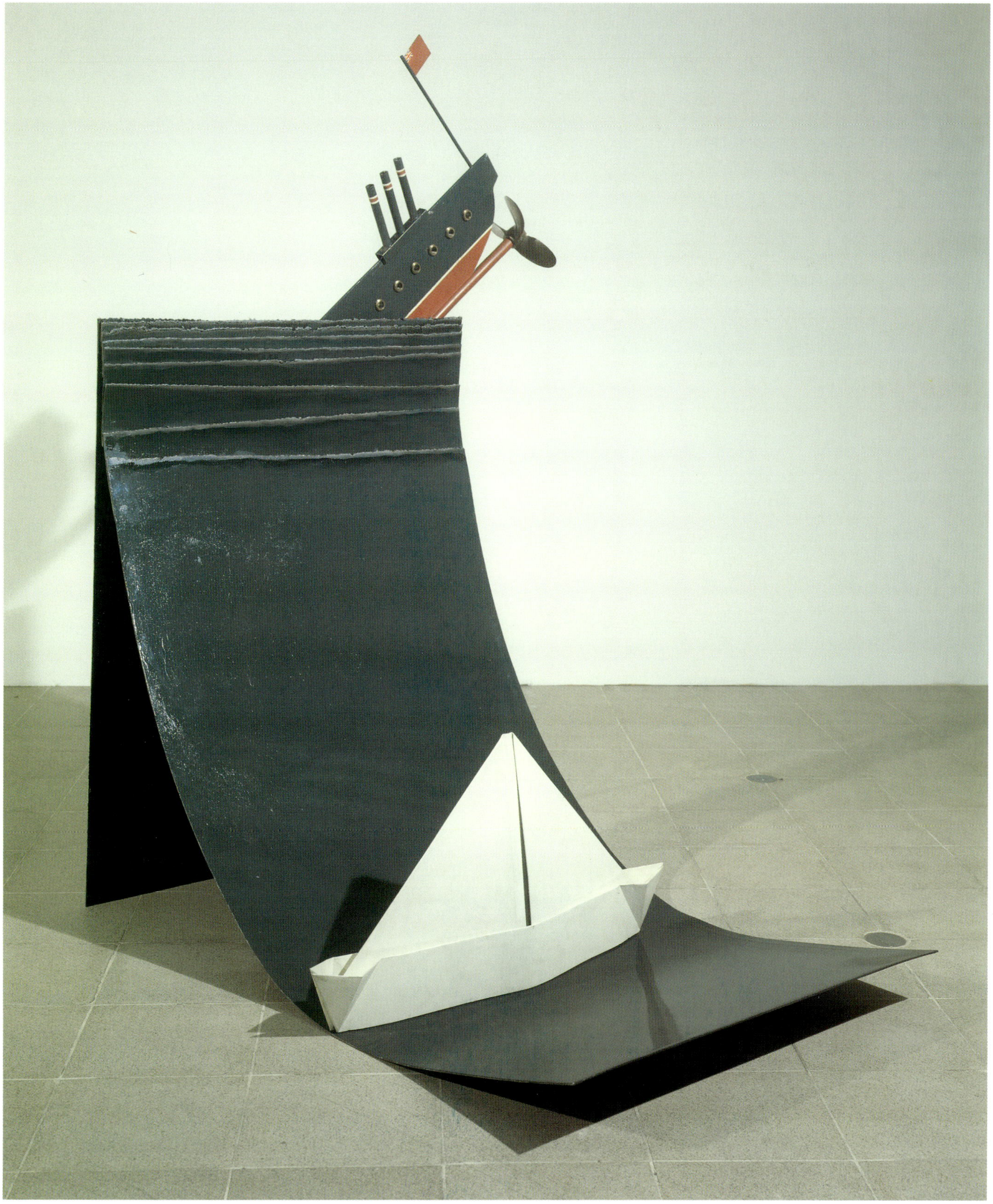

Plate 92 (Cat.79)
Forever 1969
Painted steel and brass
183 x 109 x 147 cm

Plate 93 (Cat.81)
Dream day 1970-1
Painted aluminium
96 x 175 x 48 cm

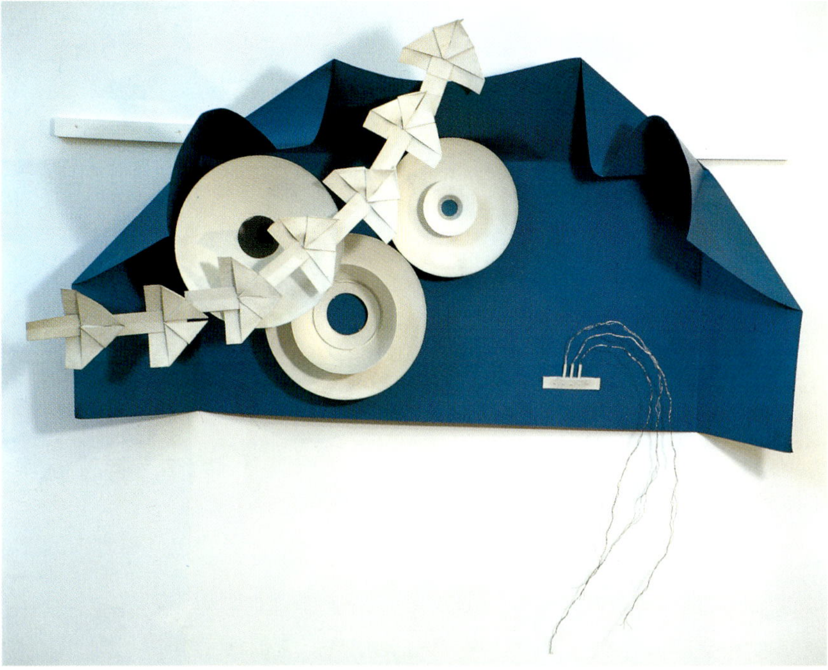

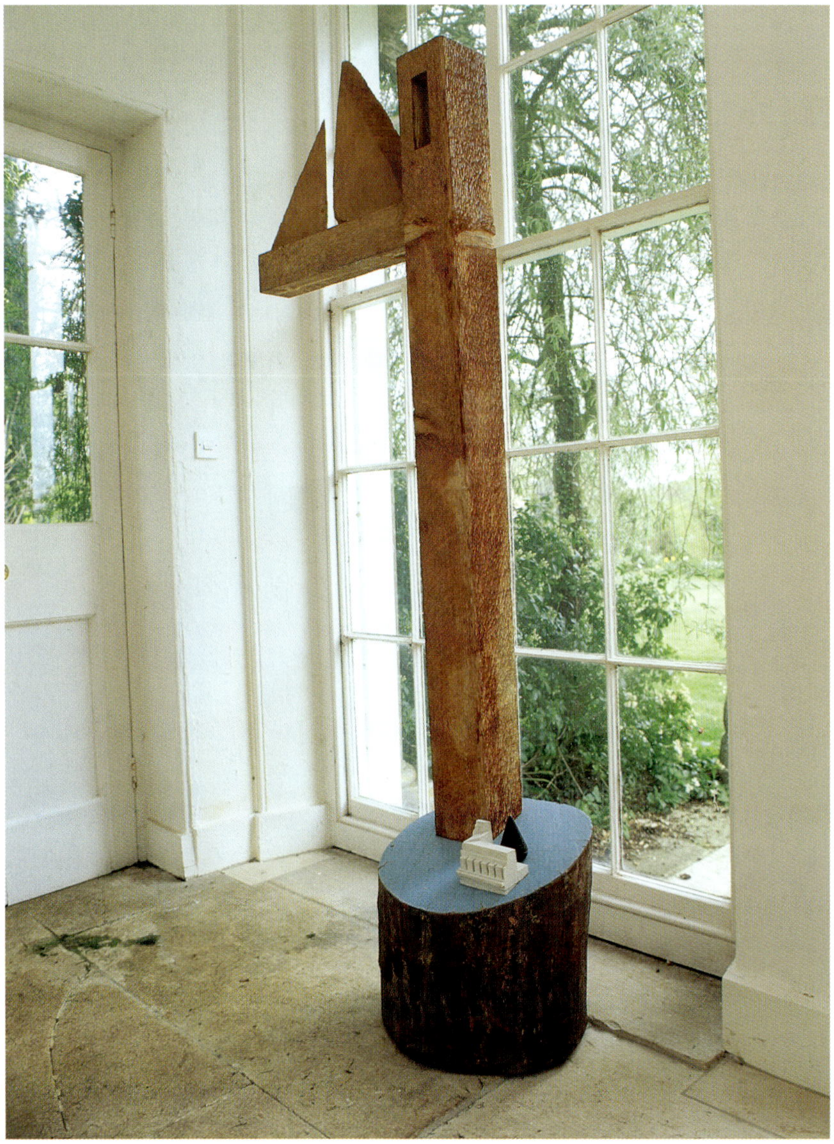

Plate 94 (Cat.77)
Location 1968
Painted wood
224 x 101 x 45 cm

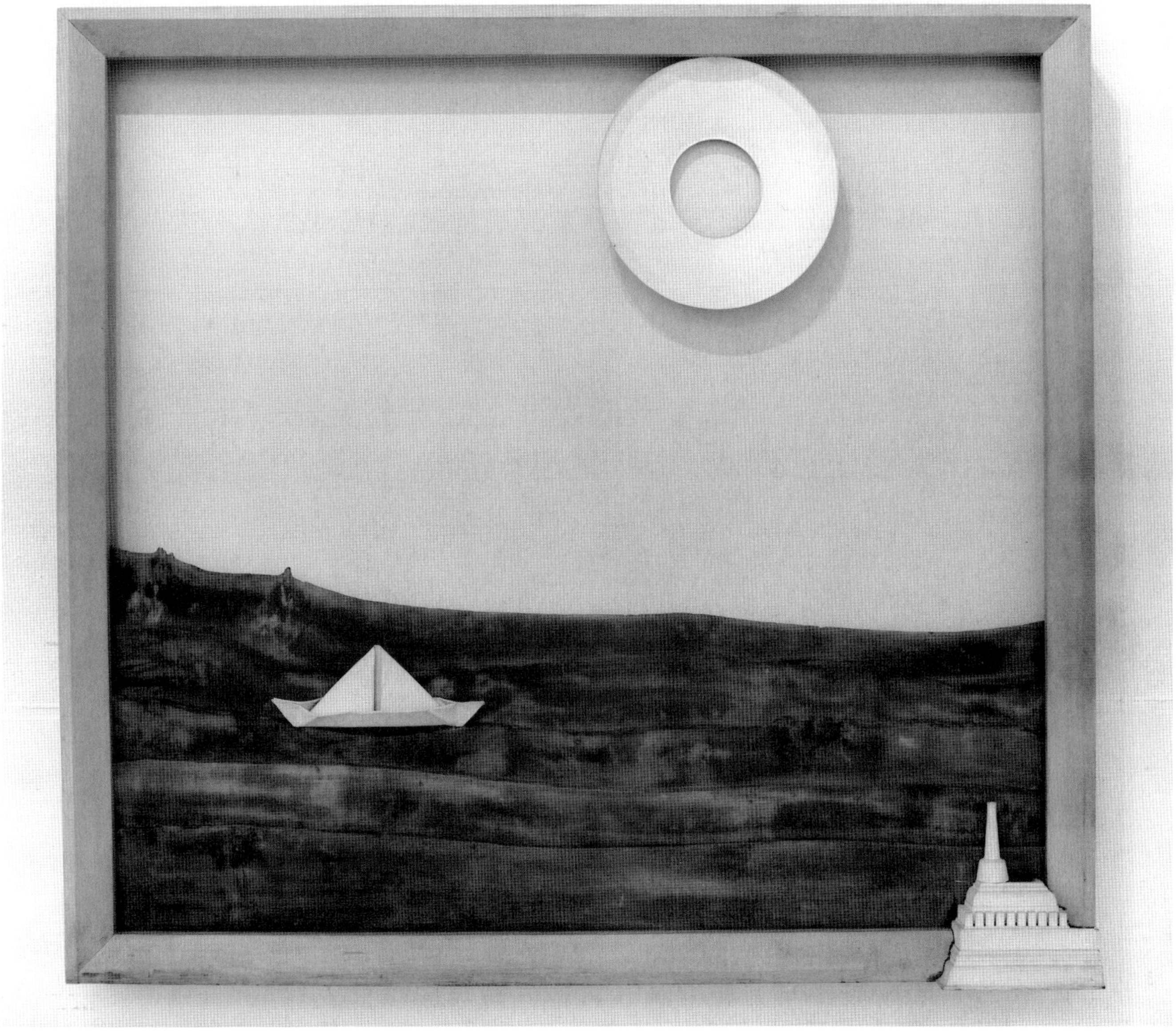

Plate 95 (Cat.80)
Long ago 1969
Painted wood, aluminium and canvas
172 x 188 x 17 cm

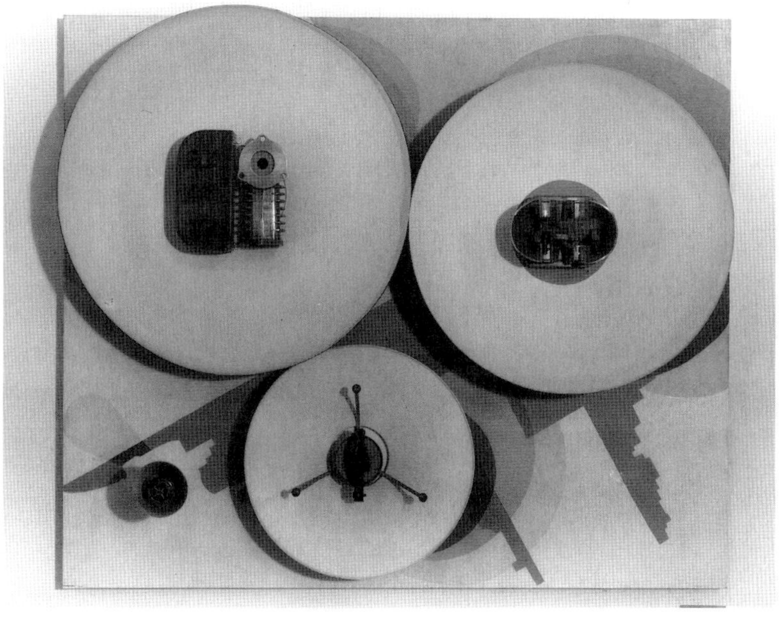

Plate 96 (Cat.75)
Flower piece 1968
Metal and wood
61 x 84 x 23 cm

was just as complicated. In particular, the *New Generation* show at the Whitechapel in 1965, which attracted unprecedented media attention, had implications for his own work and for that of his generation. Simultaneously anticipating and generating the 'hype', on the eve of the show, Bryan Robertson proclaimed it a 'revolution in British sculpture', commenting that 'visitors would find themselves on another planet altogether'.[14] The show further contributed to the acceptance and dominance of formalism and abstraction in sculpture through to the later 1960s, underpinned by Greenberg's admiration for Caro.[15] Whilst the work of Annesley, Bolus, King, Piché, Sanderson, Scott, Tucker, Witkin and Woodham was individually distinct, they shared an interest in flat fields of colour, single abstract images and industrial materials. One might identify some visual parallels between the work of these younger sculptors and that of Fullard: his rejection of sculpture as a precious object, his interest in flat colour, the reconciliation of sculpture with painting and his use of aluminium and steel. However, in his introductory comments in the Whitechapel exhibition catalogue, Robertson emphasised that these artists shared a general urge to make sculpture 'more totally abstract, non-associative, and self-contained'.[16] The subjective nature and life-orientatation of the whole range of Fullard's work, of which the sea series is the culmination, place it in a different location entirely.

There has been a consensus that Caro's influence on the British sculpture scene was considerable. In 1979, Norbert Lynton outlined how the new 'conventions' of avant-gardery had become a dogma. In his view, this new orthodoxy impeded the possibilities of discussing different sculpture as anything other than eccentricity.[17] More recently, among others, Thomas Crow has demonstrated the diversity of art in the 1960s and argued that, athough given little credence or coverage, street-level activism had taken art well beyond gallery boundaries and that this amounted to a considerable threat to the modernist position.[18] It is evident from Edward Lucie-Smith's survey of British art in 1969 that some contemporaries viewed the domination of sculpture by the 'British lightweights' – an overt reference to the New Generation sculptors – as less than healthy: 'London is essentially a province of the Greenbergians at the moment and Clement Greenberg is probably more influential than any British critic in determining the pattern of what is shown here'.[19]

Whilst it is problematic to talk of the homogeneity of a 'generation', Lucie-Smith made it abundantly clear that, in his opinion, artists of Fullard's age were coming up against particular difficulties. In a piece headed the 'plight of the older artist', he noted that the avant-garde young artists had become as much 'darlings of officialdom as they [had] of the dealers'. Identifying the severe problems which this caused for those, like Fullard, who had reached middle age without having claimed a place in the 'first rank', he noted that they were 'victims not so much of conspiracy, as of the inherent inflexibilty of the system'.[20]

In addition, the increasing commercialisation and commodification of art in the 1960s led to a growing disaffection, on Fullard's part, with the art 'system' generally. His letters of the late 1950s showed a deep distrust and distaste of the commercial arrangements for exhibiting and it is evident that

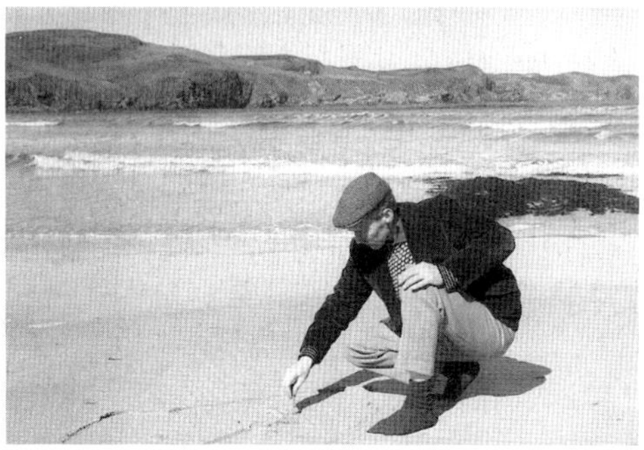

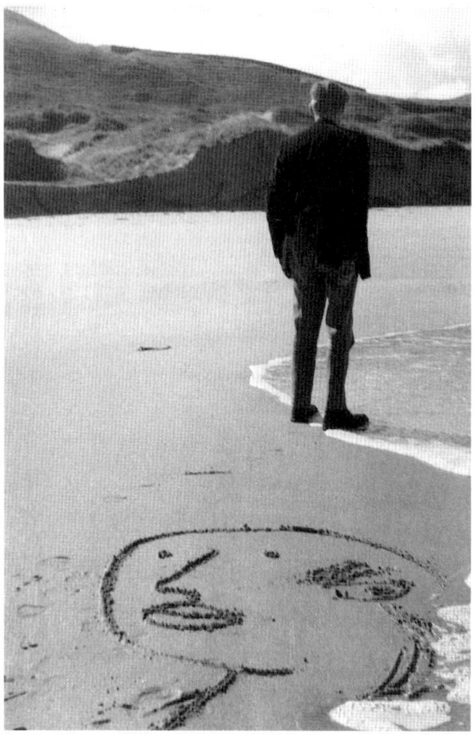

Plates 97 and 98
Fullard drawing on the sand in Sutherland in 1961

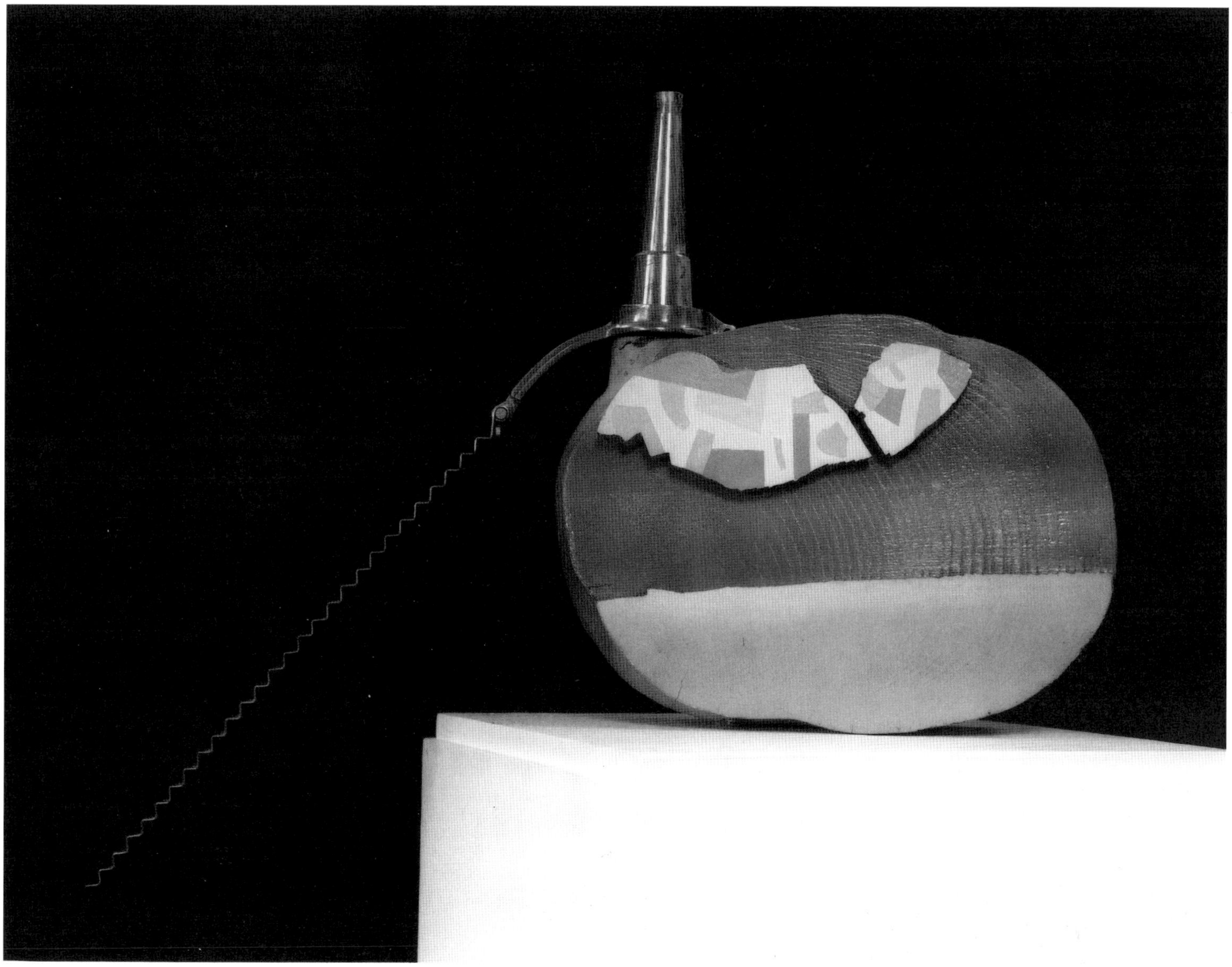

Plate 99 (Cat.72)
Small world 1967
Painted wood and brass
56 x 71 x 14 cm

Fullard regarded it as potentially destructive for art. For him, adaptation to the system offered only compromise, a kind of political betrayal of truth to oneself:

> ... the galleries are in effect a malformed 'shape' into which one is attempting to fit the finely precise key that art must be. It just will not work – what the key opens and gives access to under the present arrangements is something so far removed from art – so distorted an interpretation of one's spirit that it is in the end deadly to the artist. Without it apparently being anybody's conscious intentions the galleries are now in effect execution chambers ...[21]

Fullard's views sprang from his conviction that art must not be treated as a commodity. It is unlikely that developments in the 1960s would have provided any reassurances, as artists increasingly acquired celebrity status and art objects were 'traded' for profit. In 1960, he had purposefully tried to circumvent the system when, along with three other artists, they had set up their own exhibition, *Four One*, at the South London Gallery. Of course, Fullard could not escape the 'system' – he was just as dependent on patronage, gallery owners, dealers and critics as other artists – but it is important to stress his continued expressed ambivalence and opposition to an arrangement which he believed alienated the artist from his creative potential and from the act of artistic production.

Whilst his view of sculpture did not fit well with particular ideas dominating contemporary developments, Fullard's work did relate to a 'new strain of sculpture' emerging in Britain in the late 1960s, identified by Fenella Crichton as a new 'Romantic tradition'. She views this tendency as characterised by sculptors, such as Michael Sandle, who employed symbolic and poetic effects and brought their own personal experience to bear on the meaning of their work:

> It is a conscious decision and, unlike many artists whose search for originality is centred on the invention of new forms, these sculptors use forms which above all have a degree of personal meaning ... their work relates to their personalities, ensuring that there is always an important dimension which is private, whatever the scale.[22]

Crichton's description fits Fullard perfectly. His work was individual, poetic and symbolic. His sculpture had always related to his personal experience of the world and these last sea works have a vital private dimension.

Furthermore, a distinctly individual vision was precisely what he hoped to elicit from his own students at Chelsea. Here, his individualist views were entirely in keeping with developments in art school education in the 1960s. He became Head of Sculpture at Chelsea School of Art at a time of major expansion for art nationally, with the introduction of the new Diploma in Art and Design and measures which gave colleges unprecedented freedom to develop their own direction.[23] As a teacher, Fullard laid a pronounced emphasis on the development of an independent 'personal vision' among his students. This was reflected in the revised prospectuses at Chelsea in the 1960s and in the lasting influence his views about sculpture had on individual students. It seems that, even given the forced unconventionality of the art-school environment, Fullard was viewed as an exceptionally unconventional teacher who had a special way of engendering deep loyalty among his colleagues and students. He became immersed in work at Chelsea and later became involved in external moderation at other colleges. Nevertheless, he consciously maintained a detachment and disdain for the rarified atmosphere of such institutions. In his writings he privately despaired of students who had no 'real' experiences on which to draw.

> British contemporary art is largely geared to a kind of art-school art – a skilful facsimile or counterfeit quality – not made from real sources and not from where the artist stands in actuality, but from his relationship to art as an accepted convention....The unquestioning acceptance of 'Sculpture' is really the undemanding acceptance of social convention. Hence, an obsession with 'sculpture' and the making of it, far from producing or deepening the awareness becomes a blindfold, a restrictive process of closing off the receptive instincts.[24]

These comments serve to emphasise further a firmly held tenet and a recurrent theme of Fullard's work – that being an artist could be neither learnt nor taught.

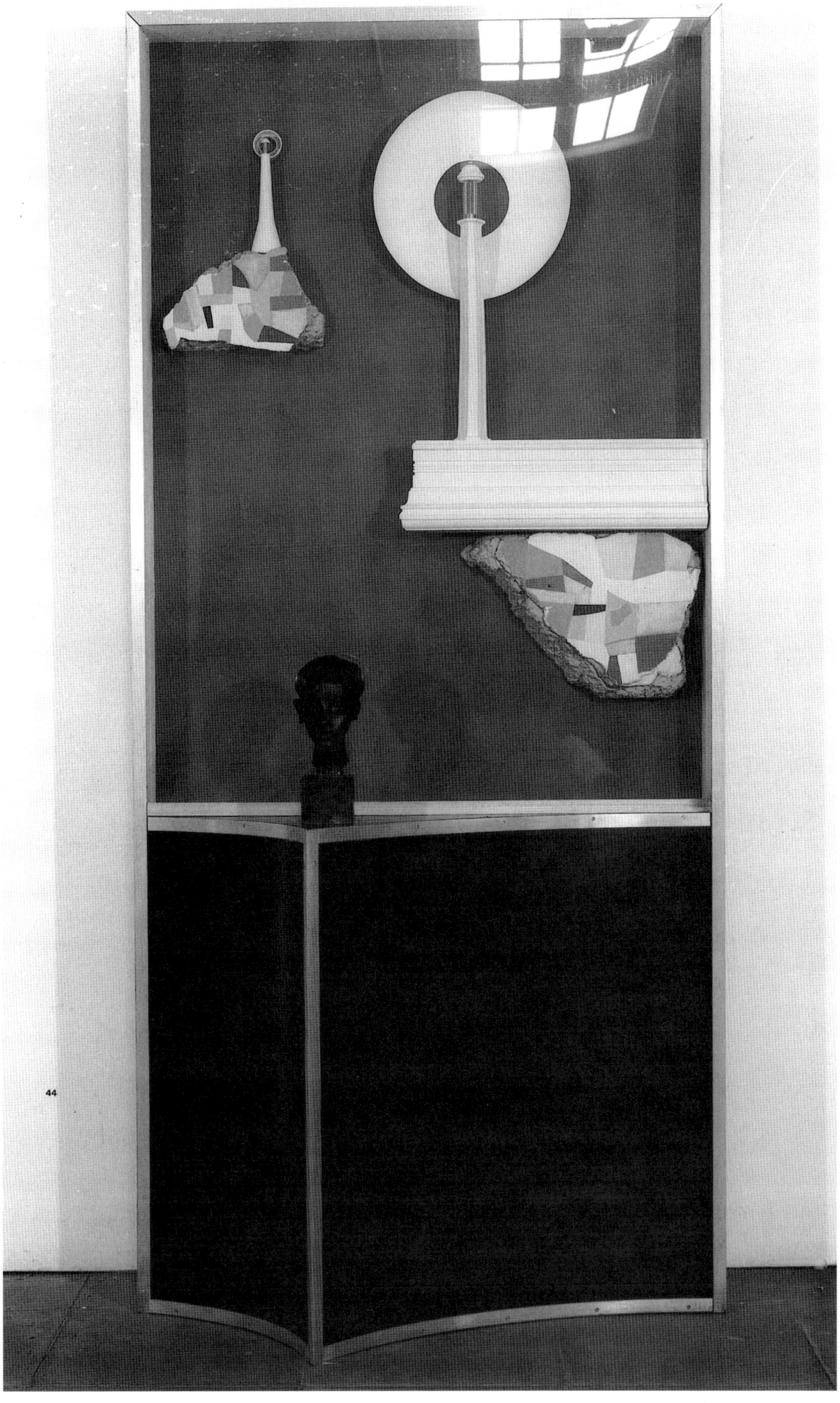

Plate 100 (Cat.71)
Ultima Thule 1967
Mixed media
241 x 112 x 48 cm

In conventional terms, the latter part of Fullard's career did not result in the fulfilment of the 'promise' he had shown in 1965. It had not been plain-sailing after all. His engagement in teaching, the type of work he produced and the particular problems faced by sculptors of his generation were all contributing factors. Undoubtedly, Fullard was disinclined to adapt to a system which was increasingly geared to the stock market rather than to the nurturing of artistic talent. Consequently, the first public showing of his sea works was not made until 1972 at the Royal Academy's *British Sculptors '72* exhibition. Whilst gradually recovering from a sudden heart attack, he gave what was to be his final solo exhibition, again featuring the sea works, at the Park Square Gallery in Leeds.

In 1974, after dismissing the sea works a couple of years earlier as 'so slight and trivial to be hardly worth considering', John Glaves-Smith, on viewing them as part of the whole body of work, wrote: 'These last works of Fullard have the impact of the final adagio of a Mahler symphony'.[25]

Frederick Brill, colleague at Chelsea and long-term friend of Fullard, speculated about the note of sadness in these sea sculptures: 'Perhaps a drowning vessel symbolizes the sad demise of some formerly precious security. Certainly the ship submerges with flag erect and all orchestras playing. It is a sinking that leaves a most memorable trace.'[26]

The final series of works which take the sea as a theme are the culmination of a complex body of work. However we decide to view these last pieces, they are meditations on time and mortality. But they are not morbid ruminations on death. Fullard may have been 'waving', he may have been 'drowning'.[27] Ever attracted to the paradoxical, he was probably doing both. In Fullard, an intense seriousness was married to a maverick individualism which could produce a tiny desert island, a cliché of a joke, as a final parting shot.

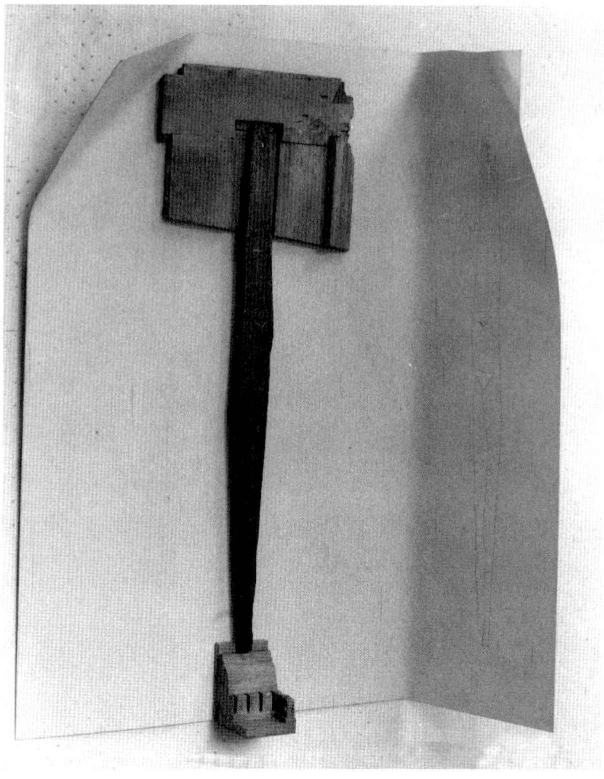

Plate 101 (Cat.74)
Relief with bronze figure 1968
Sheet steel and bronze
84 x 61 x 23 cm

NOTES

1. *Studio International*, May 1964, Vol.167, No.853, p.190.

2. The primary impact of *Private View* was visual with its exquisitely composed photographs which bestowed celebrity status on the artists, many of whom were featured with their families, homes or studios. In seeking to explain London's post-war rise to dominance in the art world, it established a directory of 'insiders' – as G. S. Whittet noted in *Studio International*, November 1965, Vol.170, No.871, p.190.

3. *Studio International*, December 1965, Vol.170, No.872.

4. The post-war success of Moore and other British sculptors and two major exhibitions of British sculpture showing in London, at the Tate and Whitechapel, provoked numerous reassessments of the current British sculpture scene. 'The Phenomenon of British Sculpture' was the title of an article by C. Spencer in *Studio International*, March 1965, Vol.169, No.863.

5. *Observer*, 2 January 1972.

6. W. Feaver, *Financial Times*, 9 August 1974, p.3.

7. Four other sculptures made after 1965 share stylistic similarities and have some thematic affinity with the sea works: *Relief with bronze figure*, *Small world*, *Flower piece*, *Location*.

8. A. Ross, 'Dream Games' in *London Magazine*, December 1974/January 1975, Vol.14, No.5, p.72.

9. Tim Scott commented 'the colour of Matisse was a counter to the high noon of Angst. Matisse influenced everybody in the Sixties, sculptors as much as painters.' Quoted in D. Mellor in *The Sixties Art Scene in London*, Barbican Art Gallery, London 1993, p.100.

10. Notes by Fullard in 'Copie-bok', private collection.

11. *Observer*, 2 January 1972, p.22.

12. *Yorkshire Post*, 13 October 1972, p.2.

13. Ross, op.cit. at note 8.

14. *The Times*, 9 March 1965, p.15.

15. Mellor stresses that Greenberg recognised Caro's 'world-historical' role. He 'apostrophised him in messianic terms ...'. Mellor, op.cit. at note 9, p.102.

16. B. Robertson (preface), *The New Generation: 1965*, exh. cat. Whitechapel Art Gallery, London 1965, p.8.

17. N. Lynton, *Hubert Dalwood – Sculptures and Reliefs*, exh. cat. Arts Council of Great Britain 1979, p.6.

18. T. Crow, *The Rise of the Sixties*, London 1996, p.111.

19. E. Lucie-Smith and P. White, *Art in Britain 1969-70*, London 1970, p.23.

20. Ibid., p.14.

21. Letter, dated 15 August 1959, from Fullard to John Warren Davis.

22. F. Crichton, 'Symbols, Presences and Poetry' in S. Nairne and N. Serota (eds), *British Sculpture in the Twentieth Century*, Whitechapel Art Gallery 1981, p.223.

23. The National Council for Diploma in Art and Design (NCDAD) had been set up to implement the Coldstream Recommendations. Its first report in 1960 recommended the setting up of new courses for the Diploma in Art and Design. Initially, in 1963, only twenty-nine colleges were given the go-ahead for the new Diploma, one of which was Chelsea. For a survey of these developments and information about attitudes of students and teachers in this transitional period see C. Madge and B. Weinberger, *Art Students Observed*, London 1973.

24. Notes, dated 3 July 1966, by Fullard. See later **Transcripts of writings by George Fullard**, private collection.

25. J. Glaves-Smith, 'George Fullard Retrospective', *Studio International*, Vol.188, No.969.

26. F. Brill (intro), *George Fullard 1923-1973*, exh. cat., Serpentine Gallery, London 1974, p.7.

27. Reviewing the Serpentine show, Feaver had concluded that, despite the wit, the sea works might have been Fullard's way of saying 'Not waving but drowning'. Feaver, op.cit. at note 6.

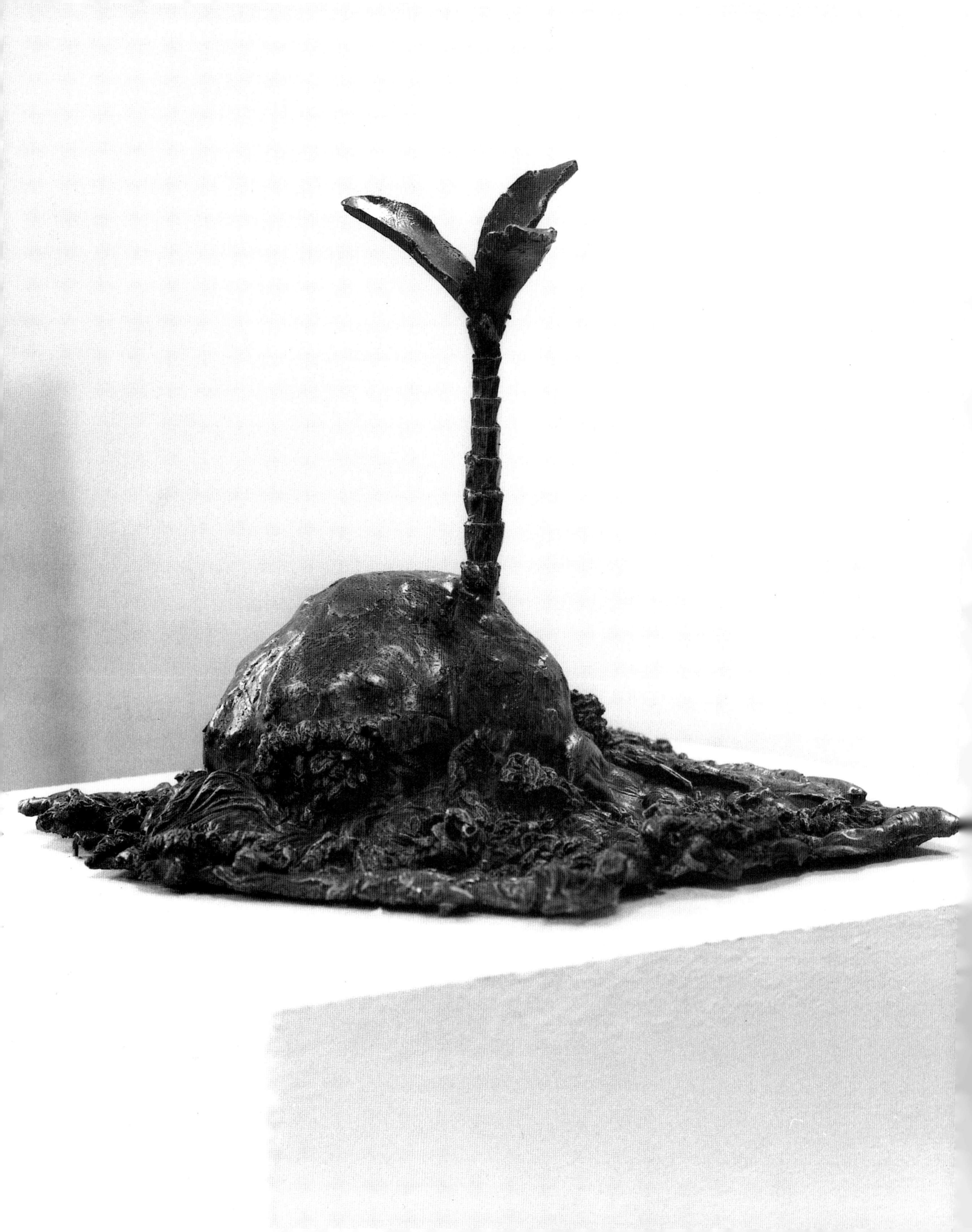

6

Overview

Plate 102 (Cat. 83)
Deserted island 1973
Bronze (edition of two)
17.7 x 23.7 x 23.7 cm

In his lifetime, Fullard's work had featured in many major exhibitions of contemporary sculpture. A few of his sculptures and drawings had been purchased for public collections: at the Marlborough show in 1964 the Arts Council bought *Fallen bastion* 1964. His work attracted critical review and he was interviewed for various journals in connection with different shows. In conventional terms, Fullard enjoyed considerable, if intermittent, success. In the latter half of the 1960s, though as we have seen, he exhibited rarely and sold even less. At his death in 1973, all his large war assemblages remained in his studio along with most of his concrete figures from the 1950s, virtually all his sea pieces and many drawings.

However, in 1974 the memorial retrospective exhibition at the Serpentine Gallery in London took everyone by surprise. One reviewer urged readers to see this 'vitally continually surprising exhibition'.[1] Critics, seeing the whole range of Fullard's work altogether for the first time, were astonished by its diversity and, simultaneously, its unity. Glaves-Smith's comments, noted earlier, were echoed elsewhere. Nigel Gosling admitted that at the Royal Academy in 1972 he had thought the sea works 'lightweight and almost frivolous' and yet, here, he found them entirely transformed. In his view, Fullard's work had been totally underestimated.[2] Willam Feaver described the show as an 'outstanding assembly of ideas and treatments ...'.[3] The tributes were belated but nonetheless they expressed a note of deep regret for the neglect of such an inventive sculptor. Twenty-five years after his death, his work has a remarkable resonance and relevance which it did not always achieve in its own time.

In the 1950s, Fullard's work had the support and admiration of Berger but the most influential post-war modernist critic, Herbert Read, viewed the sculptors who had shown at Venice in 1952 as Moore's successors. In the following decade, Fullard's acclaim was short-lived. Undoubtedly, the personal emphasis in his work – his 'quirkiness' – contravened the orthodoxy of modernism.[4] It is abundantly clear that many contemporary fellow artists admired his work and he had the support of isolated gallery owners and other individuals who considered him one of Britain's 'leading contemporary sculptors'.[5] But, for some, the war assemblages were difficult. Idiosyncratic and witty, they were perceived as lacking in gravitas – and the later sea works were either baffling or dismissed as trivia.

The intervening years have been transitional in terms of art-historical discourse and this has a bearing on the re-viewing of work by an artist such as Fullard. There is now a general consensus that political and cultural context considerably affect value judgements about art and that influential critics, dealers, selectors and policy-makers for particular collections have all shaped the received view of the development of art in the twentieth century. The 'high' modernist view, at its peak in the mid-1960s, which gave primacy to objectivity, denigrated the subjective in art and celebrated the abstract and the anonymous, was not, in fact, a given. It was the culmination of a historical process of aestheticisation of art and art objects. That view collapsed at the end of the 1960s and sculpture almost disappeared altogether – it 'dematerialised' into thin air – sometimes, literally.[6]

Of course, in the 1960s, beneath the surface of high modernism, a wealth of alternative art, counter-culture, was thriving 'underground'. The diversity of 'hidden' art of the 1950s and 1960s, from realism to happenings, has been researched and unearthed. Realist art is now a subject for serious research and is acknowledged through exhibitions. Assemblage and the use of the 'found object' has a renewed significance with so many contemporary sculptors working with objects from the built environment rather than fashioning raw materials in the traditional sense of sculpting. Whilst current views of past art are being continually refreshed, we have to be wary of making 'outsiders' into 'insiders' and vice versa. The 'eternal return of the oppressed' can become tiresome.[7]

In Fullard's case, however, the current reappraisal and revaluation is not only justified but is necessary and timely. Now, as then, his bizarre assemblages convey the idiocy of war and his facility to translate dismantled carpentry into images which are at once comic and disturbing is irrefutable. The search for the 'easy magic of the child ...' had been fruitful. William Feaver had noticed in his sculpture, the presence of '... a kind of magic in the transformation of mundane scrap into lasting imagery'.[8]

Importantly, as stylistic divergence and difference is embraced, the idiosyncratic nature of Fullard's work can now be celebrated. In Donald Kuspit's view, idiosyncracy represents the last refuge of individuality and integrity: 'Indeed, art survives only because it is idiosyncratic: it exists only to allow us to be idiosyncratic – as an escapist space for idiosyncracy in a crowded conformist world'.[9]

Fullard's work has poignancy, his sculpture is invested with human vulnerability but, ever the absurdist, he combines this always with a sense of mischief. His *Dwarf clown*, a painted plaster seated figure which he made in 1953, would probably be viewed, in the language of traditional art-historical discourse, as an early 'minor' piece. Rarely exhibited, it languishes in its bubble-wrap blanket in cold storage. Yet this is a focal work. The clown of circus and pantomime with his grotesque lips and painted suit is the descendant of fools and jesters but he also has a mischievous heritage. He is, of course, the Jungian 'trickster'. With the range of Fullard's work in mind, one peculiar

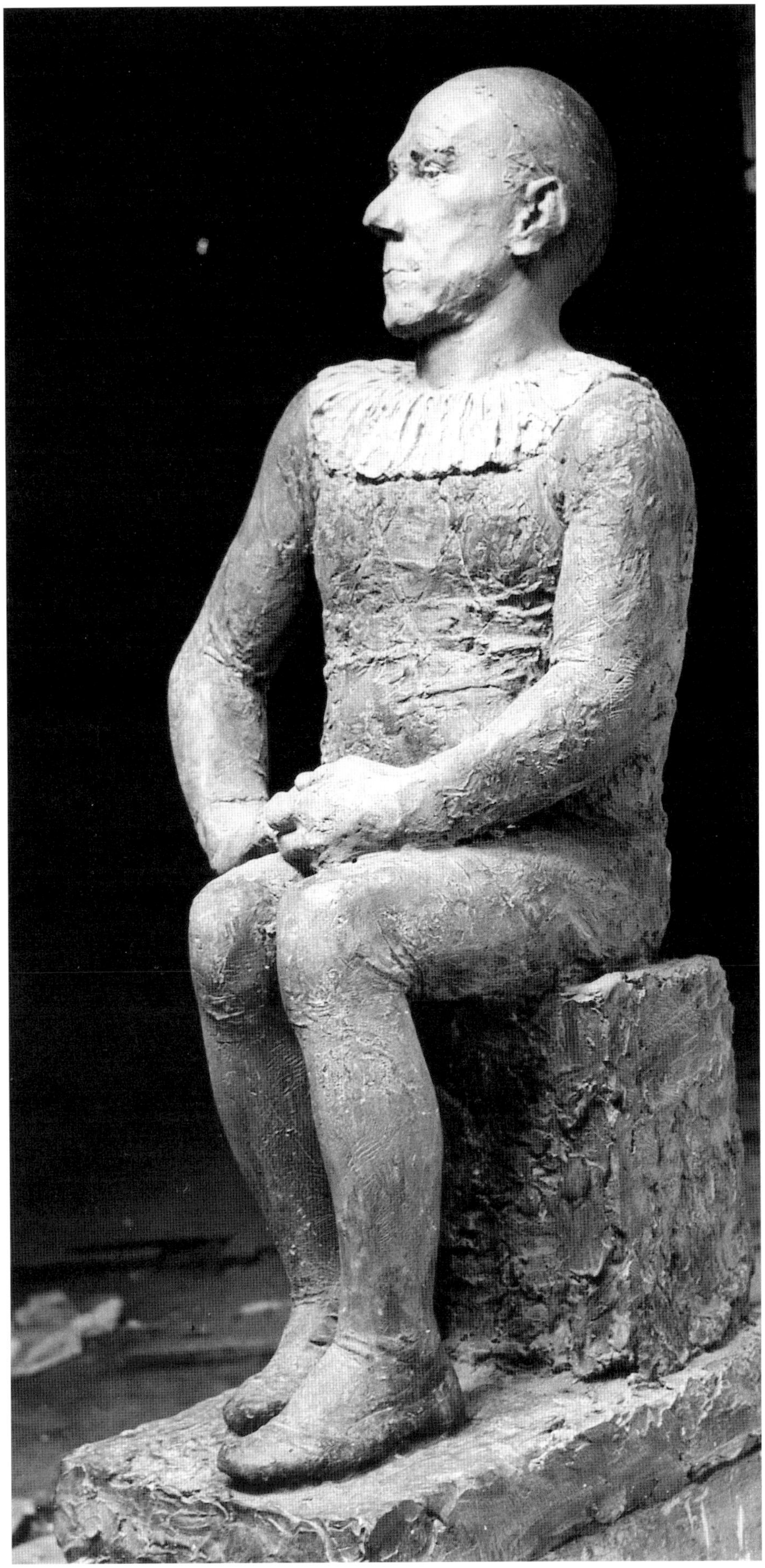

Plate 103 (Cat.13)
Dwarf clown 1953
Painted plaster
117 x 53.5 x 50 cm

attribute of the clown might be noted – 'to be the implausible invariant amid a world that desperately holds on to its own brand of sanity, to business as usual ...'.[10] Fullard's sad-happy clown is not a sculptural motif. It links directly to his later monstrous infant-machines that refuse to grow up and to that other sad mischievous dwarf, Osker. In 1974, Gosling had selected *Dwarf clown* for particular comment: '... a little plaster figure which should be horrible and is actually moving and almost beautiful. It is as though among a bunch of garden gnomes, you come across a real midget – tough, bony, dignified, suffering.'[11]

Summing up the effect that Fullard had on a younger generation of sculptors, a former student described him as a 'ruthless visionary'.[12] Fullard evidently impressed others with his strongly held views about art and life. A social and political conscience, a strong sense of comradeship and loyalty, a refusal to compromise his work in any way, the view that an artist should 'bear witness' – all these characteristics might be located with the legacy of political inolvements and war-time experiences. Certainly, Fullard was a determined non-conformist who believed in standing up for one's individual beliefs and one's own truth. He frequently wrote of the necessity for 'integrity' as an artist. Occasionally, Fullard's privately recorded views can appear self-possessed but, nevertheless, they convey ideas that were deeply experienced and felt.

Crucially though, despite its personal character, Fullard's work was never overly precious. Contradictory tension, paradox, an inherent ambivalence and ambiguity militate strongly against any such tendency. His sculpture is, at one and the same time, intellectually demanding, emotionally dense and leavened with a cavalier wit. It is complex yet immediacy is never sacrificed – surprise is a constituent element. Fullard is an intriguing quixotic artist who resists categorisation; an absurdist with a mischievous sense of humour that extended even to his own autobiography.

NOTES

1. M. Vaizey, *Sunday Times*, 28 July 1974.

2. N. Gosling, *Observer*, 28 July 1974.

3. W. Feaver, *Financial Times*, 9 August 1974.

4. See comments by F. Crichton, op.cit. at note 3 in **Introduction**.

5. As described by S. Gilchrist in correspondence and literature related to Fullard's final solo exhibition at the Park Square Gallery, Leeds in 1972. In a letter, dated 9 January 1974, to John Russell (in response to his *Sunday Times* obituary on Fullard) she wrote that 'he was a much under-estimated sculptor sadly, as you say, neglected by the London dealers, but not in Leeds'. Park Square Gallery papers, Special Collection, Brotherton Library, University of Leeds, Ref.MS 712.

6. See L. Lippard, *Six Years: Dematerialisation of Art 1966-1972*, London, 1972.

7. D. Kuspit, *Idiosyncratic Identities*, Cambridge, New York, USA 1996, p.40.

8. Feaver, op.cit. at note 3.

9. Kuspit, op.cit. at note 7, p. 4.

10. M. Gutwirth, *Laughing Matter – An Essay on the Comic*, Ithaca and London 1993, p.153.

11. Gosling, op.cit. at note 2.

12. Interview by the author with Ian Welsh, February 1998.

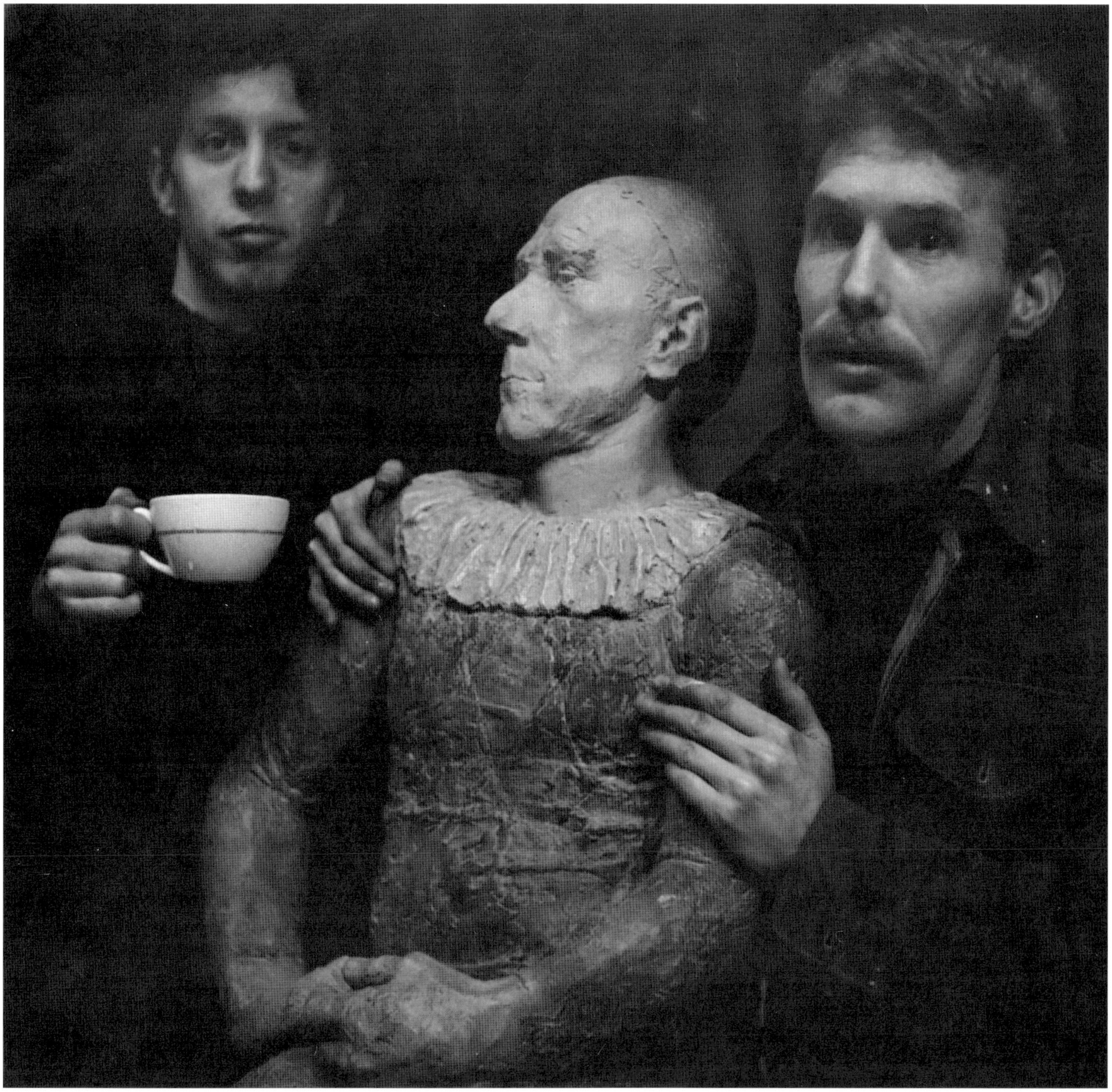

Plate 104
Fullard and Derrick Greaves with *Dwarf clown* 1953 (Cat.13).

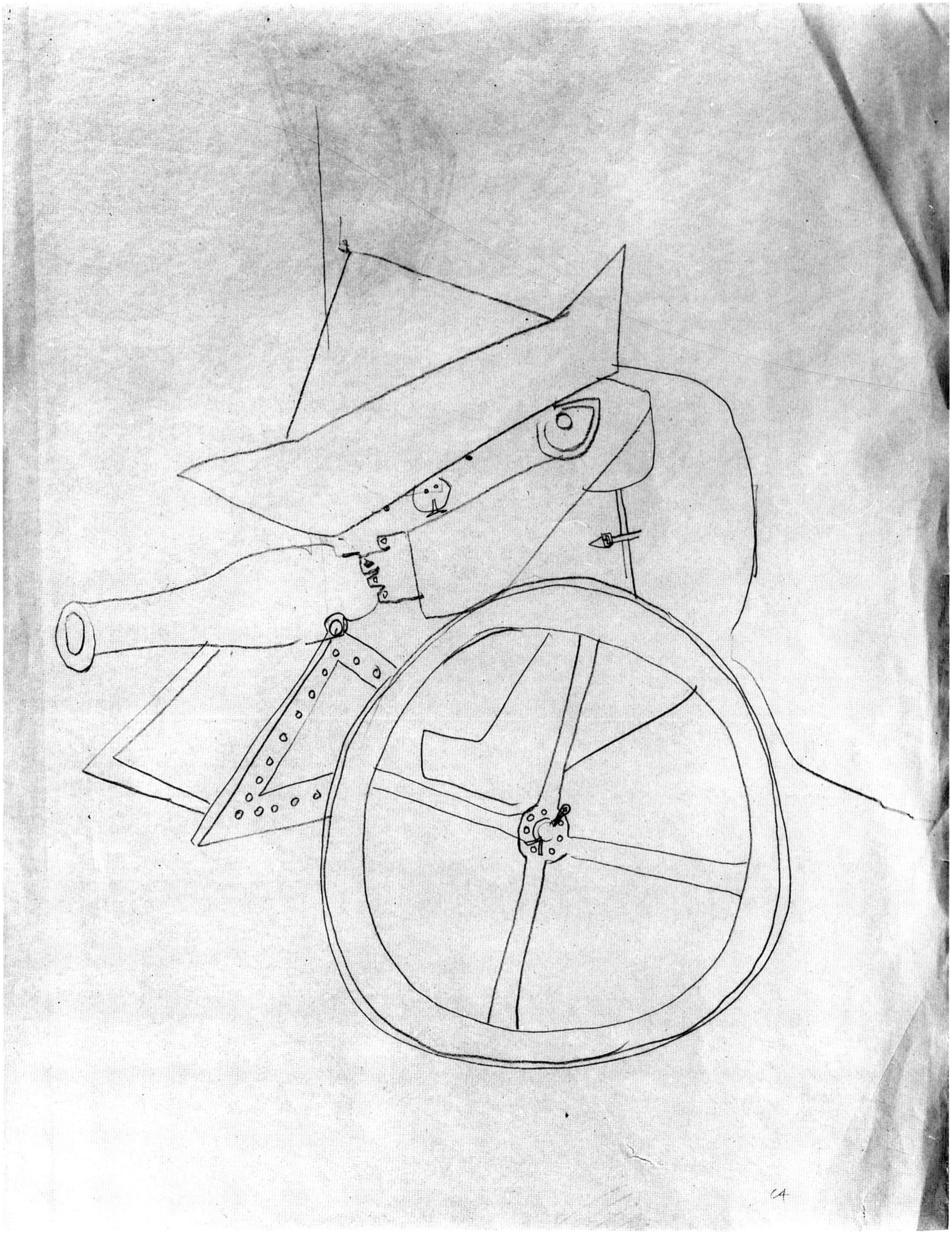
C4

7

A note on Fullard's drawings

Plate 105
Infant with cannon 1964
Pencil on paper
Private collection

For the artist drawing is discovery. And that is not just a slick phrase, it is quite literally true. It is the actual act of drawing that forces the artist to look at the object in front of him, to dissect it in his mind's eye and put it together again; or, if he is drawing from memory, that forces him to dredge his own mind, to discover the content of his own store of past observations.... A drawing is an autobiographical record of one's discovery of an event – seen, remembered or imagined.

John Berger[1]

In a brief essay which explored the process of drawing, John Berger identified its inherently private and intimate nature. He suggested that, if confronted with painting or sculpture, the viewer tends to identify with the subject-matter of the piece but in front of a drawing, one identifies with the artist – for a drawing presents the possibility of gaining 'the conscious experience of seeing as though through the artist's own eyes'. Leafing through a sheaf of an artist's drawings can be an intimate experience as there is an absence of mediation. The medium requires little in the way of materials or tools. The artist need only choose a piece of chalk and scrap of paper as the faintest marks on a surface will suffice. Fullard largely chose the simplest materials: pencil, chalk and paper, and the sparsest element – line – in the production of his many drawings, his 'auto-biographical record' as seen, remembered and imagined.

Line predominates in Fullard's drawings. Pure line drawing entails the artist expressing variations of hue, tone, form and texture through the thickness or thinness of a few lines. Line has had a particular importance for artists of the twentieth century and especially for Henri Matisse, Pablo Picasso and Paul Klee.

Fullard recognised the demands of his own concentration on line. He viewed drawing as a discipline and valued decisiveness as a crucial aspect of the medium. He stressed this in comments jotted down in a notebook: 'Drawing – uses memory – examination and inspiration teaches one to be decisive – not fuzzy ...'.[2]

Fullard's drawings, from his earliest student work in Sheffield to his later

Plate 106
Mother and child 1960
Pencil on paper
Private collection

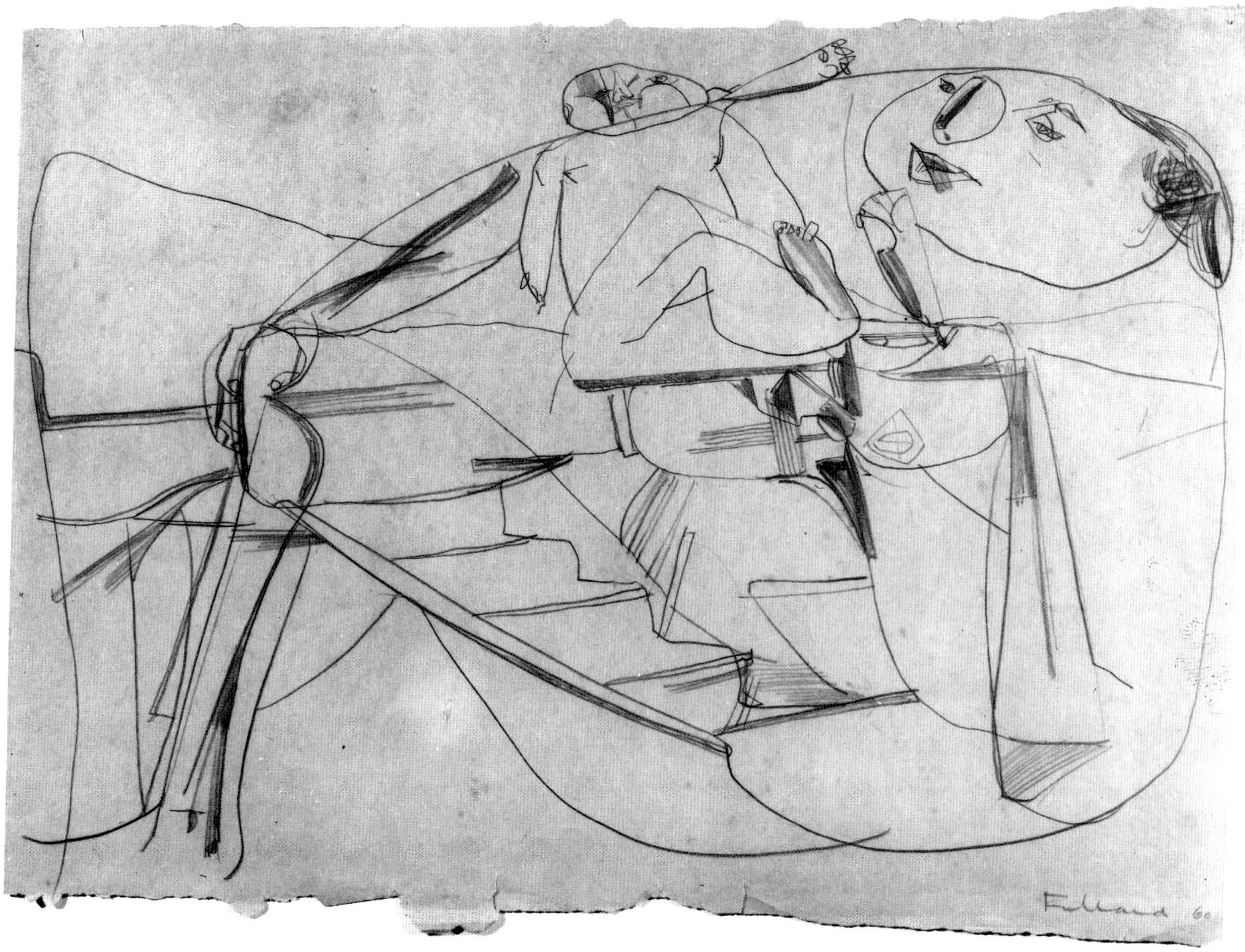

Plate 107
Dancers 1959
Pencil and ink on paper
Private collection

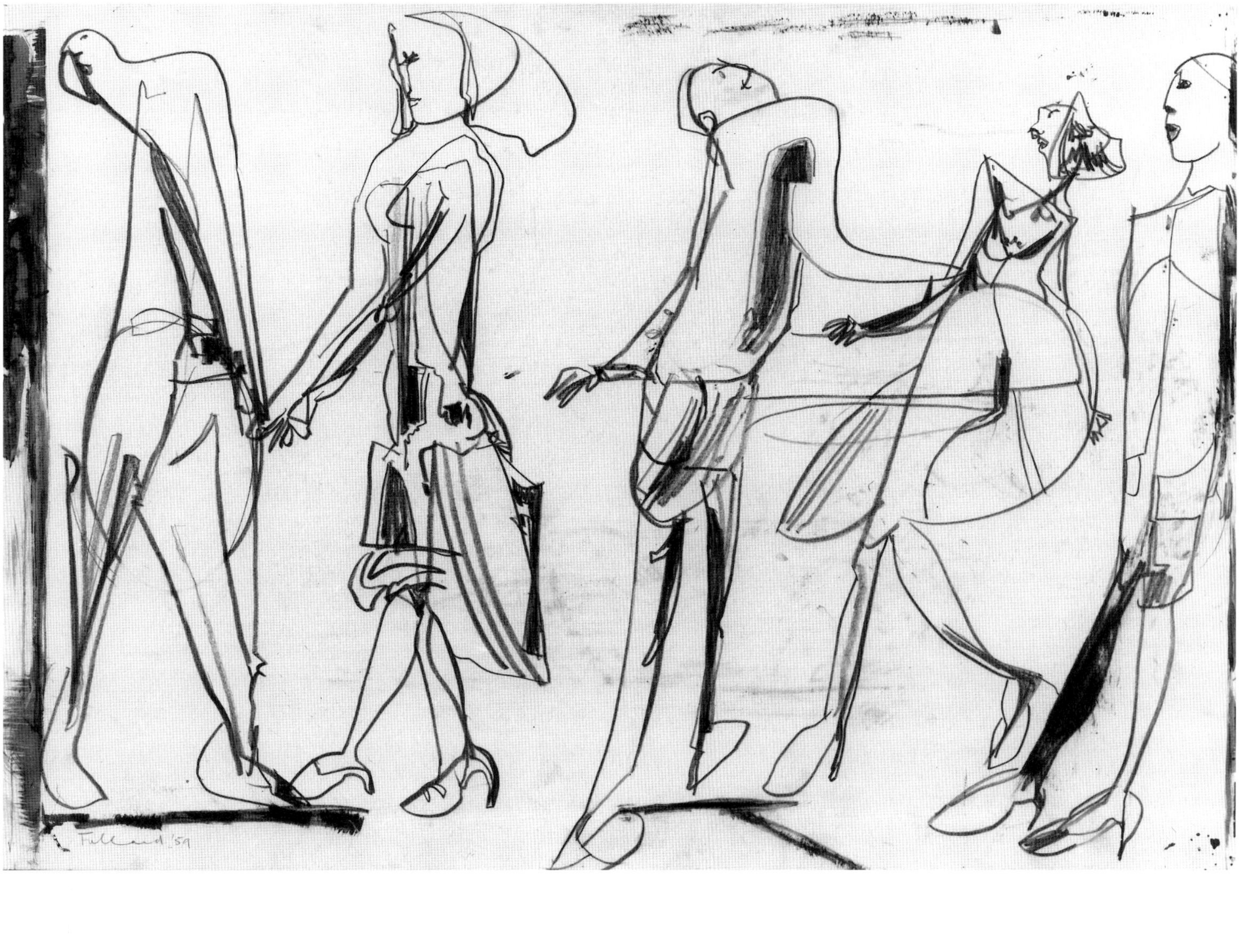

Plate 108
Dancers 1959
Pencil on paper
Private collection

OPPOSITE
Plate 109
Couple on bench 1959
Pencil on paper

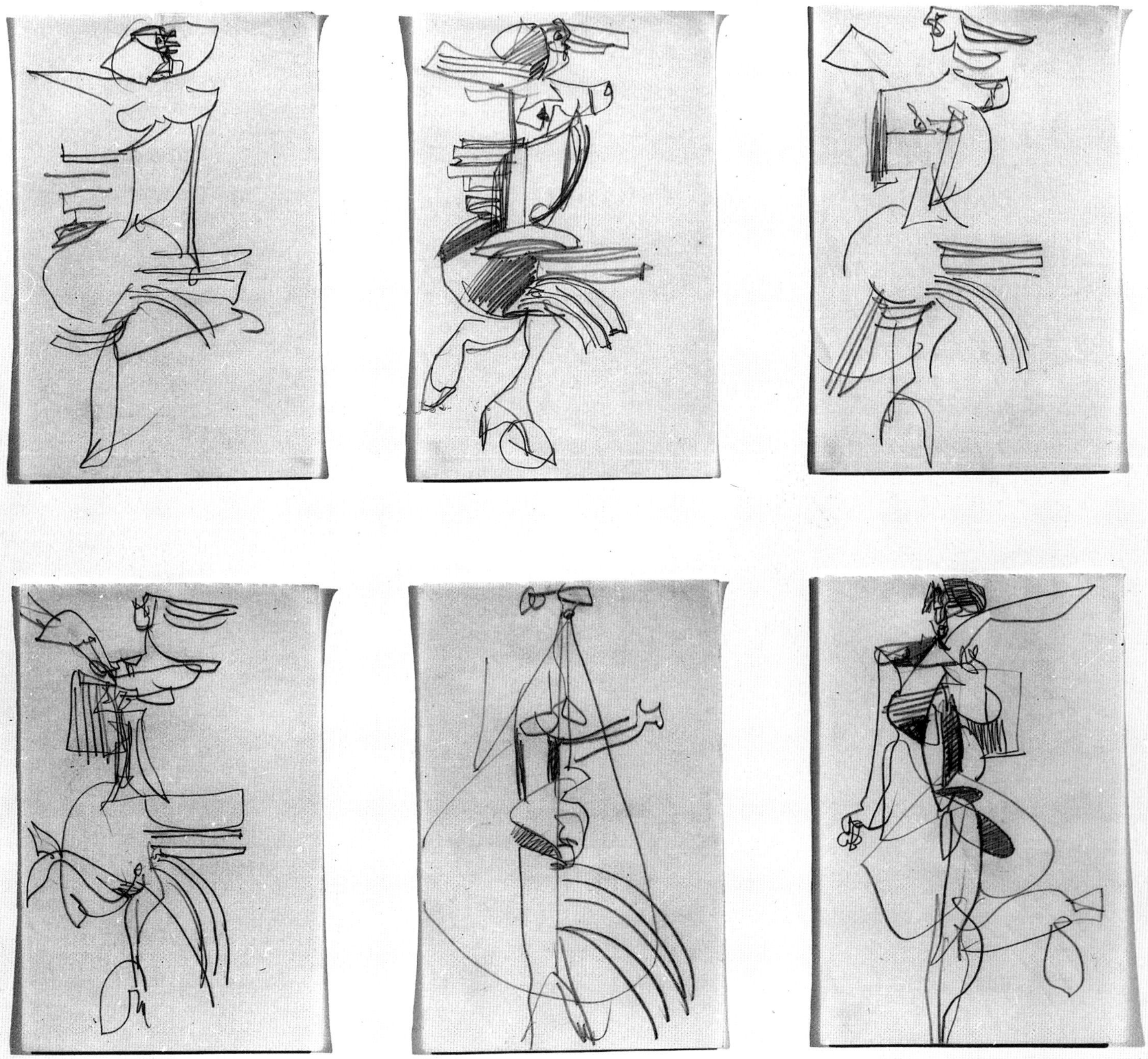

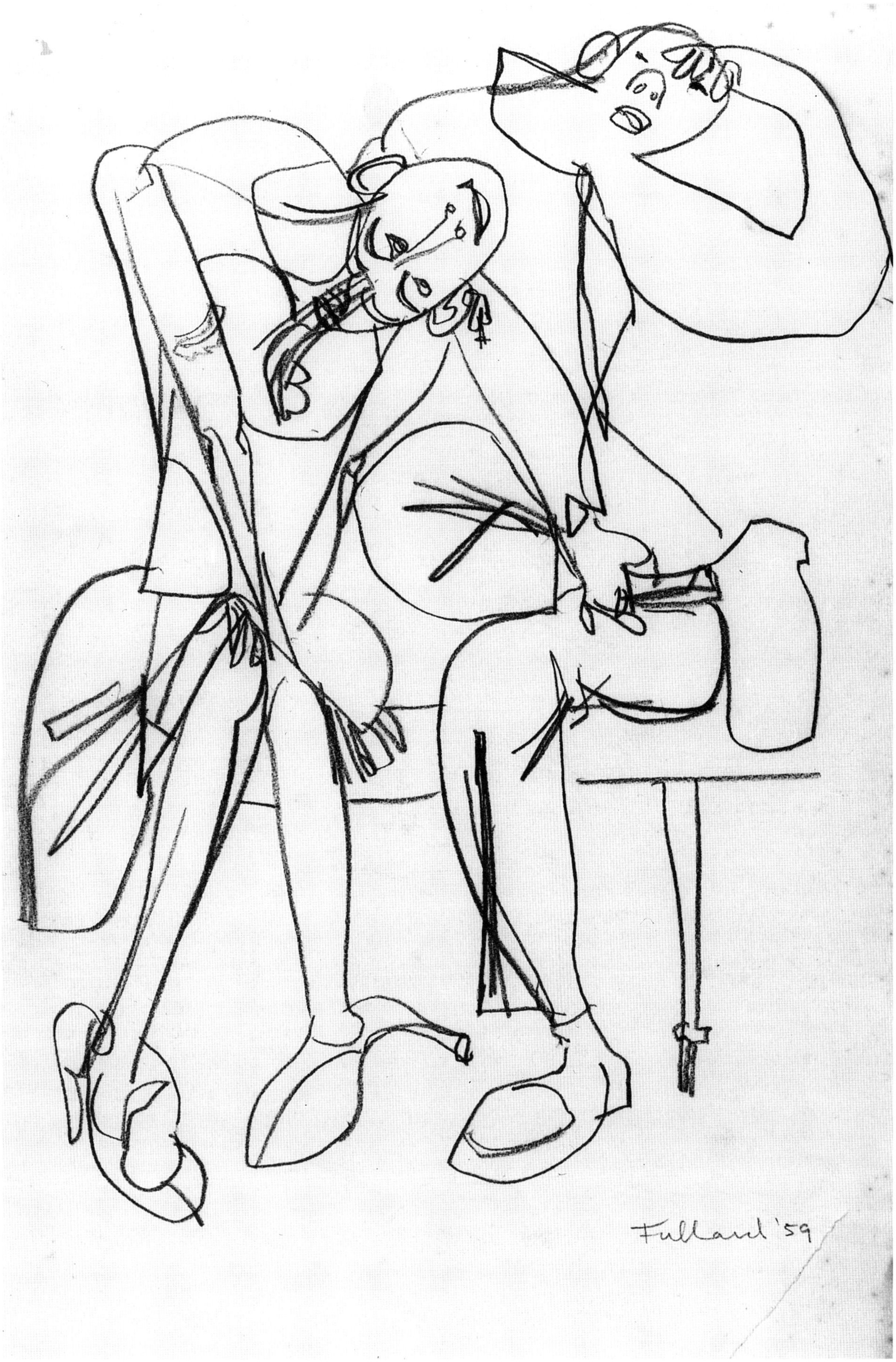
Fullard '59

figures and infant-cum-war-machines of the 1960s, maintained a strong linear quality. Among the hundreds of drawings which remain, very few have any tonal values and only a small number include any colour. The pressure of the pencil, pen and ink or charcoal is used to convey not only colour and tone but also fluently and sensually describes movement and repose. The linear quality of his own work was an aspect which Fullard identified as part of an essentially early English tradition in art. He believed that the Renaissance had disrupted the tradition of 'linear' expression and introduced notions of 'form' into art. He equated his own linear tendencies with that 'lost' tradition.[3]

Sculptors often spend a lot of time experimenting with ideas for three-dimensional works by sketching different possibilities. For contemporary sculptor Grenville Davey, drawing is a way of 'making and catching decisions for sculptures'.[4] However, Fullard rarely used drawing in this way. Once an assemblage had been completed, he would often draw for days without a break – occasionally it provided space and time to resolve a sculptural impasse. But more importantly for him, it was a vital art – 'a constant activity – like breathing'.[5] It was an activity which was separate and independent from his sculpture. Only a handful of drawings relate directly to his sculpture: two large sheets of sketches for his assemblage *War game* 1962 show that Fullard was considering a range of options, including more specific references to Monte Cassino. One of these sketches shows that, on the front of this piece, he had considered having an image of a child's torso, arms reaching out, in place of the dustbin-lid he finally used. There are other isolated examples of sketches for sculptural work but the vast majority of Fullard's drawings were not done with any further project in mind. Where drawings do have affinities with particular works of sculpture, it is likely that Fullard drew the actual sculpture after he had made it as this was a frequent practice of his – a kind of confirmation of his own work.

The drawings of the 1960s have fluidity, directness and confidence. They reflect his considerable interest in the work of Picasso but have their own distinctive character. As with his sculpture so with his drawing, Fullard's preoccupations were recurring and persistent. The human figure was an early interest which was explored in his drawings at Sheffield and the Royal College of Art. The human body continued to fascinate him and was an endless source of inspiration. Women standing, walking, dancing, sitting, nursing babies and children playing were his constant subjects. 'Falling women' feature in his sculpture and flights of steps often appear in his drawings, recalling the images of staircases left standing in bombed houses in wartime. The series of faces and heads rarely portray any particular individuals. As with his sculpture, any resemblance was coincidental and certainly not intentional. Fullard hardly ever used models, preferring to work from memory and imagination.

Drawings from the 1960s reflect Fullard's continual obsession with the idea of war. The drawings of children playing with makeshift weapons in the streets echo other artworks. A motif of a boy with arms raised in surrender brings to mind Picasso's *Massacre in Korea* of 1951 or the iconic images in Goya's paintings of rebels being shot in the Madrid rising of 1808. Fullard's drawings were done from memory, recalling earlier scenes of boyhood in Sheffield,

Plate 110
Two heads 1959
Conté crayon on paper
Private collection

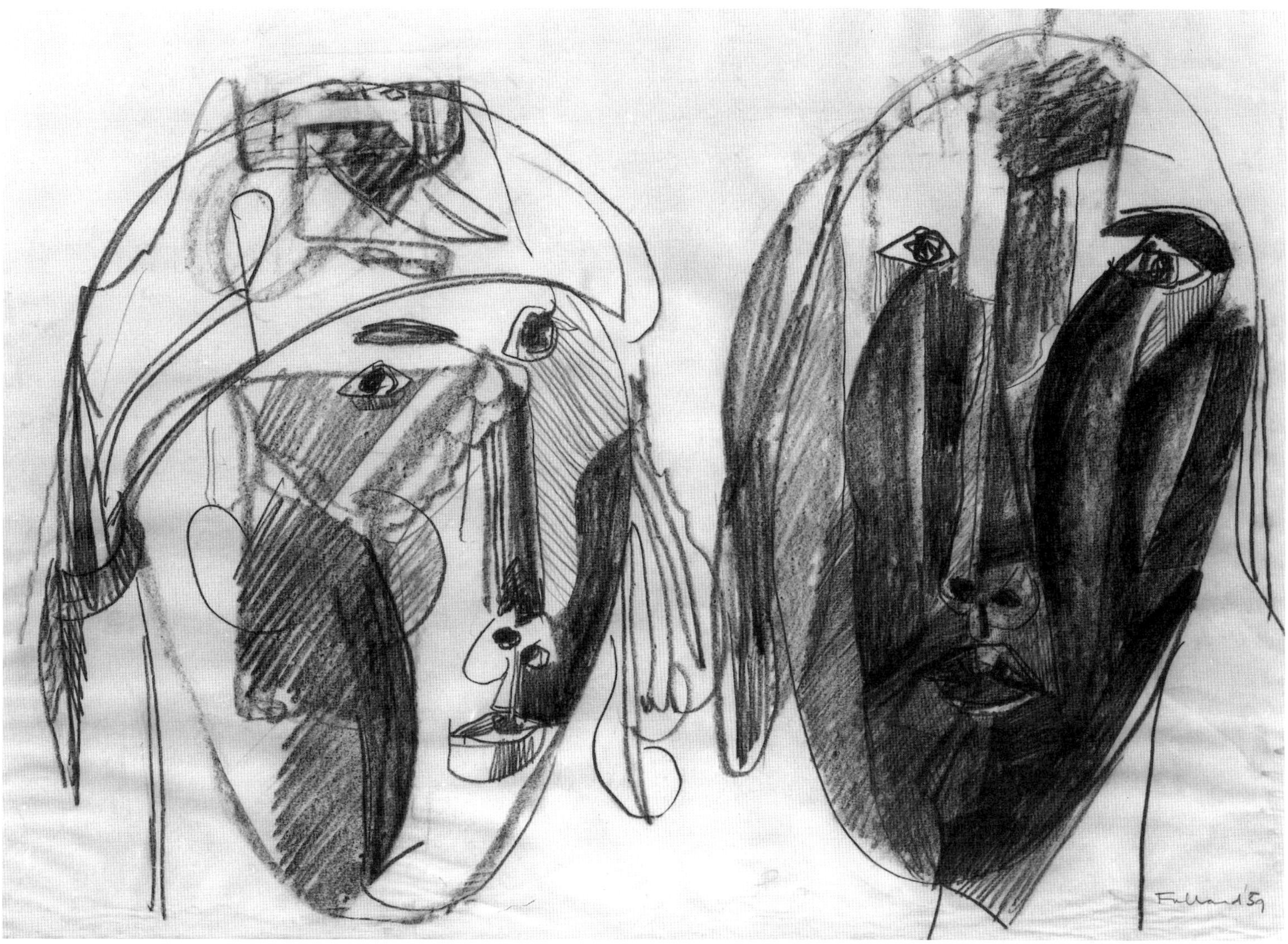

though they could equally have been inspired by children playing around the streets of Chelsea.

Although drawing was an independent activity for Fullard, undoubtedly his sculpture fed into his drawing and many drawings reflect his sculpture. Fullard's preoccupation with war and the state of infancy merge in a number of drawings of 'war-machines' of the 1960s. In the fashion of cartoons, these infant warriors mutating into war robots often have three-fingered hands as a marked characteristic. A number of drawings reveal the female body as skeletal but the bony framework is made up of what could be pieces from his earliest wooden assemblages. Equally, many of his sculptures have a strong linear and flat-frontal emphasis. This can be seen particularly in *Woman with flowers* 1959-60, *Woman* 1959 and *Mother and child* 1959. These assemblages, made up of a series of planes, invite our eyes to follow the lines of the shapes rather than be aware of the bulk or volume of the wood. Fullard's late 'sea' series of sculptures, many of which are reliefs rather than sculpture 'in the round', are even closer to the idea of drawing.

Fullard's drawing and sculpture were integrally related and yet they retain an individual coherence. But, for him, the activity of drawing in particular was always vital, never marginal.

NOTES

1. J. Berger, 'Drawing' (first published 1960) in *Selected Essays and Articles – The Look of Things*, Harmondsworth 1972, pp.165-6.

2. Notes by Fullard, private collection.

3. Ibid.

4. Grenville Davey's description as reported by P. Curtis in 'Drawing Withdrawing: The Sculptor and the Drawing', *Breaking the Mould – British Art of the 1980s and 1990s*, London 1997, p.30.

5. Notes by Fullard, private collection.

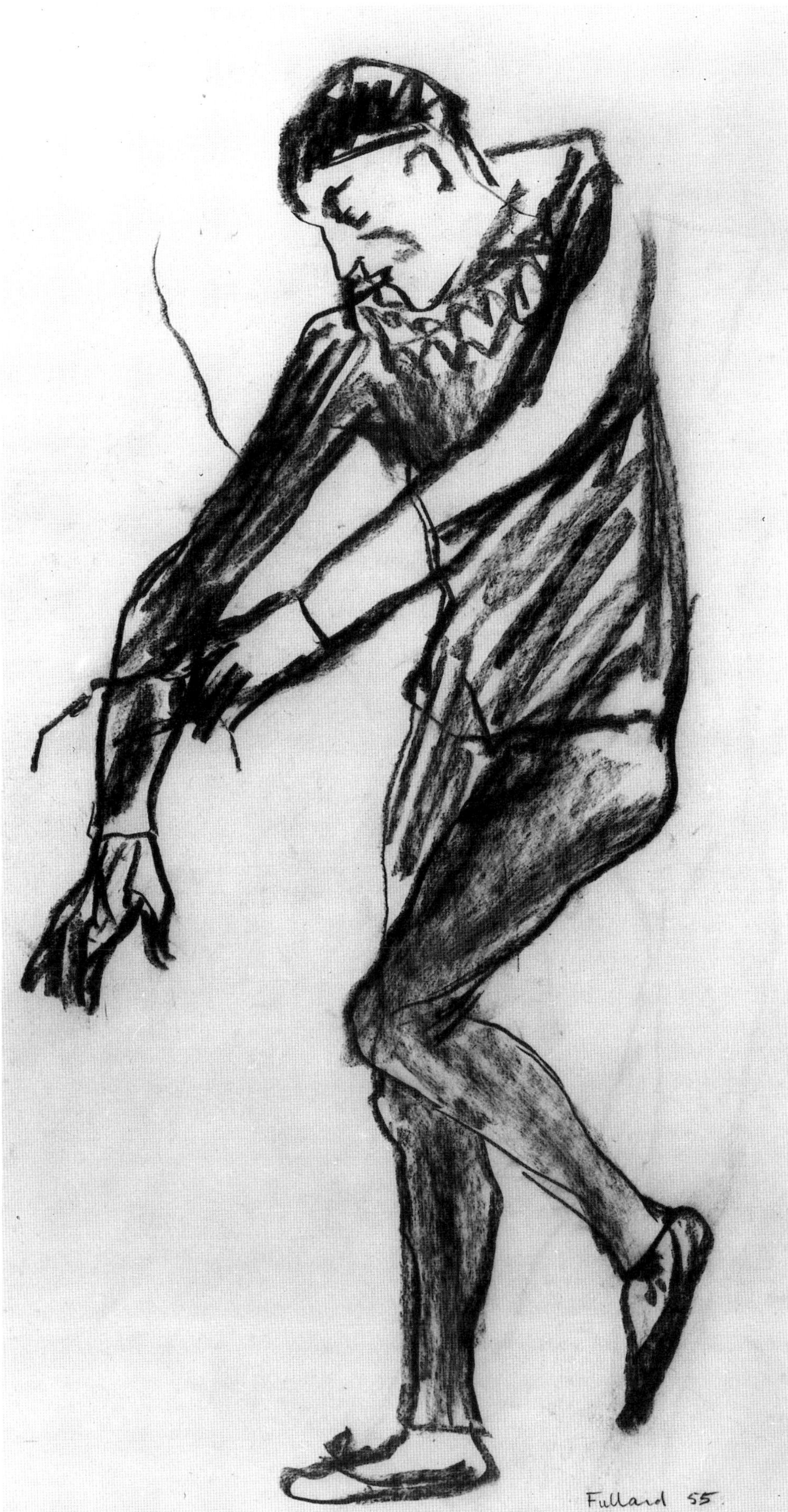

Plate 111
Clown 1955
Charcoal on paper

a face.

All too often an objective drawing made by a student is conditioned by the learned name of the object — would be more realistic to write out the word TABLE for table

The innocence of first perception that we had as children does not lie buried deep beneath acquired labels and adult responses — ~~does not require some profound~~ Does not require some profound psychoanalysis probe amused

Because → It exists in silent duality alongside acquired conventions

8

Transcripts of writings by George Fullard

1 The 'serious' artist

Plate 112
Extract from notes by Fullard, undated
Private collection

The question as to whether an artist is serious is irrelevant. The question is basically stupid – it is like asking a bird if it is serious in its singing or whether a tree is serious in its growing. It is a question that cannot be answered except by the would-be artist. (The artist never aspires – he is.)

It is the aspirant (often mistaken for the genuine artist) who regards art as evidence of his own seriousness – makes a display of sincerity and whose work publicly proclaims his private agony.

The extent to which the artist, in his work, transcends private agony and 'sings' is the measure of his success as an artist *eg* Van Gogh.

Like the bird the artist does not require an audience to provoke his singing. The bird sings whether he is heard or not and applause will in fact startle him away to another part of the forest.

(Pencil notes on paper towel, undated)

2 Space and 'military logistics'

The impossible use of space has to be made a possibility by timing. As in military logistics – the right materials in the right place at the right time. From then on the process is opposite to military operations. Instead of the material feeding a destructive quality they are directed into a constructive quality ending in a new existence, the reverse of death.

(Pencil notes on paper towel, undated)

3 Integrity

Above all the artist must have integrity in his work.

(Pencil note on back of sketch of a head, undated)

4 Sculpture as 'private poetry'

Division in sculpture – a dilemma – on one hand the attempt to make a public form (or image) and on the other, the making of a private poetry.

The two are incompatible. The attempt to make a public image which also has the aesthetic power of private poetry leads to inevitable failure by producing forms which compete with contemporary architectural context by using the same shapes. The architecture wins by sheer quantitive power and the fact that its shapes are 'true' in the sense of being dictated by function and technology. The functional sculpture is contrived.

The 'personal' element evolved in the nineteenth century disappears from this extrovert function and is replaced by a chosen style – chosen by the artist out of the many modern manners already made available.

The personal poetry approach to sculpture, on the other hand, will exist regardless of setting – wherever it happens to be. Like poetry, it exists for those who can read it.

Michelangelo's private poetry brought the sculpture off the walls. Any attempt to consciously unite the private poetic image with architecture is merely an attempt, one way or another, to stick it back on the wall again.

The individual or personal work of art serves the need of the personal and private view as now required more than ever against the all-enveloping public form – it is the psychological need for individual identity inside a fully organised society.

(Biro notes in small note-pad, undated)

NOTE: All the above are taken from material in the Tate Gallery Archive, London Ref.TGA 752. The catalogue for the Serpentine Gallery memorial exhibition held in 1974 included part of the last extract; other items previously unpublished.

5 Working with clay

Franz Kafka observed 'the beginning of every story is ridiculous at first. There seems no hope that this newborn thing, still incomplete and tender in every joint, will be able to keep alive in the completed organisation of the world, which, like every completed organisation, strives to close itself off. However, one should not forget that the story, if it has any justification to exist bears its complete organisation within itself even before it has been fully formed. It is for this reason despair over the beginning of a story is unwarranted, in a like case parents should have despair for their sucking infant for they had no intention of bringing this pathetic and ridiculous being into the world.'

Kafka's observations on the genius of a story could equally apply to any artist beginning a work in any medium and they are particularly apposite to the beginning of a work in clay. The very helplessness and fragility of clay has caused its misuse and abuse on such a scale that we are inclined to despise it and leave it alone.... And yet, whatever 'new' materials one may find or turn to in the quest to give present tempo to the work, it is the apparent worthlessness of clay which now, at this time, recurringly compels my interest.

It is as though history has worked in reverse. It is in this very worthlessness of the value of clay that the abuse and misuse of clay constitutes a process of history in reverse – subtracting from not adding to – so that clay in its worthless sense comes to us now as a medium unadorned by the trappings of tradition, therefore new in fact and containing an infinity of possibilities. To work in clay is to realise the difficulties of freedom. Everything and anything is possible – there are apparently no limitations.

A work in clay can be changed and altered in a moment – can linger temptingly in the magnificence of probabilities of ruin – before suddenly disappearing for ever in a tortuous mist of tentativeness. And in a work completed there is no finality – it can appear so untrue – the certainty of its completeness invites destruction ... and the death sentence can be carried out with one blow of the fist. Failure hovers constantly.

Freedom does not allow the half-truth of preconception – it demands the highest point of realisation. So it is with clay. Formless, shapeless without natural tension, clay does not permit substitution and it offers no refuge of established technique. The freedom of clay is in fact the freedom to realise and manifest the quality of here and now – the truth of that event is made not from a conglomeration of accidents but through the complexities of inevitability.

(*Pencil notes on folded drawing paper, undated*)

NOTE: Previously unpublished, private collection.

6 About 'being' a sculptor

As an artist I am known as a sculptor but I do not intend to talk about sculpture – for three reasons.

Firstly, I don't know what it is. Each time I come to work on an idea it is that sense of newness, of not knowing how to do it – that sense of being always the first time which provides the impulse and the desire.

Secondly, sculpture is not for me a point of commencement but the central point of conclusion – it is what one ends with – what emerges as an inevitable survivor from a relentless process of realisation, recognition and even desperation – I have often said that of work as a last desperate resort – fortunately one grows more desperate each time.

Thirdly, I believe that art is not worth talking about – though it might be worth doing – by the right person.

What I can talk about are some of the elements of being a sculptor that make sculpture my own personal process – that feeds the restlessness and discontent – not personal discontent but an organic discontent and leads me to that need to tell – the impulse of the artist to tell about that for which there are no words....

... At the same time, because I believe truth to be found where one might least expect it, I disassociate truth from that form of pretentious intellectualism which the word 'culture' connotates. I do not believe that art now should require of the spectator a specially conditioned mind, that self-conscious high-mindedness which is determined to understand art and find it interesting – Art isn't interesting – it *is*.

Such minds are only formed by retrospective thinking – of looking at art as it was – something that has been – when they look at something new they look for things that will remind them of art and of what they know – a form of self-flattery....

... This attitude of course contains some risk. People educated to the idea of art as a means of making them feel high-minded – and that includes most critics – feel bereft with any art form which overtly refers to primary recognition and doesn't require their educated minds to give it credence – minds that are limited to word labels. Since the work doesn't require their seriousness they will automatically believe the artist is not serious, his work will be regarded as whimsey, of joke-making. Fortunately, as we say – time will tell – it does in art and that which is good survives its critics....

... The making process in art is important only as a paradox – it is necessary in order to bring about that fleeting essence. For that reason the actual making process is again paradoxically all the more complex. And making not just in the physical sense but in all the moods, visual and intellectual recognitions and contradictory energies that contribute too.

Perhaps the eventual inevitability that emerges from all the realities of making, should have the power of the phantom. Phantoms – more powerful in their evocation than the reality....

... Innocence. Seeing things before we knew their names – reappraisal of the familiar ... All too often an objective drawing made by a student is conditioned by the learned name of the object – would be more realistic to write out the word TABLE for table.

The innocence of first perception that we had as children does not lie buried deep beneath acquired labels and adult responses – does not require some profound psychological probe because it exists in silent amused duality alongside acquired conventions of seeing and living. It is not required in the practicalities of living. Indeed it would be positively dangerous in the area of normality, for example on the street or buses.... But the awareness of the artist is in being not living. Indeed the operative process, the real sphere of aesthetic action is not so much in making art but in being an artist. It is in the sphere of being that our innocent perception is released from its dormant duality.

Its seriousness is the seriousness only to be found in playing – in the game – that for me is true seriousness – that calls forth great concentration until one is lost to reality *eg* children playing etc....

... Art school – academic – classical – mediterranean – incongruity even incompatibility with my own personal background. But again paradoxical – perhaps I need the values of classic art to reveal its opposite.

(*Extracts from biro notes, probably for a visiting lecture, undated*)

NOTE: Previously unpublished, private collection.

Plate 113
Fullard with his wife Irena in 1962.

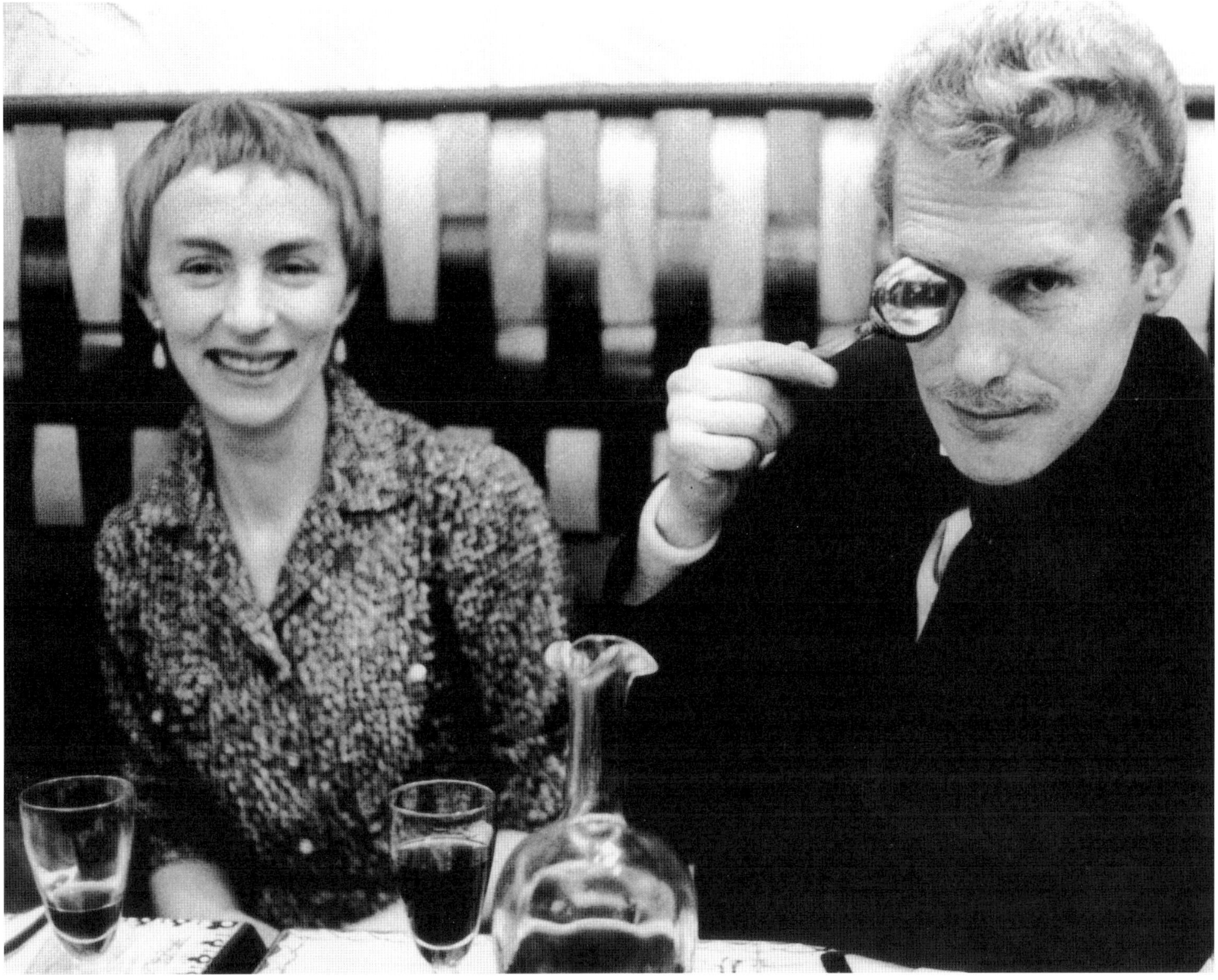

7 'Copie-bok'

This large old Swedish accounts book was given to Fullard by Ernest Adsetts in the 1950s. In the 'Copie-bok', he intermittently jotted down ideas, made notes about books and films and pasted newspaper cuttings. Interleaved between the notes, are a few line drawings in pencil which look like the working through of ideas for war assemblages.

19 June 1966

This is the basis of work – to plan, and produce around a conscious 'idea' (or subject) really in order to permit the entry of the unexpected for me. This also has to do with the significance of 'follow-through' – As in sport, so in art, the ultimate fragment of 'follow-through' – which has no purpose, but without which the action is merely action and not art, and is therefore without 'style' – is everything.

Follow-through concludes the action not by a chronological process but by using qualitatively all that has preceded – by moving the meaning, at a tangent, to a different level or dimension.

3 July 1966

'Sculpture' has become an accepted form – a convention, in a general context of art appreciation – (a belated appreciation) in England. The causes of this belated appreciation stem from several historical and sociological sources. Historically, the deprived middle class are forced into an acquisition of 'Art' as a means of reassurance and consolation. 'Art' provides a role as directors, hopeful 'impresarios' and critics who otherwise have no social or historical function since Britain can no longer place them in the administrative and military service of an Empire.

Art also provides the illusion that Britain is still great – that this greatness has now a cultural form ('another great renaissance'). The fallacy of this hopeful illusion is in the fact that it is based on art appreciation – not art and that the idea of Britain is synonymous with bourgeois.

Aesthetically, the result is puerile – British contemporary art is largely geared to a kind of art-school art – a skilful facsimile or counterfeit quality – not made from real sources and not from where the artist stands in actuality, but from his relationship to art as an accepted convention.

The unquestioning acceptance of 'Sculpture' is really the undemanding acceptance of a social convention. Hence, an obsession with 'sculpture' and the making of it, far from producing or deepening the awareness becomes a blindfold, a restrictive process closing off the receptive instincts.

The production of a piece of 'sculpture' is no longer conclusive evidence that the producer is an artist – the convention is available to all – and sociologically producing art is a therapy in an increasingly neurotic social context.

The operative process – the real sphere of aesthetic action is in being a sculptor rather than in making sculpture. Thus one's identity to everything is through this process of being – being a sculptor. All that comes into one's orbit is realised and transformed by one being a sculptor. I, consequently, do not operate through a pre-determined set of technical, material or aesthetic requirements, but I make from what there is.

Undated entry

History

Art is the means of discovering it – of posing the question, what is history? What do we mean by history? A re-examination of our concept of it, leading to a re-examination of our concept of the artist. History in the conventional sense is merely tangible evidence. Tangible evidence is the means by which all can be proved guilty – not just the murderer. 'If the truth were told' as the saying goes, the real truth cannot be formed into rational evidence – it is the lost facts of life outside that which could be recorded as history – History, the known evidence then, is hardly of interest in itself, but only to the extent to which it gives clues to the truth outside the evidence.

The truth behind history is not 'known' it cannot be 'told', but it can be realised and the realisation can be manifest. This is not 'evidence' – in the sense of history – but it is a kind of testimony – therefore 'the secret history of our times' is what the artist is manifesting and concerned with. This is true of all 'artists' in all ages – is evident in the work for all to see.

'The secret history of our times' is the means by which innocence (as opposed to guilt) is revealed.

December 1966

'Culture' versus the artist.

'I am not a cultured man; I am a fastidious primitive.'

April 67

Again, as last year in interviewing candidates for studentships, one is struck by the fact that from the evidence of their work we are confronted by a race of young people who have been born, bred and permanently confined to an art gallery. No evidence of personal being and their own physical existence on this planet.

NOTE: Previously unpublished; the 'Copie-bok' is in a private collection.

'Sculpture and Survival'

by George Fullard

Sculpture is not made from the respectful processing of dead materials – fragments of fractured mountain, felled tree or exhumed clay– but from the making of a new high-speed history for these materials, a context of action in which they undergo a vitally compressed experience. I believe it is the attempt at what is apparently impossible which produces the circumstances of this experience. That is, to find the sound of silence, to physically manifest the intangible and incalculable; to reveal through a sense of moments not consecutive but simultaneous and integrated into a single totality of the instant.

There is no method and no intention to speak of; there is only imagination and the facts learned so far from working. A completed work is not made, it emerges as a survivor out of a phase of action, struggling through the infinity of possibilities to reach the challenge of impossibility. This means a progress of failure in which the quality of the survivior is ultimately dependent on the speed and vitality of the phantoms which precede it – that succession of manifestations which appear and disappear in their own tempo and direction; an exorcising of certainties until nothing remains but the uncertainty of beginning – the initiation of a process of self-subjection to realisation on all dimensions; a freedom of availability which will not permit the half-truths of pre-conception.

As in life, the survivor lands, without luggage. For the impact of the survivor's appearance is not in the quantity of his own possessions, but in the quality of vanished experience that projected him. The power of the survivor is the power of presence in contradiction of what was possible.

In practice, the sculptor is required to couple his state of being with physical decision. For the sculptor's space is the vastness that exists between poetic realisation and action. Despite, indeed, because of all aesthetic reasoning to the contrary, the quality of this vastness makes the idea of the 'insignificant' human figure in sculpture an inescapable challenge. The challenge lies in the complexity and contradiction inherent in the idea of the human figure as a presence for the particular realities that occupy art – those realities produced by life but immeasurable and unidentified in living, and denied existence by organised society.

Figurative work in this sense recognises the fact of art and life as parallel but separate realities and the requirement is not for intentional resemblance to life, but for the phenomenon of coincidental significance. This is a requirement quite disconnected from that appalling appeal to public sentiment which so often disguises itself as figurative art. It is disconnected also from that work which so pointedly proclaims the artist's identity with life. Such a proclamation at this time, carries with it the implication that life is in some way better than art; the complete irrelevance of the comparison only reveals the originator's basic lack of conviction in what he is doing – such a person has no place in art.

The need of art is that the artist attains absolute conviction of the inevitable occurrence of miracles through the power of instinct and imagination. Just as the child, without effort, slips out of life to make a man of a pepper-pot, or the heaving deck of a ship-wreck of a placid pavement, so the artist works towards the miracle of making visible that which apparently could not exist. And it is precisely the depth of conviction with which the creator enters the imagined reality – not its outward shape or appearance – which in the end communicates truth.

But the easy magic of the child is an element of life. To find the parallel in art demands the total attendance of consciousness. And at the heart of the innocent, new infancy for which the artist works, lies the core of humility – humility not as a profound secret. The discovery of this secret is not the privilege of the amateur or the professional; it is the responsibility of the possessed – in art. Not for love or loot, but for Life.

NOTE: This article was first published in *The Painter and Sculptor*, summer 1959, Vol.2, No.2 pp.9-12.

Catalogue of Sculpture

1 **Female head 1947** (Plate 7)

Clay
Height 34.3 cm (13½ in)
Destroyed

2 **Young bather 1947** (Plate 8)

Clay
Dimensions unknown: approx. life-size
Destroyed

NOTES: Diploma piece made at the Royal College of Art.

3 **Male torso 1946-7**

Plaster
Dimensions unknown: approx. life-size
Destroyed

NOTES: This life study was made at the Royal College of Art where Fullard cast it.

4 **Reclining nude 1947** (Plate 12)

Plaster
Dimensions unknown
Destroyed

5 **Portrait of Andy Tittensor 1948** (Plate 22)

Bronze (edition of two)
35.6 x 22.9 x 25.7 cm (14 x 9 x 10 in)
Ownership: Private collections

Exhibitions: *The Forgotten Fifties*, Graves Art Gallery, Sheffield 1984

NOTES: This head of sculptor and friend, Annesley Tittensor, is the only known extant portrait made by Fullard. Plaster extant.

6 **Mother and child 1949** (Plate 20)

Clay
Height 175.3 cm (69 in)
Destroyed

7 **Politicians early 1950s** (Plate 30)

Clay
Dimensions unknown
Destroyed

8 **May Queen early 1950s**

Concrete and metal
Dimensions unknown: approx. life-size
Destroyed

Exhibitions: *Looking at People*, South London Gallery and Moscow 1957

9 **Dead Christ 1951** (Plate 72)

Mixture of cement and metal powder
Height 208.3 cm (82 in)
Destroyed

NOTES: Fullard was not pleased with the finish of this cast as the metal content showed up in streaky patches and marred the form.

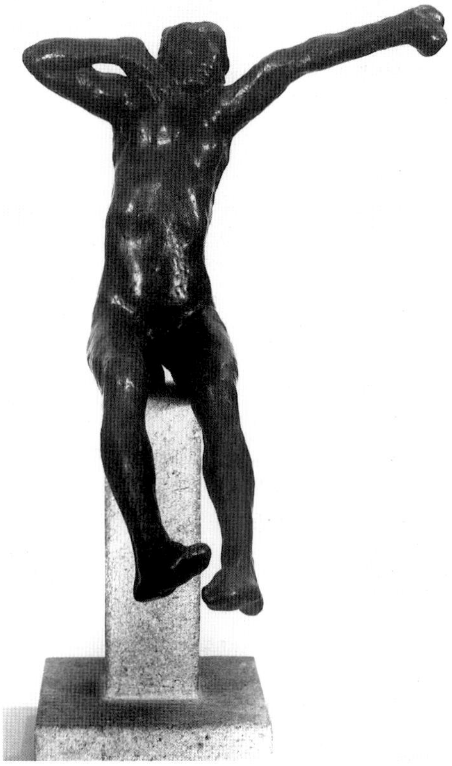

Plate 114 (Cat.10) **Girl stretching** 1952

10 **Girl stretching 1952** (Plate 114)

Bronze (edition of four)
25.5 x 19 x 23 cm (10 x 7½ x 9 in)
Ownership: Sheffield Galleries and Museums Collections; private collections

Exhibitions: Serpentine Gallery, London 1974; *The Forgotten Fifties*, Graves Art Gallery, Sheffield 1984; Hatton Gallery, University of Newcastle 1984; New Art Centre, London 1986; *The Age of Bronze*, Mappin Art Gallery, Sheffield 1995; *Playing with Paradox*, Mappin Art Gallery, Sheffield and Kettle's Yard, Cambridge 1998

NOTES: Originally cast by John Galizia & Son Ltd; purchased by Sheffield City Art Galleries in 1974.

11 **Goalkeeper 1953** (Plate 39)

Plaster
Dimensions unknown
Destroyed

Exhibitions: *Football and the Fine Arts*, Park Lane House, London 1953

12 **Goalmouth 1953** (Plate 38)

Plaster
Dimensions unknown
Destroyed

Exhibitions: *Football and the Fine Arts*, Park Lane House, London 1953

13 **Dwarf clown 1953** (Plate 103)

Painted plaster
117 x 53.5 x 50 cm (46 x 21 x 19¾ in)
Ownership: On loan to Sheffield Galleries and Museums Collections from private collection

Exhibitions: Serpentine Gallery, London 1974

14 **Young girl 1954-5** (Plate 11)

Plaster
Height 165 cm (66 in)
Destroyed

15 **Skipping girl 1955** (Plate 3)

Bronze (edition of three)
33.7 x 15.5 x 15 cm ($13^{1/4}$ x 6 x $5^{1/2}$ in)
Ownership: Art Gallery of South Australia, Adelaide; private collections

Exhibitions: *Looking at People*, South London Gallery and Moscow 1957; Serpentine Gallery, London 1974; *George Fullard – A Fastidious Primitive*, Yorkshire Sculpture Park 1997; *Playing with Paradox*, Mappin Art Gallery, Sheffield and Kettle's Yard, Cambridge 1998

NOTES: Frank Monaco, photographer friend of Fullard's, took this piece to be cast in a foundry in Rome in the mid-1950s. On a buying trip to England in 1956, the Director of the National Gallery of South Australia purchased a cast from the artist. It was featured in the *Bulletin of the National Gallery of South Australia* in October 1956, in which Fullard was described as 'a young British sculptor associated with the neo-realist painters Jack Smith and Edward Middleditch'.

16 **Dancing girl 1955-6** (Plate 115)

Plaster
Dimensions unknown: approx. life-size
Destroyed

NOTES: Mary Farnell photographed this and other work in progress at Fullard's Fawcett Yard studio in the mid-1950s.

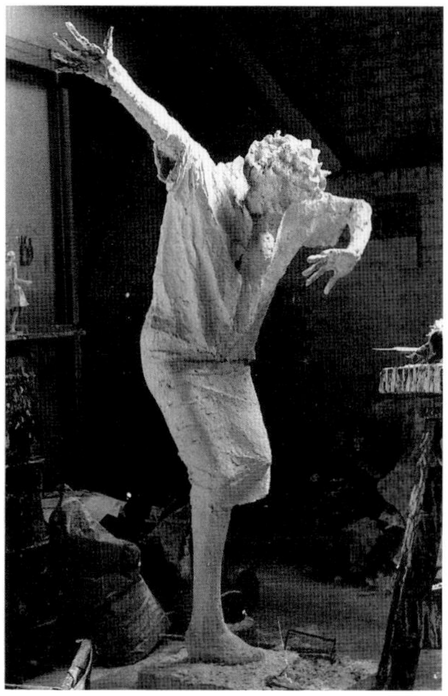

Plate 115 (Cat.16) **Dancing girl** 1955-6

17 **Torso 1956** (Plate 37)

Plaster for bronze
116 x 36 x 30 cm ($45^{3/4}$ x 14 x $11^{3/4}$ in)
Ownership: Private collection

18 **Head 1956** (Plate 35)

Plaster
Height 45.7 cm (18 in)
Destroyed

NOTES: The artist made this and another female head immediately after being confined to bed through illness in 1956. Both were made in clay and cast in plaster, since destroyed.

19 **Mother and child 1956** (Plates 14 and 21)

Concrete
142 x 59 x 37 cm (66 x 23 x $140^{1/2}$ in)
Ownership: Private collection

Exhibitions: *Contemporary British Sculpture*, Arts Council of Great Britain tour 1958

20 **Mother and child 1956** (Plate 33)

Bronze
67.3 x 37 x 28 cm ($26^{1/2}$ x $14^{1/2}$ x 11 in)
Ownership: Private collection

Exhibitions: *Looking at People*, South London Gallery and Moscow 1957; *Contemporary British Sculpture*, Arts Council tour 1960; Serpentine Gallery, London 1974; *Playing with Paradox*, Mappin Art Gallery, Sheffield and Kettle's Yard, Cambridge 1998

NOTES: Concrete version shown in 1957; Fullard obtained an Arts Council grant to fund the cast of a bronze, at John Galizia & Son Ltd, which was shown in 1960.

21 **Mother and child 1956** (Plate 23)

Bronze
163 x 66 x 66 cm (64 x 26 x 26 in)
Ownership: Sheffield Galleries and Museums Collections

Exhibitions: *Looking at People*, South London Gallery and Moscow 1957; *Contemporary British Sculpture*, Arts Council tour 1958; Hatton Gallery, University of Newcastle 1984

NOTES: Donated to Sheffield by Irena Fullard, cast 1985 at Morris Singer Foundry Ltd, sited in the grounds of Upper Chapel, Norfolk Street, Sheffield.

22 **Glancing woman 1956** (Plate 50)

Bronze
33 x 25.5 x 12.7 cm (13 x 10 x 5 in)
Ownership: Private collection

Exhibitions: *Looking at People*, South London Gallery and Moscow 1957; Woodstock Gallery, London 1958; Serpentine Gallery, London 1974

23 **Head of a worker 1957** (Plate 34)

Ciment fondu
33.2 x 22.2 x 23 cm (13 x $8^{3/4}$ x 9 in)
Ownership: Private collection

Exhibitions: *Looking at People*, South London Gallery and Moscow 1957; *Playing with Paradox*, Mappin Art Gallery, Sheffield and Kettle's Yard, Cambridge 1998

24 **Head 1957** (Plate 116)

Concrete
99 x 52 x 40.7 cm (39 x $20^{1/2}$ x 16 in)
Ownership: Private collection

Exhibitions: Woodstock Gallery, London 1958; Serpentine Gallery, London 1974

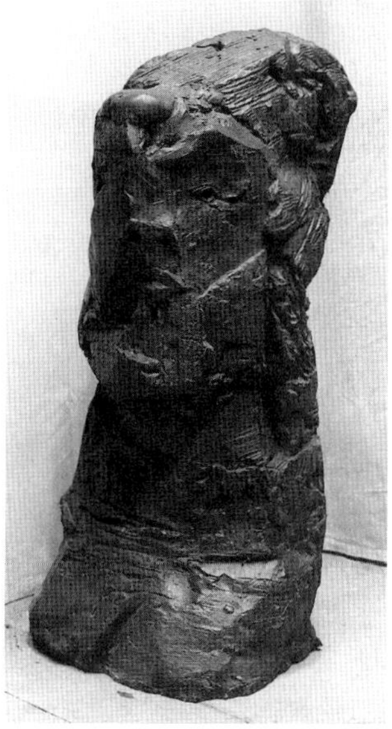

Plate 116 (Cat.24) **Head** 1957

25 Old woman 1957 (Plates 48 and 49)

Ciment fondu
108.5 x 38.5 x 8.5 cm ($42\frac{3}{4}$ x $15\frac{1}{4}$ x $3\frac{1}{4}$ in)
Ownership: Stoke-on-Trent City Museum and Art Gallery

Exhibitions: *Looking at People*, South London Gallery and Moscow 1957; Woodstock Gallery, London 1958; *George Fullard's Old Woman*, Stoke-on-Trent City Art Gallery and Museum 1986-7

NOTES: Purchased by the Contemporary Art Society and presented to Stoke in 1961.

26 Walking man 1957 (Plates 1 and 117)

Bronze
183 x 24 x 48.3 cm (72 x $9\frac{1}{2}$ x 19 in)
Ownership: Sheffield Galleries and Museums Collections (bronze and ciment original on loan from private collection)

Exhibitions: *Looking at People*, South London Gallery and Moscow 1957; Royal College of Art exhibition in gardens of Natural History Museum, London 1958; Serpentine Gallery, London 1974; Yorkshire Sculpture Park 1977; *The Forgotten Fifties*, Graves Art Gallery, Sheffield 1984; *Playing with Paradox*, Mappin Art Gallery, Sheffield and Kettle's Yard, Cambridge 1998

NOTES: First cast by Ray Arnatt in 1974; purchased 1983 and publicly sited in Sheffield City Centre.

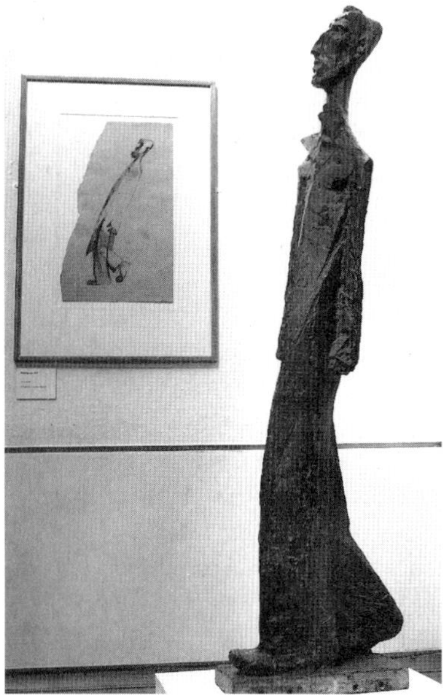

Plate 117 (Cat.26) **Walking man** 1957

27 Storm 1957 (Plate 26)

Bronze (edition of three)
49.5 x 22.3 x 12.7 cm ($19\frac{1}{2}$ x $8\frac{3}{4}$ x 5 in)
Ownership: Private collections

Exhibitions: Woodstock Gallery, London 1958; Serpentine Gallery, London 1974; *The Forgotten Fifties*, Graves Art Gallery, Sheffield 1984; Hatton Gallery, University of Newcastle 1984; *George Fullard – A Fastidious Primitive*, Yorkshire Sculpture Park 1997

NOTES: Cast by Steve Hurst.

28 Running woman 1957 (Plate 25)

Bronze
213.5 x 122 x 85 cm (84 x 48 x $33\frac{1}{2}$ in)
Ownership: Sheffield Galleries and Museums Collections

Exhibitions: *1st John Moores Liverpool Exhibition*, Liverpool 1957-8 (Junior Prizewinner); Hatton Gallery, University of Newcastle 1984

NOTES: Donated by Irena Fullard, cast 1985 at Morris Singer Foundry Ltd, sited in the grounds of Upper Chapel, Norfolk Street, Sheffield.

29 Infant with flower 1958 (Plate 32)

Bronze
76.2 x 42 x 38 cm (30 x $16\frac{1}{2}$ x 15 in)
Ownership: Tate Gallery, London

Exhibitions: Woodstock Gallery, London 1958; *Four One*, South London Gallery 1960; *Northern Artists*, Arts Council tour 1960; *Contemporary British Sculpture*, Arts Council tour 1961; Gimpel Hanover Galerie, Zurich 1963; Royal Academy of Arts, London 1973; Serpentine Gallery 1974; *Playing with Paradox*, Mappin Art Gallery, Sheffield and Kettle's Yard, Cambridge 1998

NOTES: Unique cast by John Galizia & Son Ltd in 1960. Plaster extant. Purchased from the artist by the Trustees of the Chantrey Bequest 1973.

30 Angry woman 1958 (Plates 2, 27 and 55)

Bronze
213.5 x 122 x 85 cm (84 x 48 x $33\frac{1}{2}$ cm)
Ownership: Sheffield Galleries and Museums Collections

Exhibitions: Woodstock Gallery, London 1958; *Four One*, South London Gallery 1960; Serpentine Gallery 1974; *The Forgotten Fifties*, Graves Art Gallery, Sheffield 1984; Hatton Gallery, University of Newcastle 1984; *Recalling the Fifties – British Painting and Sculpture 1950-60*, Serpentine Gallery, London 1985

NOTES: Donated by Irena Fullard, cast 1985 at Morris Singer Foundry Ltd, sited in the grounds of Upper Chapel, Norfolk Street, Sheffield.

31 Mother and child 1958 (Plates 28 and 47)

Bronze
163 x 66 x 66 cm (64 x 26 x 26 in)
Ownership: Norfolk Museums Service (Norwich Castle Museum)

Exhibitions: Woodstock Gallery, London 1958; Serpentine Gallery, London 1974

NOTES: Donated by Irena Fullard to Norfolk Arts Society in 1974, cast at John Galizia & Son Ltd, publicly sited in 1974 in Cathedral Close, Norwich.

32 Mother and child 1958 (Plate 118)

Bronze (edition of two)
58.5 x 17.7 x 5 cm (23 x 7 x 2 in)

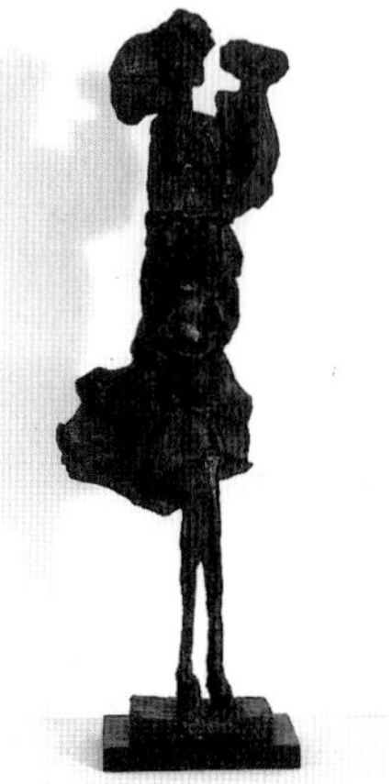

Plate 118 (Cat.32) **Mother and child** 1958

Ownership: Arts Council of Great Britain (lost/stolen); private collection

Exhibitions: Woodstock Gallery, London 1958; Serpentine Gallery, London 1974

33 Three women 1958 (Plate 29)

Bronze
55.7 x 55.7 x 33 cm (22 x 22 x 13 in)
Ownership: Private collection

Exhibitions: Woodstock Gallery, London 1958; Serpentine Gallery, London 1974; *British Sculpture in the Twentieth Century*, Whitechapel Art Gallery, London 1981; *The Forgotten Fifties*, Graves Art Gallery, Sheffield 1984; Hatton Gallery, University of Newcastle 1984; *George Fullard – A Fastidious Primitive*, Yorkshire Sculpture Park 1997; *Playing with Paradox*, Mappin Art Gallery, Sheffield and Kettle's Yard, Cambridge 1998

NOTES: Cast at John Galizia & Son Ltd; plaster extant.

34 Pregnant woman 1959 (Plate 45)

Bronze (edition of two plus original wooden assemblage)
61 x 27 x 13 cm (24 x 10½ x 5 in)
Ownership: Bronzes in private collections (one on loan to Hove Museum); original wooden assemblage in private collection

Exhibitions: *Four One*, South London Gallery 1960; Gallery One, London 1961; Gimpel Hanover Galerie, Zurich 1963; Serpentine Gallery, London 1974; Hatton Gallery, University of Newcastle 1984; *George Fullard – A Fastidious Primitive*, Yorkshire Sculpture Park 1998; *Playing with Paradox*, Mappin Art Gallery, Sheffield and Kettle's Yard, Cambridge 1998

NOTES: Cast at Mancini Foundry, Edinburgh in 1959.

35 Striding woman and child 1959 (Plate 46)

Bronze (edition of two plus original wooden assemblage)
80 x 31 x 24 cm (31½ x 12¼ x 9½ in)
Ownership: One bronze in private collection (the location of the other bronze cannot be traced); original wooden assemblage Sheffield Galleries and Museums Collections

Exhibitions: *Four One*, South London Gallery 1960; Gallery One, London 1961; New Art Centre, London 1986; *George Fullard – A Fastidious Primitive*, Yorkshire Sculpture Park 1997; *Playing with Paradox*, Mappin Art Gallery, Sheffield and Kettle's Yard, Cambridge 1998

NOTES: First cast, location unknown, at John Galizia & Son Ltd, later cast at Morris Singer Foundry Ltd.

36 Stick figure 1959 (Plate 119)

Bronze (edition of two)
68.5 x 5 x 7 cm (27½ x 2 x 2½ in)
Ownership: Private collection

Exhibitions: Serpentine Gallery, London 1974; Hatton Gallery, University of Newcastle 1984

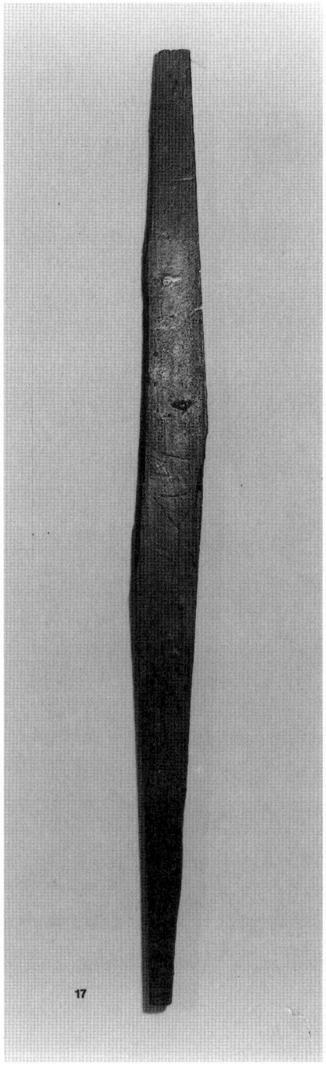

Plate 119 (Cat.36) **Stick figure** 1959

NOTES: This was cast from an old piece of wood which the artist had inscribed with features of a female head and body. Another cast also forms part of *Relief with bronze figure* 1968 (cat.74).

37 Mother and child 1959 (Plates 64 and 69)

Assemblage of various wooden items
195 x 110 x 49 cm (76¾ x 43¼ x 19¼ in)
Ownership: Manchester City Art Galleries

Exhibitions: *2nd John Moores Liverpool Exhibition*, Liverpool 1959-60; *Four One*, South London Gallery 1960; Gallery One, London 1961; Hanover Gallery, London 1961; Serpentine Gallery, London 1974; *British Sculpture in the Twentieth Century*, Whitechapel Art Gallery, London 1981; Hatton Gallery, University of Newcastle 1984; *Playing with Paradox*, Mappin Art Gallery, Sheffield and Kettle's Yard, Cambridge 1998

NOTES: This work was first exhibited under the title *Survivors*. Described as 'wood for bronze' in Gallery One catalogue 1961, this piece incorporates pieces of wood carved by the artist with bits of ornately carved picture frames and old wooden furniture. Purchased by Manchester City Art Galleries in 1991.

38 Woman 1959 (Plates 51 and 65)

Assemblage of various wooden items
229.2 x 43.2 x 81.3 cm (90¼ x 17 x 32 in)
Ownership: Arts Council Collection, Hayward Gallery, London

Exhibitions: *Four One*, South London Gallery 1960; *3rd John Moores Liverpool Exhibition*, Liverpool 1961-2; Serpentine Gallery, London 1974; *Flesh and Stone*, Arts Council tour 1983; *Questions about Sculpture*, Arts Council tour 1984; *Here and Now*, Serpentine Gallery, London 1995; *George Fullard – A Fastidious Primitive*, Yorkshire Sculpture Park 1997; *Playing with Paradox*, Mappin Art Gallery, Sheffield and Kettle's Yard, Cambridge 1998

NOTES: This work was first exhibited under the title of *Freya*. This figure is made up of bits of old wooden furniture (chairs and tables), doors, picture frames and pieces of wood carved by the artist. Purchased from the artist in 1966.

39 **Woman with flowers 1959-60** (Plate 66)

Assemblage of various wooden items
244 x 101.5 x 38.2 cm (96 x 40 x 15 in)
Ownership: Sheffield Galleries and Museums Collections

Exhibitions: *Four One*, South London Gallery 1960; Gallery One, London 1961; Hanover Gallery, London 1962; Serpentine Gallery, London 1974; Hatton Gallery, University of Newcastle 1984; *George Fullard – Student to Sculptor*, Graves Art Gallery, Sheffield 1993; *Playing with Paradox*, Mappin Art Gallery, Sheffield and Kettle's Yard, Cambridge 1998

NOTES: Figure made up of assorted pieces of old wooden furniture, including parts of an old door and wood carved by the artist.

40 **The patriot 1959-60** (Plate 68)

Assemblage of mainly painted wooden items
178 x 214.5 x 31.7 cm (70 x 84½ x 12½ in)
Ownership: Southampton City Art Gallery

Exhibitions: Gallery One, London 1961; Marlborough New London Gallery 1964; *Aspects of Twentieth Century Art*, Marlborough New London Gallery 1964; Serpentine Gallery, London 1974; Hatton Gallery, University of Newcastle 1984; *Playing with Paradox*, Mappin Art Gallery, Sheffield and Kettle's Yard, Cambridge 1998

NOTES: Purchased from private owner by Southampton City Art Gallery in 1978 on the advice of Dr David Brown of the Tate Gallery, who, at the time, considered *The patriot* to be the most important work of an artist whose reputation was increasing rapidly. Describing it as a sculpture of 'great tenderness and resonance with references back to Schwitters, bringing the "real" world into art', he particularly drew attention to Fullard's early use of the Union Jack.

41 **Phoenix 1960** (Plate 120)

Assemblage of various metal items
27.3 x 38 x 28 cm (10¾ x 15 x 11 in)
Ownership: Private collection

Exhibitions: Gallery One, London 1961; Serpentine Gallery, London 1974

NOTES: This piece is made from a kettle, old forks, decorative lock panels, spanners and a carving-fork for a tail.

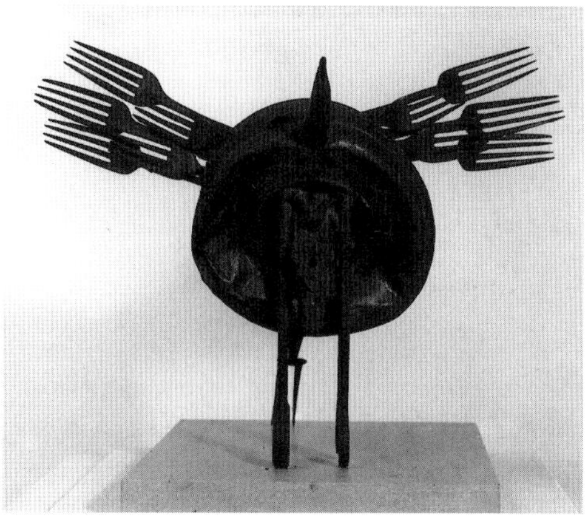

Plate 120 (Cat.41) **Phoenix** 1960

42 **Head 1960** (Plate 58)

Bronze
69 x 84 x 31 cm (27¼ x 33 x 12¼ in)
Ownership: On loan to Sheffield Galleries and Museums Collections from private collection

Exhibitions: Gallery One, London 1961; *Sculptors Today*, Midland Group Gallery, Nottingham 1962; *Contemporary British Sculpture*, Arts Council tour 1962; Brook Street Gallery, London 1963; Serpentine Gallery, London 1974; Yorkshire Sculpture Park 1977; *Mind Over Matter*, Arts Council tour 1983; *George Fullard – A Fastidious Primitive*, Yorkshire Sculpture Park 1997; *Playing with Paradox*, Mappin Art Gallery, Sheffield and Kettle's Yard, Cambridge 1998

NOTES: Cast at John Galizia & Son Ltd; plaster extant.

43 **Head 1960** (Plates 41 and 59)

Bronze
66 x 32 x 30 cm (26 x 12½ x 11¾ in)
Ownership: Private collection

Exhibitions: Gallery One, London 1961; *Alive To It All*, Arts Council tour 1983; Royal Academy Summer Exhibition 1974; *George Fullard – A Fastidious Primitive*, Yorkshire Sculpture Park 1997; *Playing with Paradox*, Mappin Art Gallery, Sheffield and Kettle's Yard, Cambridge 1998

NOTES: Cast at John Galizia & Son Ltd; plaster extant.

44 **Head 1960** (Plate 56)

Bronze
33 x 30 x 19.5 cm (13 x 11¾ x 7¾ in)
Ownership: Private collection

Exhibitions: Gallery One, London 1961; *Playing with Paradox*, Mappin Art Gallery, Sheffield and Kettle's Yard, Cambridge 1998

NOTES: Cast at John Galizia & Son Ltd; plaster extant.

45 **Head 1960** (Plate 57)

Bronze
28 x 46.5 x 23.5 cm (11 x 18¼ x 9¼ in)
Ownership: Private collection

Exhibitions: Gallery One, London 1961; *Sculptors Today*, Midland Group Gallery, Nottingham 1962; Gimpel Hanover Galerie, Zurich 1963; Serpentine Gallery, London 1974; *Alive To It All*, Arts Council tour 1983; *George Fullard – A Fastidious Primitive*, Yorkshire Sculpture Park 1997; *Playing with Paradox*, Mappin Art Gallery, Sheffield and Kettle's Yard, Cambridge 1998

NOTES: Cast at John Galizia & Son Ltd; plaster extant.

46 **Head 1960** (Plates 40 and 60)

Bronze (edition of two)
26 x 9.5 x 5 cm (10¼ x 3¾ x 2 in)
Ownership: Private collections

Exhibitions: Gallery One, London 1961; Serpentine Gallery, London 1974; *George Fullard – A Fastidious Primitive*, Yorkshire Sculpture Park 1997; *Playing with Paradox*, Mappin Art Gallery, Sheffield and Kettle's Yard, Cambridge 1998

NOTES: Cast at John Galizia & Son Ltd.

47 Head 1960 (Plate 60)

Bronze (edition of two)
17 x 10 x 7.5 cm (6¾ x 4 x 3 in)
Ownership: Private collections

Exhibitions: Gallery One, London 1961; Brook Street Gallery, London 1963; Serpentine Gallery, London 1974; *Alive To It All*, Arts Council tour 1983; *Playing with Paradox*, Mappin Art Gallery, Sheffield and Kettle's Yard, Cambridge 1998

NOTES: Cast at John Galizia & Son Ltd; plaster extant.

48 Head 1960

Bronze (edition of two)
14 x 11 x 9 cm (5½ x 4¼ x 3½ in)
Ownership: Private collections

NOTES: Cast at the Royal College of Art. Fullard made four other similarly small 'heads' – three of these were cast into bronze by the artist.

49 Head 1960 (Plate 60)

Bronze (edition of two)
17.7 x 7.5 x 9 (7 x 3 x 3½ in)
Ownership: Private collections

Exhibitions: Gallery One, London 1961; Serpentine Gallery, London 1974; *Alive To It All*, Arts Council tour 1983

NOTES: Cast at John Galizia & Son Ltd; Plaster extant.

50 Head 1961 (Plate 42)

Bronze
47.5 x 23.7 x 33 cm (18¾ x 9 x 13 in)
Ownership: Private collection

Exhibitions: Gallery One, London 1961; Arthur Tooth Gallery, London 1962; Serpentine Gallery, London 1974; Hatton Gallery, University of Newcastle 1984; *George Fullard – A Fastidious Primitive*, Yorkshire Sculpture Park 1997

NOTES: Fullard made and cast this into bronze, with the assistance of John Clinch, whilst teaching at the Royal College of Art. Plaster extant.

51 Head 1961 (Plate 43)

Bronze
20.3 x 40.4 x 16.5 cm (8 x 16 x 16½ in)
Ownership: Private collection

Exhibitions: Gallery One, London 1961; Serpentine Gallery, London 1974; Hatton Gallery, University of Newcastle 1984; *George Fullard – A Fastidious Primitive*, Yorkshire Sculpture Park 1997; *Playing with Paradox*, Mappin Art Gallery, Sheffield and Kettle's Yard, Cambridge 1998

NOTES: Cast at John Galizia & Son Ltd; plaster extant.

52 Head 1961 (Plate 44)

Bronze (edition of two)
24.2 x 19 x 10.2 cm (9½ x 7½ x 4 in)
Ownership: Private collections

Exhibitions: Serpentine Gallery, London 1974; Hatton Gallery, University of Newcastle 1984; *George Fullard – A Fastidious Primitive*, Yorkshire Sculpture Park 1997

NOTES: Cast by Steve Hurst.

53 Falling woman (1) 1961 (Plate 121)

Bronze
16.5 x 28 x 19 cm (6½ x 11½ x 7½ in)
Ownership: Private collection

Exhibitions: Gallery One, London 1961; Serpentine Gallery, London 1974

NOTES: Cast at John Galizia & Son Ltd; plaster extant.

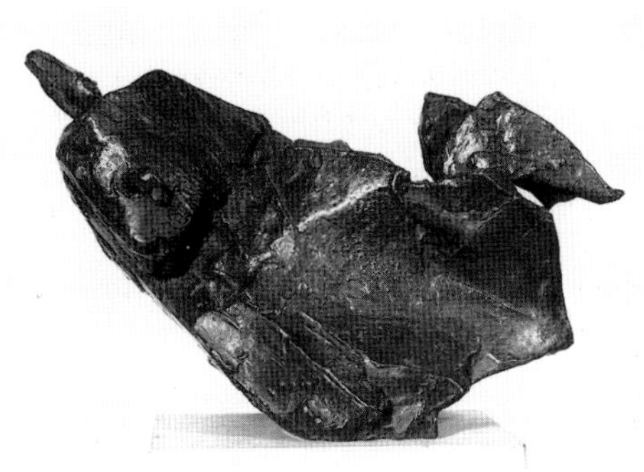

Plate 121 (Cat.53) **Falling woman (1)** 1961

54 Falling woman (2) 1961 (Plate 122)

Ciment fondu
89 x 175.5 x 46 cm (35 x 69 x 18 in)
Ownership: On loan to Manchester City Art Galleries from private collection

Exhibitions: Gallery One, London 1961; Serpentine Gallery, London 1974

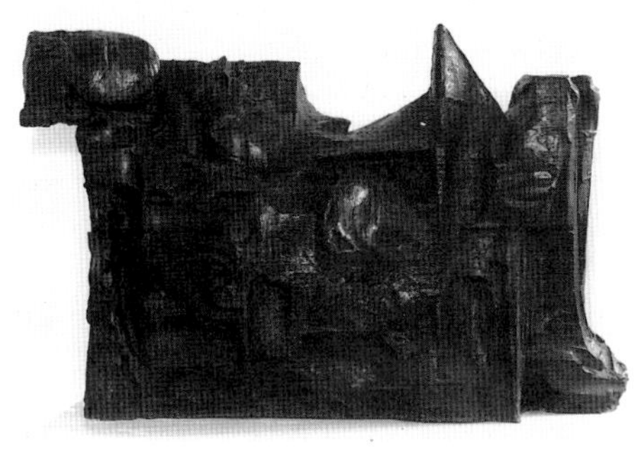

Plate 122 (Cat.54) **Falling woman (2)** 1961

55 Falling woman (3) 1961 (Plate 61)

Bronze
Length 42 cm (16½ in)
Ownership: Purchased by West Riding of Yorkshire Education Department in 1964, now part of Bretton Hall University College Collection, Wakefield

Exhibitions: Gallery One, London 1961

NOTES: Cast at John Galizia & Son Ltd; plaster extant.

56 Falling woman (4) 1961

Plaster
Length 122 cm (48 in)
Destroyed

Exhibitions: Gallery One, London 1961

NOTES: This was very similar to the small *Falling woman (1)* (cat.53).

57 War ghost 1961 (Plates 73 and 74)

Assemblage, mainly steel
139.7 x 155 x 78.5 cm (55 x 61 x 41 in)
Ownership: On loan to Sheffield Galleries and Museums Collections from private collection

Exhibitions: London County Council, *Sculpture in the Open Air*, Battersea Park 1963; Marlborough New London Gallery 1964; Serpentine Gallery, London 1974; Hatton Gallery, University of Newcastle 1984; *George Fullard – Student to Sculptor*, Graves Art Gallery, Sheffield 1993; *Playing with Paradox*, Mappin Art Gallery, Sheffield and Kettle's Yard, Cambridge 1998

NOTES: Assembled from an old trader's sack barrow, half a British soldier's 'tin' helmet, part of a gun mechanism and a piece of sheet steel from an old milk tank collected from a bomb-site in Chelsea.

58 War game 1962 (Plates 53, 62, 71 and 80)

Bronze (cast 1998); ciment fondu from assemblage of various items
148 x 146 x 71 cm ($58^{1/2}$ x $57^{1/2}$ x 28 in)
Ownership: Sheffield Galleries and Museums Collections (bronze); ciment fondu on loan to Hatton Gallery, University of Newcastle from private collection

Exhibitions: Marlborough New London Gallery 1964; Serpentine Gallery, London 1974; *Playing with Paradox*, Mappin Art Gallery, Sheffield and Kettle's Yard, Cambridge 1998

NOTES: In making this piece, Fullard impressed various objects (including fragments of basketwork, corrugated roofing, pieces of wood, old picture frames, brickwork, steps, an old door, wooden beams) into soft clay. Once hardened, positive casts were then made in more clay and the whole piece assembled, possibly with other objects incorporated. A plaster mould was made and finally a ciment fondu version produced. The dustbin-lid is thought to have been modelled by the artist. Donated by Irena Fullard, the new bronze cast is to be located on a public site in Sheffield city centre in 1998.

59 The infant St George 1962-3 (Plate 67)

Assemblage of wooden objects
211.5 x 115.5 x 124.5 cm ($83^{1/2}$ x $45^{1/2}$ x 49 in)
Ownership: On loan to Aberdeen City Art Gallery from private collection

Exhibitions: Marlborough New London Gallery 1964; Serpentine Gallery, London 1974; *Playing with Paradox*, Mappin Art Gallery, Sheffield and Kettle's Yard, Cambridge 1998

NOTES: There are two figures in this sculpture. The 'infant', with a small wooden 'gun' at the front, has carved wooden head with wooden pegs for hair, golf-clubs for feet, its 'body' is made up of slatted wooden shuttering and sections of parquet flooring, the whole is mounted on cartwheels. The tall figure at the rear is made of wooden mouldings and a section of door-panelling which has been painted cream.

60 Mounted infant 1963 (Plates 79 and 80)

Bronze cast from assembled objects
195 x 91.4 x 117 cm (77 x 36 x 44 in)
Ownership: Sheffield Galleries and Museums Collections

Exhibitions: Marlborough New London Gallery 1964; *British Sculpture in the Sixties*, Tate Gallery, London 1965; *Six Sheffield Artists*, Graves Art Gallery, Sheffield 1966; Serpentine Gallery, London 1974; *Alive To It All*, Arts Council tour 1983; Hatton Gallery, University of Newcastle 1984; *The Age of Bronze*, Mappin Art Gallery, Sheffield 1995; *Playing with Paradox*, Mappin Art Gallery, Sheffield and Kettle's Yard, Cambridge 1998

NOTES: The 'legs' were cast from a kitchen table (originally belonging to Jack Smith) which was in general domestic use at the Fullard's Park Walk residence. The 'infant' has a helmet made from paper, stiffened by plaster, its head was modelled in clay, the 'body' is made of sections of a cane-fronted cupboard. Inside the drawer there is a row of pegs. Purchased by Sheffield City Art Galleries with Victoria & Albert Museum Grant Aid in 1979.

61 Death or Glory 1963-4 (Plate 75)

Assemblage of various wooden objects
188 x 191 x 97 cm (74 x $75^{1/4}$ x $38^{1/4}$ in)
Ownership: Tate Gallery, London

Exhibitions: Marlborough New London Gallery 1964; Serpentine Gallery, London 1974; *British Sculpture in the Twentieth Century*, Whitechapel Art Gallery, London 1981; *Playing with Paradox*, Mappin Art Gallery, Sheffield and Kettle's Yard, Cambridge 1998

NOTES: The wall at the front of this piece, edged with parts of old picture frames, was a section of flooring from a derelict house near Park Walk, Chelsea. The reverse of the sculpture is clad with shuttering salvaged from a butcher's shop in Fulham Road. The 'shield', complete with 'leopards' stencilled by the artist, is a sculptor's modelling banker. The horseshoes and toy sword were especially made for the piece. The horse's eye is represented by a metal drawer-pull. The little cannons are made from toy kits and other items. Purchased 1975.

62 Fallen bastion 1964 (Plate 76)

Assemblage, including stone and steel
17.1 x 28.6 x 21.6 cm (7 x $11^{1/4}$ x $8^{1/2}$ in)
Ownership: Arts Council Collection, Hayward Gallery, London

Exhibitions: Marlborough New London Gallery 1964; *Sculpture from the Arts Council Collection*, Arts Council tour 1965; Serpentine Gallery, London 1974; Hatton Gallery, University of Newcastle 1984; *Playing with Paradox*, Mappin Art Gallery, Sheffield and Kettle's Yard, Cambridge 1998

NOTES: Purchased from the Marlborough New London Gallery in 1964.

63 The Cross of St George 1964 (Plate 78)

Assemblage of various objects
298.5 x 115 x 95.4 cm ($117^{1/4}$ x $45^{1/4}$ x $37^{1/4}$ in)
Ownership: On loan to the Tank Museum, Bovington from private collection

Exhibitions: Marlborough New London Gallery 1964; Greater London Council open-air exhibition, Battersea Park 1966; Serpentine Gallery, London 1974

NOTES: The base is made from a Post Office Telephones cable drum, resting on a pair of cartwheels. The cut-out at the front has chains hanging down, resembling the type of chain 'curtains' used in tanks and on some helmets. At the rear of the barrel is a miniature cannon. The tall column is made of pieces of metal shelf-support and chunks of old masonry with scraps of wallpaper on them. There are military-type vehicles in two of the apertures on the column, one of which contains a damaged Airfix model of a German Tiger tank.

64 **Lost patrol 1964** (Plate 82)

Assemblage of various items
33.6 x 24.4 x 10.8 cm (13¼ x 9½ x 4½ in)
Ownership: Private collection

Exhibitions: Marlborough New London Gallery 1964; *British Sculpture in the Sixties*, Tate Gallery, London 1965; *Six Sheffield Artists*, Graves Art Gallery, Sheffield 1966; Serpentine Gallery, London 1974; *George Fullard – A Fastidious Primitive*, Yorkshire Sculpture Park 1997; *Playing with Paradox*, Mappin Art Gallery, Sheffield and Kettle's Yard, Cambridge 1998

NOTES: This piece is formed from half a wooden 'pattern' of the type used in the engineering industry. At the front, in each of the six separated boxes, there is a prone toy soldier. A background landscape is provided by a piece cut from a French magazine, inverted, showing war-time tanks on the top of cliffs.

65 **The first war dream 1964** (Plate 81)

Assemblage of various items
19 x 27.9 x 6.9 cm (7½ x 11 x 2¾ in)
Ownership: Private collection

Exhibitions: Solo show at Marlborough New London Gallery 1964; *Aspects of Twentieth Century Art*, Marlborough New London Gallery 1964; Serpentine Gallery, London 1974; *Playing with Paradox*, Mappin Art Gallery, Sheffield and Kettle's Yard, Cambridge 1998

NOTES: This boxed piece, lined with mottled wallpaper, has three burnt-out cigarette packets. One toy soldier lies at the bottom of the frame.

66 **The second war dream 1964** (Plate 83)

Assemblage of various objects, mainly metal
26 x 14 x 22.2 cm (10¼ x 5½ x 8¾ in)
Ownership: Private collection

Exhibitions: Solo show at Marlborough New London Gallery 1964; *Aspects of Twentieth Century Art*, Marlborough New London Gallery 1964; *British Sculpture in the Sixties*, Tate Gallery, London 1965; Serpentine Gallery, London 1974; *George Fullard – A Fastidious Primitive*, Yorkshire Sculpture Park 1997; *Playing with Paradox*, Mappin Art Gallery, Sheffield and Kettle's Yard, Cambridge 1998

NOTES: This piece, mounted on wheels, includes a brass chimney, black plastic gun (probably part of an Airfix kit) and sets of tiny black plastic gates. Two toy soldiers are inside the 'machine'.

67 **The third war dream 1964** (Plate 70)

Assemblage of various objects
63.5 x 32 cm (25 x 12½ in)
Ownership: Palm Beach Community College, Florida, USA

Exhibitions: Pittsburgh International, Carnegie Institute, USA

NOTES: Mounted on wheels, with a small cannon at the front, this piece is formed from a fragment of masonry with wallpaper. Purchased by the Lannan Foundation, Chicago 1964.

68 **Captive 1964** (Plate 77)

Boxed assemblage of various items, including a drawing
72 x 46.5 x 13.5 cm (28¼ x 18¼ x 5¼ in)
Ownership: Private collection

Exhibitions: Marlborough New London Gallery 1964; *British Sculpture in the Sixties*, Tate Gallery, London 1965; *Six Sheffield Artists*, Graves Art Gallery, Sheffield 1966; Serpentine Gallery, London 1974; Hatton Gallery, University of Newcastle 1984; *George Fullard – A Fastidious Primitive*, Yorkshire Sculpture Park 1997; *Playing with Paradox*, Mappin Art Gallery, Sheffield and Kettle's Yard, Cambridge 1998

NOTES: The wall fragments in this piece were salvaged from refuse skips. The 'infant' drawn on the piece of plaster has a 'paper-helmet' made from a French newspaper cutting which shows a Panther tank.

69 **Night crossing 1966** (Plate 89)

Painted wood and brass
56 x 56 x 15 cm (22 x 21 x 6 in)
Ownership: Ferens Art Gallery, Hull

Exhibitions: *British Sculptors '72*, Royal Academy of Arts, London 1972; Serpentine Gallery, London 1974; Park Square Gallery, Leeds 1978; *Ship-shape 1880-1980*, Glynn Vivian Gallery, Swansea 1980; Hatton Gallery, University of Newcastle 1984; *Hull Maritime Paintings from the Ferens Art Gallery*, Stoke-on-Trent City Museum and Art Gallery 1986; *Surrealism in Hull*, Hull University 1989; *Playing with Paradox*, Mappin Art Gallery, Sheffield and Kettle's Yard, Cambridge 1998

NOTES: A painted drawer forms the basis of this piece. On the left, there is a specially made brass propeller. Inside is a boat shaped from pieces of wood and a box in which there is a toy tram with three candelabra funnels. Purchased from the artist in 1972.

70 **First voyage 1966** (Plate 90)

Painted wood and bronze
91 x 91 x 20 cm (36 x 36 x 8 in)
Ownership: On loan to Glynn Vivian Gallery, Swansea from private collection

Exhibitions: *British Sculptors '72*, Royal Academy of Arts, London 1972; Park Square Gallery, Leeds 1972; Serpentine Gallery, London 1974

NOTES: This perspex-fronted box includes painted wooden shapes. One of these suggests the deck of a ship with two bronze Cycladic figures (modern casts made by Geoff Dudley from ancient originals); another red shape has three white 'funnels' and black 'portholes', as on an ocean liner.

71 Ultima Thule 1967 (Plate 100)

Mixed media
241 x 112 x 48 cm (95 x 44 x 19 in)
Ownership: On loan to Chelsea School of Art from private collection

Exhibitions: Pittsburgh International, Carnegie Institute, USA 1967-8; *British Sculptors '72*, Royal Academy of Arts, London 1972; Park Square Gallery, Leeds 1972; Serpentine Gallery, London 1974; Hatton Gallery, University of Newcastle 1984

NOTES: The lower part of this large work suggests the prow of a ship. On this curved section there is a small bronze Egyptian bust (modern cast made by Geoff Dudley). Above, there are two fragments of painted plaster walls which resemble rocks. Each has a 'lighthouse' structure made from white wood, brass and perspex.

72 Small world 1967 (Plate 99)

Painted wood and brass
56 x 71 x 14 cm (22 x 28 x 5¼ in)
Ownership: Private collection

Exhibitions: Park Square Gallery, Leeds 1972; Serpentine Gallery, London 1974; Hatton Gallery, University of Newcastle 1984

73 Near and far 1968 (Plate 91)

Painted steel
198 x 183 x 15 cm (78 x 72 x 6 in)
Ownership: On loan to Glynn Vivian Gallery, Swansea from private collection

Exhibitions: *British Sculptors '72*, Royal Academy of Arts, London 1972; Park Square Gallery, Leeds 1972; Serpentine Gallery, London 1974

NOTES: This assemblage shows a painted sea, a navy blue and orange boat with portholes and three black and orange funnels and a large flag on a pole.

74 Relief with bronze figure 1968 (Plate 101)

Sheet steel and bronze
84 x 61 x 23 cm (33 x 24 x 9 in)
Ownership: On loan to Sheffield Galleries and Museums Collections from private collection

Exhibitions: Park Square Gallery, Leeds 1972; Serpentine Gallery, London 1974

NOTES: A bronze figure is mounted onto a piece of folded sheet-metal, originally painted white. The feet of the bronze figure are set into a small piece of wood. The head is set onto a wooden shape, painted pink and pale yellow. On the bent side of metal, there is a pencil line-drawing of the figure. Also see *Stick figure* 1959 (cat.36).

75 Flower piece 1968 (Plate 96)

Metal and wood
61 x 84 x 23 cm (24 x 33 x 9 in)
Ownership: Private collection

Exhibitions: Park Square Gallery, Leeds 1972; Serpentine Gallery, London 1974

76 Valentine 1968 (Plate 86)

Mixed media
33 x 22.3 x 7.5 cm (12 x 8¾ x 3 in)
Ownership: Private collection

Exhibitions: Serpentine Gallery, London 1974

NOTES: This piece has three discs, painted red, white and blue. A heart-shaped piece of flint, an object found by the artist, is placed at the centre.

77 Location 1968 (Plate 94)

Painted wood
224 x 101 x 45 cm (88 x 40 x 18 in)
Ownership: New Art Centre Sculpture Park, Roche Court, Salisbury

Exhibitions: *British Sculptors '72*, Royal Academy of Arts, London 1972; Park Square Gallery, Leeds 1972; Serpentine Gallery, London 1974

78 Voyage home 1968 (Plate 88)

Mixed media
107 x 41 x 18 cm (42 x 16 x 7 in)
Ownership: On loan to Sheffield Galleries and Museums Collections from private collection

Exhibitions: *British Sculptors '72*, Royal Academy of Arts, London 1972; Park Square Gallery, Leeds 1972; Serpentine Gallery, London 1974.

NOTES: In this work, an Airfix kit steamship has been mounted onto a large piece of folded sheet-metal. Pencil lines suggest the movement of the ship through the water. The whole sculpture was originally painted white.

79 Forever 1969 (Plates 85 and 92)

Painted steel and brass
183 x 109 x 147 cm (72 x 43 x 58 in)
Ownership: Arts Council Collection, Hayward Gallery, London

Exhibitions: *British Sculptors '72*, Royal Academy of Arts, London 1972; Park Square Gallery, Leeds 1972; Serpentine Gallery, London 1974; *Ship-shape 1880-1980*, Glynn Vivian Gallery, Swansea 1980; *A Mansion of Many Chambers*, Arts Council tour 1981-2; Hatton Gallery, University of Newcastle 1984; *George Fullard – A Fastidious Primitive*, Yorkshire Sculpture Park 1997; *Playing with Paradox*, Mappin Art Gallery, Sheffield and Kettle's Yard, Cambridge 1998

NOTES: The front section of this large sculpture is a curved steel sheet, painted blue; the back is a flat sheet of steel, painted green. Inserted between these two sheets is a flat 'ship' with six brass rings for portholes, a small propeller and a tiny maroon flag with the Union Jack insignia. A white-painted steel 'paper' boat stands at the base of the front curve. Purchased in 1977.

80 Long ago 1969 (Plate 95)

Painted wood, aluminium and canvas
172 x 188 x 17 cm (68 x 74 x 7 in)
Ownership: On loan to Stoke-on-Trent City Museum and Art Gallery from private collection

Exhibitions: *British Sculptors '72*, Royal Academy of Arts, London 1972; Park Square Gallery, Leeds 1972; Serpentine Gallery, London 1974; *Ship-shape 1880-1980*, Glynn Vivian Gallery, Swansea 1980; Hatton Gallery, University of Newcastle 1984; *Playing with Paradox*, Mappin Art Gallery, Sheffield and Kettle's Yard, Cambridge 1998

NOTES: This large framed relief has a small aluminium painted 'paper' boat and 'waves' represented by overlapping slats of wood. On the outside of the frame is a wooden construction, resembling a lighthouse.

81 Dream day 1970-1 (Plate 93)

Painted aluminium
96 x 175 x 48 cm (38 x 69 x 19 in)
Ownership: On loan to Bristol City Art Gallery from private collection

Exhibitions: *British Sculptors '72*, Royal Academy of Arts, London 1972; Park Square Gallery, Leeds 1972; Serpentine Gallery, London 1974; Hatton Gallery, University of Newcastle 1984; *Playing with Paradox*, Mappin Art Gallery, Sheffield and Kettle's Yard, Cambridge 1998

82 Ebb tide 1971 (Plate 87)

Aluminium
198 x 102 x 23 cm (78 x 40 x 9 in)
Ownership: Private collection

Exhibitions: *British Sculptors '72*, Royal Academy of Arts, London 1972; Park Square Gallery, Leeds 1972; Serpentine Gallery, London 1974

83 Deserted island 1973 (Plate 102)

Bronze (edition of two)
17.7 x 23.7 x 23.7 cm (7 x 9 x 9 in)
Ownership: Private collections

Exhibitions: Serpentine Gallery, London 1974; *George Fullard – A Fastidious Primitive*, Yorkshire Sculpture Park 1997; *Playing with Paradox*, Mappin Art Gallery, Sheffield and Kettle's Yard, Cambridge 1998

NOTES: The wax model was cast by Ray Arnatt in 1974.

Chronology

1923 Born 15 September, Sheffield

1937-42 Sheffield College of Arts and Crafts

1942-4 War service with 17/21st Lancers, North Africa and Italy

1945-7 Royal College of Art, Ambleside and London

1946 Marriage to Irena Corcoran

1947 Awarded travel scholarship to study in Paris

Taught part-time at Brighton School of Art

1950 Moved to Stanley Studios, Park Walk, Chelsea

1950s Taught part-time at St Martins School of Art, Camberwell and Hammersmith

1957-62 Taught two days per week at St Albans School of Art

1960-1 Taught at Royal College of Art

1962-3 Chelsea School of Art (part-time)

1963-73 Head of Sculpture at Chelsea School of Art

1973 Associate of Royal Academy

Died 25 December, London

Solo exhibitions

1958 30 August - 14 September, Woodstock Gallery, London

1959 29 June - 18 July, Woodstock Gallery, London (drawings only)

1961 October, Gallery One, London

1964 November - December, Marlborough New London Gallery, London

1972 11 October - 4 November, Park Square Gallery, Leeds

1974 27 July - 18 August, *George Fullard 1923-1973*, memorial retrospective at Serpentine Gallery, London and Mappin Art Gallery, Sheffield, later touring to Hull, Leicester, Aberdeen, Whitehaven, Durham, Swansea, Bristol and Reading

1982 9-31 October, *George Fullard Drawings*, Midland Arts Centre, Birmingham (Arts Council of Great Britain exhibition) and tour, including Leeds University Art Gallery 7-23 March 1984

1984 6 October - 10 November, *Fullard Drawings, Paintings, Sculptures*, Hatton Gallery, University of Newcastle upon Tyne.

1990 Redfern Gallery, London (drawings only)

1993 3 July - 2 October, *George Fullard – from Student to Sculptor*, Graves Art Gallery, Sheffield

1997 22 August - 16 November, *George Fullard – A Fastidious Primitive*, Yorkshire Sculpture Park, Wakefield

1998 9 May - 20 July, *Playing with Paradox*, Mappin Art Gallery, Sheffield and 8 August - 20 September, Kettle's Yard, Cambridge

Group exhibitions

1953 October, *Football and the Fine Arts*, Park Lane House, London

1956 18 April - 5 May, *Looking Forward*, South London Art Gallery

12 July - 11 August (Part 1) and 23 August - 22 September (Part 2), *Artists of Fame and Promise*, Leicester Galleries, London

1957 26 April - 15 May, *Looking at People*, South London Art Gallery and tour to Pushkin Museum of Fine Arts, Moscow

10 November - 11 January 1958, *1st John Moores Liverpool Exhibition*, Liverpool (junior prizewinner)

1958 *An Exhibition of Graphic Work chosen by John Berger*, Hampstead, London

31 May - 22 June, *Contemporary British Sculpture*, Leamington Spa (Arts Council of Great Britain open-air exhibition) touring to Shrewsbury and Cardiff

4-16 August, *Sculpture and Drawings*, Woodstock Gallery, London

15-27 September, *Sculpture*, Woodstock Gallery, London

November, Natural History Museum (gardens), London

December, *Graphic art/painters & sculptors*, Partisan Café, London

29 December - 17 January 1959, *Sculpture*, Woodstock Gallery, London

1959 4-30 April, *George Fullard – Michael Fussell*, Portal Gallery, London

19 November – 17 January 1960, *2nd John Moores Liverpool Exhibition*, Liverpool

1960 7-27 February, *Four One*, South London Gallery

April, Hanover Gallery, London

30 April - 14 May, *Contemporary British Sculpture*, Cannon Hill Park, Birmingham (Arts Council of Great Britain open-air exhibition) touring to Barnsley, Manchester, Stratford-upon-Avon, Edinburgh and Cheltenham

16 July - 7 August, *Northern Artists*, City Art Gallery, Manchester (Arts Council of Great Britain exhibition) touring to Sheffield, Newcastle upon Tyne, Bolton, Bradford and Carlisle

1961 22 April - 13 May, *Contemporary British Sculpture*, Cannon Hill Park, Birmingham (Arts Council of Great Britain open-air exhibition) touring to Eastbourne, Cirencester, Nottingham, Edinburgh and Bradford

21 June - 2 September, *Sculpture and Drawings*, Hanover Gallery, London

16 November - 14 January 1962, *3rd John Moores Liverpool Exhibition*, Liverpool

1962 9-22 January, *One Year of British Art*, Arthur Tooth & Sons Ltd, London

28 April - 12 May, *Contemporary British Sculpture*, Caerphilly Castle (Arts Council of Great Britain open-air exhibition) touring to Stevenage, Chester and Edinburgh

3 July - 1 September, *Sculpture*, Hanover Gallery, London

18 August - 8 September, *Sculptors Today*, Midland Group Gallery, Nottingham

1963 May - September, *Sculpture in the Open Air*, London County Council exhibition, Battersea Park, London

July - October, *Summer Exhibition – Modern Sculpture and Sculptor's Drawings*, Brook Street Gallery, London

19 August - 6 September, *Ten Years On*, Gallery One, London

30 August - 28 September, *Englische Maler und Bildhauer*, Gimpel-Hanover Galerie, Zurich

1964 22 April - 28 June, *Painting and Sculpture of a Decade*, Tate Gallery, London

July - August, *Aspects of Twentieth-Century Art*, Marlborough New London Gallery, London

30 October - 10 January 1965, *Pittsburgh International*, Carnegie Institute, Pittsburgh, USA

1965 *Sculpture from the Arts Council Collection*, Arts Council of Great Britain touring exhibition

25 February - 4 April, *British Sculpture in the Sixties*, Tate Gallery, London

1966 *Six Sheffield Artists*, Mappin Art Gallery, Sheffield

20 May - 30 September, *Sculpture in the Open Air*, Greater London Council exhibition, Battersea Park, London

1967 27 October - 7 January 1968, *Pittsburgh International*, Carnegie Institute, Pittsburgh, USA

1972 *British Sculpture*, Redfern Gallery, London

8 January - 5 March, *British Sculptors '72*, Royal Academy of Arts, London

1973 Royal Academy of Arts, Summer Exhibition

1977 2 June - 4 September, *A Silver Jubilee Exhibition of Contemporary British Sculpture 1977*, Greater London Council exhibition, Battersea Park

24 September - 27 November, inaugural exhibition at Yorkshire Sculpture Park, Wakefield

1978 Park Square Gallery, Leeds

1980 4-25 October, *Ship-shape 1880-1980*, Glynn Vivian Gallery, Swansea

1981 *A Mansion of Many Chambers: Beauty and other works*, Arts Council of Great Britain touring exhibition

11 September - 24 January 1982 (in two parts), *British Sculpture in the Twentieth Century*, Whitechapel Art Gallery, London

1982 9-30 January, Mayor Gallery, London

1983 *Alive To It All*, Arts Council of Great Britain touring exhibition

29 October - 20 November, *Flesh and Stone*, Southampton Art Gallery (Arts Council of Great Britain exhibition) touring to Bradford, Stoke-on-Trent and Sheffield

1984 *Questions about Sculpture*, Arts Council of Great Britain touring exhibition

7 January - 5 February, *Mind over Matter*, Southampton Art Gallery (Arts Council of Great Britain exhibition) touring to Bradford, Stoke-on-Trent and Sheffield

31 March - 13 May, *The Forgotten Fifties*, Graves Art Gallery, Sheffield (Arts Council of Great Britain) touring to Norwich Castle Museum, Herbert Art Gallery and Museum Coventry and Camden Arts Centre, London

1985 2 February - 3 March, *Recalling the Fifties – British Painting and Sculpture 1950-1960*, Serpentine Gallery, London

1986 22 May - 5 July, *British Sculpture 1950-1965*, New Art Centre, London

13 December - 1 February 1987, *George Fullard's 'Old woman'*, Stoke-on-Trent City Museum and Art Gallery

1995 10 June - 15 October, *The Age of Bronze*, City Museum and Mappin Art Gallery, Sheffield

19 June - 2 July, *Here and Now*, Serpentine Art Gallery, London

Public collections

Many of Fullard's works are in private collections.
Public collections include:

Arts Council Collection, Hayward Gallery, London
Art Gallery of South Australia, Adelaide
British Museum, London
Ferens Art Gallery, Hull
Manchester City Art Galleries Collection
New Art Centre Sculpture Park, Roche Court, Salisbury
Norfolk Museums Service (Norwich Castle Museum)
Palm Beach Community College, Florida, USA
Sheffield Galleries and Museums Collections
Southampton City Art Gallery
Stoke-on-Trent City Museum and Art Gallery
Tate Gallery, London
Victoria & Albert Museum, London

Select bibliography

The following is not a bibliography of books and other material referred to in the section notes. Instead, it concentrates on listing the best sources of information about the artist and his work and these are generally exhibition catalogues and contemporary journal articles. The first section includes useful general reading on sculpture in the post-war period.

General reading

Archer, M., *Art Since 1960*, London 1997
Causey, A., *Sculpture since 1945*, Oxford 1998
Crow, T., *The Rise of the Sixties*, London 1996
Curtis, P., *Modern British Sculpture*, Tate Gallery, Liverpool 1988
Fineberg, J., *Art Since 1940 – Strategies of Being*, London 1995
Hammacher, A. M., *Modern English Sculpture*, London 1967
Janis, H. and Blesh, R., *Collage – Personalities, Concepts, Techniques*, Philadelphia, USA 1962
Lindey, C., *Art in the Cold War*, London 1990
Mellor, D., *The Sixties Art Scene in London*, Barbican Art Gallery, London 1993
Nairne, S. and Serota, N. (eds), *British Sculpture in the Twentieth Century*, Whitechapel Art Gallery, London 1981
Read, H., *Contemporary Modern Sculpture*, London 1964
Robertson, B., Russell, J. and Lord Snowden, *Private View*, London 1965
Walden, D., *Collage, Assemblage and the Found Object*, London 1992

Exhibition catalogues

Alston, D. and Kirby, J., in broadsheet for *George Fullard – Student to Sculptor*, Sheffield 1993
Brill, F. (intro.), *George Fullard 1923-1973*, Serpentine Gallery, London 1974
Spalding, J. (ed.), with contributions from others, including Baines, H., Francia, P. de, Berger, J., *The Forgotten Fifties*, Sheffield 1984
Spalding, J., *George Fullard Drawings*, Arts Council of England 1982
Sutton, K. (intro.), *George Fullard*, Gallery One, London 1961
Whiteley, G., *George Fullard – A Fastidious Primitive*, Yorkshire Sculpture Park, Wakefield 1997
Whiteley, G. (essay) in J. Kirby and A. Middleton (eds), *Playing with Paradox: George Fullard 1923-1973*, Sheffield Hallam University 1998

Articles in journals and newspapers

Berger, J., 'George Fullard', *New Statesman*, 6 September 1958, Vol.56, No.1434, pp.274-6
Berger, J., 'Social Realism and the young', *New Statesman and Nation*, 30 July 1955, Vol.50, No.1273, pp.133-4
Brill, F., 'George Fullard', *Motif*, 1967, No.13
Burr, J., 'The power of paradox', *Apollo*, August 1974, Vol.100, No.150
Cherry, D. and Steyn, J., 'The moment of realism 1952-1956', *Artscribe*, June 1982, No.35
Duncan, S., 'Tension and vitality – figurative sculpture of the fifties', *Artscribe*, June 1982, No.35
Feaver, W., *Financial Times*, 9 August 1974, p.3
Fuller, P., 'George Fullard', *Connoisseur*, October 1974, No.187
Glaves-Smith, J., 'George Fullard retrospective', *Studio International*, Vol.188, No.969
Gosling, N., *Observer*, 16 November 1964
Greaves, D., 'Except the Kitchen Sink', *Art Review*, June 1994, Vol.XLVI, p.18
Jones, M., 'Art in a cold climate', *Tribune*, 10 August 1956
Observer, 2 January 1972, p.22
Oliver, W. T., *Yorkshire Post*, 13 October 1972, p.2
Reichardt, J., 'George Fullard and the menacing baby saint', *Metro* 1965, No.9, pp.27-9
Ross, A., 'Dream games', *London Magazine*, December 1974/January 1975, Vol.14, No.5, p.72
Russell, J. (obituary), *The Times*, 5 January 1974
Spencer, C. S., 'Sculptor in search of the labyrinth', *Studio International*, July 1963, Vol.166, No.843, pp.8-9
Spencer, C. S., 'The phenomenon of British sculpture', *Studio International*, March 1965, Vol.169, No.863
Thiemann, E., 'George Mathias Fullard', *Das Kunstwerk*, November 1964, No.5, XVIII, p.12
Weekend Telegraph, 19 February 1965, p.24
Whiteley, G., 'The impact of the survivor: the sculpture of George Fullard (1923-1973)', *The Sculpture Journal*, Public Monuments and Sculpture Association, London 1997

Archive material

The Tate Gallery Archive has a selection of Fullard's writings, drawings and papers: Ref.TGA 752. The Victor Musgrave papers, also held in the Tate Archive, contain useful material, including a scrapbook of newspaper cuttings about exhibitions at Gallery One: Ref.TGA 8714.

Inter-active resource

Sheffield Hallam University's ongoing CD-ROM project, *George Fullard – Complexity and Contradiction*, provides students and researchers with access to Fullard's drawings and sketchbooks from his period at Sheffield College of Arts and Crafts. A range of secondary source material relating to the artist and images of later sculpture are also included. Information about the project can be obtained on the Web at http://www.shu.ac.uk/services/lc/people/psalter2.htm

Index of Works

Numbers in italics refer to pages on which illustrations appear

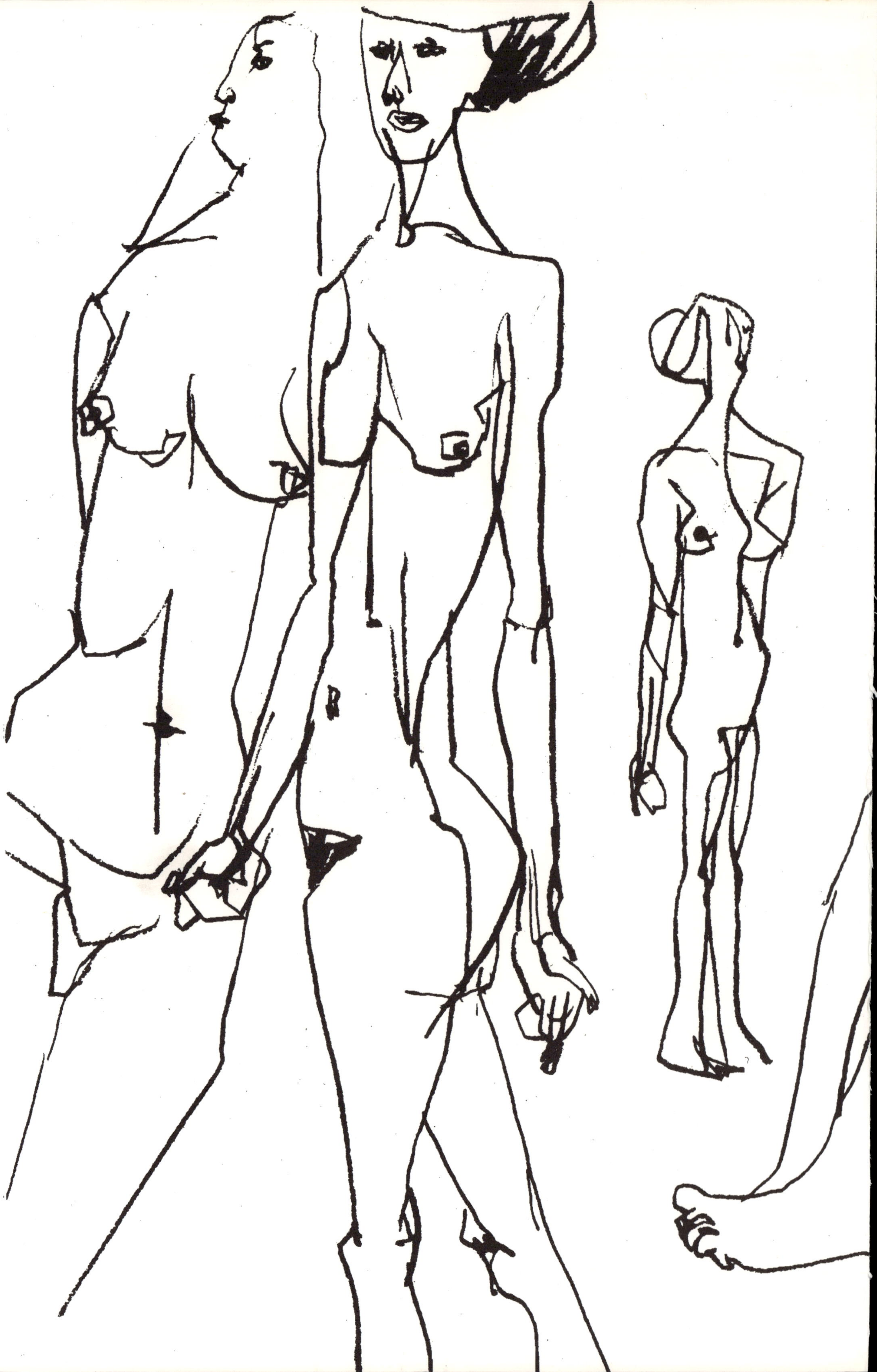